Jerome Bruner

Language, Culture, Self

Jerome Bruner
Language, Culture, Self

Edited by

David Bakhurst and Stuart G. Shanker

SAGE Publications
London • Thousand Oaks • New Delhi

First published 2001

SAGE Publications Ltd
6 Bonhill Street
London EC2A 4PU

SAGE Publications Inc
2455 Teller Road
Thousand Oaks, California 91320

SAGE Publications India Pvt Ltd
32, M-Block Market
Greater Kailash - I
New Delhi 110 048

British Library Cataloguing in Publication data

A catalogue record for this book is
available from the British Library

ISBN 0 7619 5531 3
ISBN 0 7619 5532 1 (pbk)

Library of Congress catalog card number available

Typeset by SIVA Math Setters, Chennai, India
Printed and bound in Great Britain by Athenaeum Press,
Gateshead

Contents

Contributors

David Bakhurst is Professor of Philosophy at Queen's University at Kingston, Ontario. He is the author of *Consciousness and Revolution in Soviet Philosophy* (1991) and co-editor, with Christine Sypnowich, of *The Social Self* (1995).

Michael Beran is a graduate student in psychology at Georgia State University, where he conducts research at the Language Research Center.

Jane R. Brown earned her Ph.D. in Human Development and Family Studies at Penn State University. She currently works as an evaluation consultant to programmes and agencies serving children and families in Monterey County, California.

Jerome Bruner is University Professor at New York University. He has held the G.H. Mead University Professorship at the New School for Social Research, New York, and the Watts Chair of Psychology at Oxford. He has written extensively on questions of perception, language and education, and on the significance of culture to psychology. His books include *Child's Talk* (1983), *Actual Minds, Possible Worlds* (1986), *Acts of Meaning* (1990), *The Culture of Education* (1996) and (with Anthony Amsterdam) *Minding the Law* (2000).

Judy Dunn is MRC Research Professor at the Institute of Psychiatry in London. Her research explores children's social, cognitive and communicative development, in the context of their close relationships. Her books include *The Beginnings of Social Understanding* (1988) and, with Robert Plomin, *Separate Lives: Why Siblings are so Different* (1990).

Christopher Elder studied at the Language Research Center at Georgia State University and is now Research Specialist in the Department of Neurology in the Emory University School of Medicine. He is currently investigating the effects of deep brain stimulation on Parkinson's disease.

Howard Gardner is John H. and Elisabeth A. Hobbs Professor of Cognition and Education and Adjunct Professor of Psychology at Harvard University. Trained as a cognitive-developmental psychologist, Gardner has also conducted research in the areas of neuropsychology, educational reform and ethics in the professions. He is the author of many books and articles including, most recently, *The Disciplined Mind* and *Intelligence Reframed*, both published in 1999.

Clifford Geertz is an anthropologist and Harold F. Linder Professor of Social Science in the School of Social Science, Institute for Advanced Study, Princeton. He is author of a number of books, including *The Interpretation of Cultures, Local Knowledge* (1973) and *After the Fact* (1995). He has done extensive fieldwork in both Indonesia and Morocco.

Rom Harré is Emeritus Fellow of Linacre College, Oxford, Professor of Psychology at Georgetown University, and Adjunct Professor of Philosophy at American University, Washington, DC. His published work includes *Varieties of Realism* (1986) and *Great Scientific Experiments* (1981), both studies in the philosophy of the natural sciences, and the trilogy *Social Being* (1979), *Personal Being* (1983) and *Physical Being* (1991), which explores the role of rules and conventions in various aspects of human cognition. His most recent book is *The Singular Self* (1998). He holds honorary doctorates from the universities of Helsinki, Aarhus and Lima.

David R. Olson is University Professor, University of Toronto, and Professor of Applied Cognitive Science at OISE/UT. He is author of *The World on Paper* (1994) and editor, with Nancy Torrance, of *Handbook of Education and Human Development* (1996). Bruner's *The Culture of Education* (1996) is dedicated to Olson.

Edward S. Reed was Associate Professor of Psychology at Franklin & Marshall College from 1991 until his untimely death in February 1997. During that period he received a Guggenheim Fellowship, which enabled him to complete his final three books: *Encountering the World* (1996), *The Necessity of Experience* (1996) and *From Soul to Mind: the Emergence of Psychology, 1815–1890* (1997).

Duane Rumbaugh is currently director of the Language Research Center of the College of Arts and Sciences at Georgia State University, where he held a chair of Psychology from 1971 to 1989. His research interests lie in comparative studies of cognition.

Stuart G. Shanker is Professor of Psychology and Philosophy at Atkinson College, York University, Toronto. His recent publications include *Wittgenstein's Remarks on the Foundations of AI* (1998) and, with S. Savage-Rumbaugh and Talbot J. Taylor, *Apes, Language and the Human Mind* (1998).

John Shotter is Professor of Interpersonal Relations, and chair of the Department of Communication of the University of New Hampshire. His long-term interest is in the social conditions conducive to people having a voice in the development of participatory democracies and civil societies. His books include *Social Accountability and Selfhood* (1984), *Cultural Politics of Everyday Life* (1993) and *Conversational Realities* (1993).

Talbot J. Taylor is the Louise G.T. Cooley Professor of English and Linguistics at the College of William and Mary Virginia. He is, with Roy Harris, co-editor of the journal *Language & Communication*. His recent publications include *Theorizing Language* (Pergamon Press, 1998) and, with S. Savage-Rumbaugh and S. Shanker, *Apes, Language and the Human Mind* (Oxford, 1998).

Michael Tomasello taught at Emory University and worked at Yerkes Primate Center (USA) from 1980 to 1998. Since 1998, he has been Co-Director, Max Planck Institute for Evolutionary Anthropology, Leipzig, Germany. His research focuses on processes of social cognition, social learning, and language and communication in human children and great apes. His recent publications include *Primate Cognition*, with Josep Call (1997), and *The Cultural Origins of Human Cognition* (1999).

Acknowledgements

The editors are grateful to the Social Sciences and Humanities Research Council of Canada for grants facilitating their respective contributions to this project. In addition, thanks are due to Atkinson College, York University, for supporting Stuart Shanker's research, and to the Advisory Research Committee of Queen's University for its support of David Bakhurst's work.

INTRODUCTION: BRUNER'S WAY

David Bakhurst and Stuart G. Shanker

The subject of this book is Jerome Bruner's contribution to our understanding of the mind. Although Bruner has often concerned himself with
concrete and practical issues, such as education (Bruner, 1960, 1966, 1996),
child development (1983a) and, mostly recently, the law (Amsterdam and
Bruner, 2000), he has always been an intensely theoretical thinker, a man
fascinated by ideas. His writings have been constantly informed by
broadly philosophical themes, drawn not just from philosophy itself, but
from linguistics, literary theory, anthropology and other disciplines (see
Bruner, 1979, 1986). No matter how small or matter-of-fact his subject,
Bruner is always keen to explore what it tells us about the nature of
psychological studies in general and their contribution to our understanding of ourselves. His prodigious influence is in part due to the theoretical
profundity of his work and the light it has cast on the central concepts and
methods of psychology. For this reason we have chosen to focus this
volume on Bruner the philosophical psychologist and philosopher of
psychology.

The book is not a *Festschrift*.[1] Although the contributors' admiration
for Bruner is evident in every chapter, their primary concern is not to
celebrate his legacy, but to use his work as a lens through which to see
contemporary debates in psychology and cognate disciplines, debates
about mind and culture, language and communication, identity and
development. The sheer scope of Bruner's contribution over the decades
makes him an apt figure for this purpose. There is hardly a major area of
psychology on which Bruner has not written, and no area to which his
work is not relevant. This is evidenced by the range of topics addressed by
our contributors, which include language and its development, pragmatics
and the emotions, education, memory, rules and normativity, discourse,
dialogue, and the self.

Another reason why Bruner is an ideal focus is his role in two crucial
paradigm shifts in twentieth-century psychology. In the 1950s, he was
an instrumental figure in the cognitive revolution, which restored to
psychology the inner life of the mind after decades of arid behaviourist
objectivism. Cognitive psychology prospered and, in league with other
fields, evolved into 'cognitive science', conceived as a systematic interdisciplinary approach to the study of mind (see Gardner, 1985). Bruner,

however, gradually grew more and more dissatisfied with what cognitivism had become. In 1990, he published *Acts of Meaning*, in which he argued that the cognitive revolution had betrayed the impulse that had brought it into being. The revolution's principal concern, Bruner argued, had been to return the concept of meaning to the forefront of psychological theorizing. But cognitivism had become so enamoured of computational models of the mind that it had replaced behaviourism's impoverished view of the person with one no better: human beings as information processors. In response, Bruner argued forcefully that meaning is not a given, but something made by human beings as they negotiate the world. Meaning is a cultural, not computational, phenomenon. And since meaning is the medium of the mental, culture is constitutive of mind.

In many ways, Bruner's objection was familiar. It had often been lamented that mainstream psychology was individualistic and scientistic, representing minds as self-contained mental atoms and ignoring the social and cultural influences upon them. In the last decade, however, this well-known critique has really been gaining momentum. Besides Bruner, both Richard Shweder (1990) and Michael Cole (1996) have sounded the call for a new 'cultural psychology'. Assorted versions of 'constructionist' and 'discursive' psychology have appeared on the scene, joining a veritable chorus of diverse voices urging that psychology treat the mind as a sociocultural phenomenon (e.g., Edwards and Potter, 1992; Harré and Gillett, 1994; Gergen, 1999). It is particularly striking that these voices no longer come exclusively from the margins. Just as the left/right divide is collapsing in political theory, so the dichotomy between mainstream 'individualistic/scientistic/Cartesian' psychology and radical 'communitarian/interpretative/post-Cartesian' psychology has become outmoded. Cognitive scientists and philosophers of mind now commonly acknowledge that no plausible account of the mind can be indifferent to the context in which we think and act, and some significant works have appeared devoted to the cultural origins, and social realization, of human mentality (e.g., Donald, 1991). A psychologist interested in culture is no longer a counter-cultural figure.

For all that, however, there is no consensus about exactly how to accommodate culture within psychology. Shweder's and Cole's respective visions of cultural psychology differ significantly from each other and from Bruner's. And while some thinkers believe that psychology must embrace the cultural as an alternative (or as an antidote) to scientific theories of mind, others seek to incorporate the study of culture's influence on mind into scientific psychology.

It is thus an excellent time to take stock of this 'cultural turn' in psychology and of the various conceptual presuppositions behind it. Bruner's work is perfectly situated for such an enquiry. His status as a disaffected cognitivist means that he has a fine understanding of the positions he now criticizes. Moreover, although Bruner increasingly strikes a radical posture, drawing on literary-critical and 'postmodern' sources, his attitude to cognitive science is basically reconciliatory. Bruner sees himself as pursuing the same theoretical goals that motivated the original cognitive revolution and he is no enemy of systematic theory or experimental enquiry. He is thus someone capable of entering into fruitful dialogue with everyone in the debate, another fact that explains his considerable influence on so many diverse thinkers.

A further reason to focus on Bruner is this. We can make progress on such issues as the fate of the cognitive revolution, and the relation of culture and mind, only by addressing some intensely theoretical questions about the fundamentals of psychological explanation. Cognitive science prides itself on being *science*, but it is driven by strong conceptual commitments, which seem to invite philosophical criticism on purely conceptual grounds. How are we to understand the relation between, on the one hand, empirical, psychological enquiry and, on the other, philosophical reflection on the nature of the mind? Here Bruner's work is particularly enlightening. As we remarked above, he has always been a distinctively philosophical psychologist, both in his appreciation and use of certain philosophical ideas, and in his supremely reflective and speculative approach to psychological study. At the same time, Bruner continually seeks to deploy conceptual analysis to assist the construction of empirically supported theories of genuine practical import. In what follows, we argue that Bruner's approach offers an instructive illustration of the fruitful interplay of empirical and philosophical enquiry. It is a model from which psychologists, cognitive scientists and philosophers of mind have much to learn.

To make this case, however, it is important to formulate the distinction between empirical and conceptual enquiry properly. We should not make it seem, of course, as if we must choose between empirical studies uninformed by reflection upon their conceptual foundations or conceptual speculation utterly indifferent to empirical findings. Neither strategy is serious. What is at issue is whether, and to what degree, the nature of mind is best revealed by empirical theories, grounded in observation and experiment, of the kind propounded by the natural sciences. Or can part of the mind's nature only be captured by philosophical reflection on our concepts of mind and mental phenomena?

This issue, which is as difficult as it is fascinating, has haunted the relation of philosophy and psychology since the latter's emergence in the mid-nineteenth century. Before turning to Bruner, it is worth considering the two disciplines' tense relationship in more detail.

Philosophy and psychology

What is the relation between philosophy and psychology? What should it be? Philosophy is a variety of conceptual enquiry that involves speculative reflection upon our fundamental concepts, beliefs and forms of thought, principally with the aim of elucidating the relation of mind and world and the nature of value. Psychology, in contrast, aspires to study the mind empirically and scientifically. The history of philosophy, of course, contains many views of the nature of philosophy itself and its relation to empirical enquiry. For all their variety, they may be grouped into two main kinds. The first, illustrated famously by Descartes and Kant, casts philosophy in a normative, foundational role. The philosopher's task is to legitimate the conceptual framework of empirical enquiry by grounding our fundamental concepts, beliefs and forms of explanation. The second, seen in Locke and Hume, portrays the philosopher as describing and clarifying our fundamental conceptions, rather than as justifying them. Many exponents of the first approach represent themselves as defenders of the sciences, though the pretension that philosophy writes permissions has often irritated scientists, who do not perceive their claims as needing an external warrant. Theorists of the second sort tend to be more subservient to science. Witness Locke's famous self-effacing portrayal of the philosopher as the 'underlabourer' for the sciences, engaged 'in clearing the ground a little, and removing some of the rubbish, that lies in the way to knowledge' (Locke, 1979: 10). Yet proponents of conceptual clarification usually conceive of themselves as defining limits to knowledge or intelligible discourse and thereby as setting constraints on empirical enquiry. To clarify our conceptions, the philosopher establishes criteria to distinguish the meaningful from the meaningless, sense from nonsense. Here again is potential for conflict between the philosopher and the scientist. Even the logical positivists, who were as enamoured of science as any philosophers could be, were keen to tell scientists what could or could not be said. Naturally, scientists tend to resist these incursions, reasoning that where there is no conflict between philosophy and science, philosophy leaves science where it is, and where the two are in tension, it is only the progress of science that will reveal whether the philosopher's qualms are justified.

Thus however much philosophers cast themselves as underwriters or handmaidens of empirical enquiry, the potential for conflict between philosophy and science is always real. And this is especially so when the science in question is psychology, for both disciplines lay claim to the mind as their primary object of investigation. Having largely conceded the world to the natural sciences in the early modern period, philosophers were not about to give up the mind. So when psychology began to emerge in the nineteenth century, many philosophers resisted the idea that mental phenomena could be captured in the net of scientific explanation. Even William James, so often heralded as the father of American psychology, confessed to a colleague at Harvard that he regarded psychology as 'a nasty little subject' because 'all one cares to know lies outside' the bounds of empirical research (Fancher, 1979: 166). James's distaste issued from the fact that the new science of psychology was deeply committed to a mechanist paradigm, whereas the primary task of philosophy, as he conceived it, was to explain and preserve those aspects of human existence that render us distinctly human, such as the higher emotions and freedom of the will.

The deterministic conceptions James abhorred recurred in many species of twentieth-century psychology: first in the overwhelming spread of behaviourism, which promised to transform psychology into a branch of social engineering; then in the explosion of Artificial Intelligence in the mid-1950s, which rendered the mind a computational device; and, more recently, in the dominance of genetic determinism, which sees the development of our 'species-typical behaviours' as a matter of biological maturation. In addition, where psychology has not simply ignored the higher emotions, it has reduced them either to chemical and motor processes inherited from our distant forebears or to 'socially conditioned behaviours'. Finally, the development of neuro-imaging techniques has opened up the prospect of tracking the chain of neural events from impulse to action, seemingly rendering discussions of 'free will' a quaint philosophical pastime. James would not have been amused.

Philosophers have reacted to these assaults on their fiefdom in various ways. Many have been impressed by the power of empirical approaches, especially Artificial Intelligence, and have sought to bring the philosophy of mind into line (AI, of course, inspired influential functionalist philosophies of mind). A few have gone further and embraced scientism, arguing that the philosophy of mind is obsolete. The majority, however, have continued to insist on the primacy of philosophical theories for establishing the parameters of psychological research, and some have sought to rein in the pretensions of psychology. Wittgensteinians, for example, have argued that psychologistic and cognitivist theories misconstrue the logical grammar of psychological concepts. While the physical processes that underlie our mental lives are open to scientific investigation, the nature of the mental can be disclosed only by elucidating our psychological concepts, especially as they are expressed in our language practices. Of course, there are many facts about the way in which people think and act which are open to empirical scrutiny, but these are not facts of a kind that can be regimented into scientific explanations. They are simply too infused with normativity. Human mentality and behaviour must be understood 'from within', and this involves acute observation and description, sensitive to the variety and complexity of our practices, rather than the subsumption of human behaviour under supposedly explanatory laws. While this Wittgensteinian response represents one, perhaps extreme, rejection of scientific psychology, philosophers of many different stripes would assent to parts of it.

Thus, all things considered, the relation between philosophy and psychology in the twentieth century was characterized more often by a spirit of conflict than of cooperation. Moreover, the divergence between the two fields was thoroughly institutionalized. Philosophy is often taught as a largely historical discipline, with great emphasis placed on prominent individuals and influential schools. In this, little attention is paid to the leading figures in the history of psychology (or other sciences) and even less to current psychological writings and debates. The student is typically required to master the tools of informal and formal logic, and to reflect on abstract questions in the philosophy of science, but little attention is paid to mastering the techniques of scientific reasoning and theory construction. And while philosophy graduates may be adept at identifying problems implicit in the questions psychologists ask, they are usually ignorant of the complexities involved in constructing well-considered experiments, designing psychological research projects, or interpreting empirical data in light of a developing theory.

Psychology, in contrast, is usually taught as an ahistorical discipline. The standard textbooks make only brief mention of the important figures of the past, and include virtually no discussion of philosophical concepts or methods. The emphasis is placed squarely on the specific problems studied by the various sub-branches of psychology, and on the research methods whereby theories and hypotheses can be rigorously tested. Thus psychology students become skilled at gathering and interpreting data, but not nearly so proficient at discussing the broader implications of their findings.

At least until recently, matters have been hardly more promising at the professional level. Joint conferences organized around some common theme often degenerate into polarized affairs with each camp regarding the other as an alien culture with a peculiar and opaque idiom. Philosophers tend to see rank and file psychologists as theoretically unsophisticated, blind to the conceptual issues that *really* matter; psychologists, in contrast, often tolerate philosophical speculation only for its instrumental value in the construction of experimentally testable research projects. The psychologist tells the philosopher, 'These thoughts are all well and good, but how can we operationalize them?', to which the philosopher replies, 'That you wish to "operationalize" such thoughts merely reveals the artificiality of your approach.' In short, little has come of the widespread desire for cross-fertilization between philosophy and psychology.

Fortunately, however, this unhappy circumstance is changing. In the past decade, philosophers of mind have become increasingly concerned to make their ideas gel with our best empirical theories of mental functioning. It is no longer credible to be a philosopher of mind who is uninterested in the way human minds actually work. It might be thought that this is a direct, if rather belated, effect of Quine's famous assault on the analytic/synthetic distinction. In the 1950s, Quine attacked the idea that there are 'analytic' statements true solely in virtue of the meaning of their constituents (Quine, 1953). In contrast, Quine maintained that all beliefs face 'the tribunal of experience' and belief truth may be held true 'come what may' so long as one is prepared to make radical enough alterations to the rest of one's beliefs. But if there are no analytic truths, there is no such thing as 'purely conceptual' enquiry. Thus there cannot be a division of labour between philosophers engaged in the examination of concepts and scientists who explore empirical facts. Quine therefore called for the 'naturalization' of epistemology (1969). The theory of knowledge, he argued, should be absorbed into psychology, neurophysiology and related empirical disciplines.

Quine's arguments have been enormously important, though their influence on the present scene is rather oblique. Quine himself rejected the dogma of analyticity as part of a wholesale attack on meaning and intentional states. No such phenomena, Quine argued, could have a role in a genuinely explanatory theory. There is thus a direct line from Quinean behaviourism to eliminitive materialism, the view that our everyday ways of describing and explaining mental phenomena (our 'folk psychology') are fundamentally misconceived and should be replaced by a scientific account of the mind cast in non-intentional terms. Ironically, the appearance of eliminitivism in the 1960s, and its resurgence in the 1980s in the hands of Stephen Stich (1983) and the Churchlands (Patricia Churchland, 1986; Paul Churchland, 1989), helped intensify the traditional conviction that there *is* a role for purely conceptual reflection in the philosophy of mind, for eliminitivism seems flawed precisely on the grounds that it does violence to our *concept* of the mental. Quine's arguments, however, were an important impetus for the broadly naturalistic views that now dominate the philosophical scene. In epistemology, philosophy of mind, and many other branches of their discipline, the majority of philosophers now declare themselves to be 'naturalists', and although conceptions of naturalism vary, everyone seems agreed that it requires that philosophical theories be compatible with the findings of the natural sciences. In this climate, it is unsurprising that many philosophers take an interest in what science has to say about the mind.

Though the rise of naturalism is an important contributing factor, other recent developments have also helped stimulate fruitful interplay between philosophy and psychology. First, the past 15 years have seen renewed interest in cognitive science conceived as a coherent, systematic 'interdiscipline'. This interest was the result of a number of factors, including: the development of parallel distributed processing approaches that promised effective, realistic models of the kind of complex processing that occurs in animal nervous systems; the explosion of cognitive neuroscience; the growth of primatology and the renewed interest in ape language research; advances in genetic modelling; and the influence of anthropological thinking on psycholinguistics and developmental psychology. Cognitive science began to receive significant institutional recognition, and innovative programmes have been established at a number of leading universities.

Second, and perhaps most important, work of real quality is finally being done at the interface of psychology and philosophy. One excellent example is the Project on Spatial Representation supported by King's College Research Centre, the various proceedings of which show an extraordinarily fruitful interplay between conceptual and empirical approaches to fundamental questions about the self, agency and bodily awareness (Eilan, McCarthy and Brewer, 1993; Bermudez, Marcel and Eilan, 1995). Another is the mass of interesting work on 'theory of mind' in which philosophical conceptions of mind have been brought to bear in significant ways on developmental issues about children's understanding of self and other (e.g., Astingston, 1993; Gopnik and Meltzoff, 1997). Moreover, compelling work on the borders of philosophy and psychology has been presented in highly accessible ways, such as the empirically informed philosophy of mind of Daniel Dennett (e.g., Dennett, 1991) and the philosophically rich perspective of neuroscientist Antonio Damasio (1994, 1999).

However, although there are thus grounds for optimism about the prospect of further rewarding interplay between philosophy and psychology, the old controversies about the relation of the two fields have found no satisfying theoretical resolution. Indeed, the question of the relation of the conceptual and the empirical in psychological enquiry is all the more urgent. Let us see, then, what there is to learn from Bruner's legacy.

Bruner as psychologist and as philosopher

In his psychology, Bruner has always sought a judicious balance between conceptual and empirical considerations. He appreciates very well that pictures of the mind which issue from conceptual reflection, however compelling they may seem, must be faithful to the real life of the mind, while recognizing that bold empirical theories of mind must carry conviction in light of our deeply entrenched concepts of what mind is. Let us examine some examples of Bruner at work.

Consider Bruner's contribution to the nativist–empiricist debate about language, one of the great driving forces in developmental psycholinguistics over the past generation. Chomsky first mounted his attack on the behaviourist view of language development with his famous 'poverty of the stimulus' argument. According to this rationalist credo, we can only explain how, as Stephen Pinker puts it, 'children's grammar explodes into adultlike complexity in so short a time' if we credit children with innate knowledge of all the possible forms that grammar can take (Pinker, 1994: 112). Here we have a primarily conceptual argument to the conclusion that:

> Language is not a cultural artifact that we learn the way we learn to tell time.... Instead, it is a distinct piece of the biological makeup of our brains. Language is a complex, specialized skill, which develops in the child spontaneously, without conscious effort or formal instruction, is deployed without awareness of its underlying logic, is qualitatively the same in every individual, and is distinct from more general abilities to process information or behave intelligently. (Pinker, 1994: 18)

Nativists sought to find empirical support for this position by appeal to the 'degeneracy of the data' argument,[2] various language 'universals',[3] the apparent invariance of the steps through which all children proceed in the acquisition of language, and the supposed existence of structure/ functional correlations revealed by aphasias and specific language disorders. Yet, despite the force of these considerations, opponents of nativism found them too heavily informed by the framework they were invoked to justify. Paradoxically, what made nativism the dominant force in psycholinguistics was the fact that it provoked a serious response that was sympathetic to empiricism; namely, Bruner's work in the 1960s on the growth of skills, and in the 1970s on scaffolding theory.

Scaffolding theory – the idea that effective caregivers carefully monitor and adjust the amount of support they provide as a child begins to master language (and other) practices – thus affords an excellent illustration of Bruner enriching and revising powerful conceptual arguments by sensitive empirical observation. Through careful examination of the real life of language learning, Bruner arrived at the fundamentally interactionist picture of human development which has informed all of his later work. And once supplemented by a plausible account of the reality of language learning, the nativist paradigm took on a much more human, and more plausible, look.

Bruner's interactionism was not just a happy corrective to Chomsky's formalism. It was equally relevant to Piaget's massively influential views of cognitive development. Piaget's work could hardly be accused of being insensitive to empirical considerations. Nevertheless, Bruner was quick to diagnose how Piaget's theories were in the grip of entrenched conceptual presumptions that rendered them blind to the real context of development. Bruner wrote:

> The world is a quiet place for Piaget's growing child. He is virtually alone in it, a world of objects that he must array in space, time and causal relationships. He begins his journey egocentrically and must impose properties on the world that will eventually be shared with others. But others give him little help. The social reciprocity of infant and mother plays a very small role in Piaget's account of development. And language gives neither hints nor even a means of unravelling the puzzles of the world to which language applies. Piaget's child has one overwhelming problem: to bring the inner representations of mind into equilibrium with the structures of experience. Piaget's children are little intellectuals, detached from the hurly-burly of the human condition. (1983b: 138)

Such a view of children is not only unfaithful to the real circumstances of their development; it also distorts the theoretical options open to us in portraying the child's cognitive growth. For so long as the child is seen as acquiring concepts, learning a language, or building a conception of the world, by hypothesis formation, we will feel compelled to represent the child as already endowed with the wherewithal to construct and assess those hypotheses. Thus, the kind of 'intellectualism' we see in Piaget, and which is yet more evident in Chomsky's rationalism, significantly constrains the way we can represent the potential efficacy of the child's interaction with her social environment.

Bruner's interactionism, then, provided an important alternative to Chomskian and Piagetian orthodoxies. As we noted above, Bruner's scaffolding theory was seen – and was presented by Bruner himself – as a complement to the generativist paradigm, one which promised to enhance nativism with a realistic account of how language is actually acquired. What made Bruner's approach especially distinctive was his emphasis on a Vygotskian view of linguistic socialization. The Vygotskian picture, however, has two important features. First, for a Vygotskian, language and culture cannot be conceptually separated from one another: culture is the medium of language and language the vehicle of culture. Second, Vygotsky rejects the idea that the child's cognitive development proceeds through hypothesis formation. Many constituents of the child's intellectual powers are absorbed or appropriated from the culture rather than 'deduced' by the child through some form of ratiocination. These themes are not especially prominent in Bruner's early uses of Vygotsky, but they become increasingly evident in Bruner's most mature writings. It is for this reason, among others, that several contributors to this volume suggest that Bruner's efforts to complement Chomskian conceptions in fact undermine them. By teaching us to attend to the complex interactional factors involved in children's linguistic enculturation, Bruner reveals insurmountable weaknesses in nativist conceptions of language acquisition and in the whole generativist framework.

An excellent example of Bruner deploying primarily conceptual arguments against a scientific paradigm is found in the opening chapter of *Acts of Meaning* (1990), where Bruner targets the legacy of the cognitive revolution. As we noted above, Bruner argues that the cognitive revolutionaries – himself among them – aspired to oust the prevailing behaviourist orthodoxy by placing the concept of meaning at the centre of psychology. Their aim was

> to discover and to describe formally the meanings that human beings created out of their encounters with the world, and then to propose hypotheses about what meaning-making processes were implicated. [The cognitive revolution] focused upon the symbolic activities that human beings employed in constructing and making sense not only of the world, but of themselves. Its aim was to prompt psychology to join forces with its sister interpretative disciplines in the humanities and in the social sciences. (Bruner, 1990: 2)

But this noble project was undermined as cognitive psychologists became obsessed with computational models of the mind. Behaviourist talk of 'stimulus' and 'response' was succeeded by the equally one-dimensional view of minds as 'information processors'. And, in time, the behaviourists' yearning to replace our ordinary psychological vocabulary with a scientifically respectable language resurfaced in eliminativist critiques of folk psychology.

Bruner concludes that cognitivism is fraught with the same dehumanizing scientism as the behaviourism it aspired to destroy. Meaning is not a by-product of formal processing, but something 'made' or 'constructed' by real, embodied people, situated in a shared culture. Thus, psychology cannot concern itself simply with what goes on in the heads of individuals:

> It is man's participation in culture and the realization of his mental powers through culture that make it impossible to construct a human psychology on the basis of the individual alone.... To treat the world as an indifferent flow of information to be processed by individuals each on his or her own terms is to lose sight of how individuals are formed and how they function. (Bruner, 1990: 12)

We must therefore aspire to understand mind and self as aspects of a social world, which is neither an 'aboriginal reality' nor a projection of individual minds, but something essentially 'transactional'. Thus, Bruner rests his argument for cultural psychology on fundamentally conceptual premisses. A plausible psychology must respect our concepts of mind and meaning and the whole folk psychological idiom which human beings use to interpret their behaviour. Only then will it be possible for psychology to understand the life of the mind.

Our examples illustrate Bruner's adeptness with both empirical and conceptual arguments. But it is not just that Bruner appreciates the need to strike an appropriate balance between, as it were, speculation and observation. More than this, his work shows the artificiality of the very distinction between 'philosophical' and 'psychological' approaches to the study of the mind. Indeed, Bruner's attitude affirms Piaget's conviction that there really is 'no sharp division between scientific and philosophical problems' (Piaget, 1965: 18), for Bruner has always been guided by the idea that the study of the mind demands a *unity* of, on the one hand, conceptual enquiry sensitive to empirical findings and, on the other, empirical enquiry informed by constructive speculation about its conceptual orientation and foundations.

In both our examples, Bruner attacks individualist and formalist approaches to language and mind and advances a vision of psychology as a human science which pays due attention to the cultural context of our mental lives. It is important, however, that Bruner does not dismiss the idea of scientific psychology. He writes:

> I would like to urge an end to the kind of 'either-or' approach to the question of what psychology should be in the future, whether it should be entirely biological, exclusively computational, or monopolistically cultural. (1996: 160)

Bruner sees himself as enriching, supplementing and correcting the aspirations of scientific psychology, rather than as rejecting his opponents' approaches outright. He remains an advocate of cognitive science, just so long as it employs methods appropriate to its subject. Cultural psychology is thus not at odds with scientific psychology. On the contrary, Bruner concludes *The Culture of Education* with the words:

> The dilemma in the study of man is to grasp not only the causal principles of his biology and his evolution, but to understand these in light of the interpretive processes involved in meaning making. To brush aside the biological constraints on human functioning is to commit hubris. To sneer at the power of

culture to shape man's mind and to abandon our efforts to bring this power under human control is to commit moral suicide. A well-wrought psychology can help us avoid both these disasters. (1996: 184–5)

Reconciliation or (counter)-revolution?

An advocate of cognitive science might complain that Bruner's reconciliatory tone is disingenuous. After all, the whole point of *Acts of Meaning* is to assert a distinction between causal and interpretative modes of explanation and to argue for the autonomy of the latter. It follows that, for example, causal accounts of brain functioning may help explain the preconditions of mind, but brain processes are enabling conditions of our mental life, they do not constitute it. The account of what constitutes our mental life must be interpretative-hermeneutical rather than causal. Thus Bruner sets severe a priori constraints on what scientific psychology can be.

Bruner would no doubt resist this description of his approach. The distinction between interpretative-hermeneutical and causal-explanatory modes of thought has a long pedigree. Bruner is fond of citing Dilthey's division between *Natur-* and *Geisteswissenschaften,* but the origins of the distinction lie in Kant's contrast between the causal and the rational – the realms of necessity and of spontaneity. Many modern thinkers embrace the distinction in one form or another. Indeed, it is widely recognized that the criteria we use to ascribe intentional states to subjects are very different in kind from those we deploy when determining the properties of physical objects and events, and hence that our mentalistic and physicalistic forms of talk represent two distinct, and in a sense incommensurable, modes of description and explanation. When we use the former, we are involved in making sense – or interpreting – the behaviour of subjects according to norms of rationality (we figure out what someone believes by asking what it would *make sense* for them to hold true in light of what we suppose them already to believe, etc.); while deploying the latter, we explain material goings-on by subsuming them under physical laws. This is almost a commonplace in contemporary philosophy of mind, accepted both by proponents of scientific psychology and by its detractors. It is not, after all, that the interpretative mode is 'primary', for which discourse is superior depends on what it is one seeks to explain. If you want to know how a steam engine functions, or how global warming is related to climate change, you had best deploy scientific modes of explanation. If you seek to understand why your friend suspects her husband of infidelity, or why Raskolnikov committed murder, you had best deploy the interpretative mode. Such a position – which is so widely accepted – can hardly be portrayed as an a prioristic assault on scientific psychology!

Bruner's critic would not be satisfied with this response. First, the distinction is often invoked to rule out the idea that a scientific psychology can cast its explanations in terms of the states and properties that figure in our folk psychology. Yet Bruner is resolute that folk psychology is ineliminable. Second, there is a sense in which Bruner, despite his protestations, does privilege the interpretative mode of thought. The idea that the appropriateness of a mode of explanation depends on what one seeks to explain is quite compatible with the view that certain modes of explanation are more fundamental than others. Some modes of thought, it might be argued, get at 'things as they really are'. So naturalists who deploy the distinction between causal and mentalistic modes of explanation usually start from the idea that the causal-explanatory strategies of science reveal to us the world as it is. Daniel Dennett, for example, accords the deliverances of science ontological supremacy and asks how we can accommodate mental phenomena within the world as science portrays it. Our psychological modes of talk are represented as essentially (folk-) theoretical devices for explaining and predicting the behaviour of biological (and hence ultimately physical) systems, and the states psychological talk invokes are considered to be abstractions or posits rather than 'real' entities. On such a view, the interpretative mode figures in a story about the construction of the mental, and the mental must be a construct, since, given Dennett's physicalistic starting point, nothing like mind, as we typically understand it, could be straightforwardly part of nature.

In contrast, some thinkers treat the interpretative mode as paramount. They argue that science itself must be seen as a mode of interpretation; as one among the modes in which rational beings make sense of their world. The deliverances of the scientific conception, however compelling, cannot undermine our confidence in the reality of mental phenomena and intentionalistic modes of explanation, for the very power of scientific conceptions is, after all, a matter of how certain sorts of explanations meet certain norms of enquiry in a way that makes them rationally compelling. We must not forget that the scientific conception of the world is a product of our mental powers. Science doesn't give us the world; it gives us compelling representations of reality. Thus, the point of view from which explanations are cast is an ineliminable dimension of scientific enquiry. It cannot be that the deliverances of science render the mental so problematic that we are reduced to 'finding a place' for mind within nature by portraying it as *merely* a mode of interpreting or describing certain physical systems. To think that way is to focus on the results of scientific enquiry while forgetting its presuppositions.

Bruner is undoubtedly a thinker of the second kind. His point of departure is the perspective of intelligence rather than conceptions of nature. This is why, Bruner's critic will conclude, he has no hesitation in invoking conceptual arguments to keep scientific psychology in its place, for he is wedded to the idea that psychology must respect deeply entrenched elements in our conception of ourselves. But if this is a desideratum of cultural psychology, it must be an obstacle to reconciliation with a full-bloodedly naturalistic cognitive science.

We might also observe that Bruner's emphasis on reconciliation is also unlikely to impress those who welcome cultural psychology as a powerful stand against scientism. Indeed, several of the contributors to this volume argue that Bruner is too quick to portray his position as a modification of, or supplement to, mainstream cognitive science. His spirit of compromise blinds him to the really radical consequences of his own position, which is built upon premises that entail, not a return to the original ethos of the cognitive revolution, but its outright rejection. This kind of criticism is a theme in the chapters by Geertz, Harré, Shotter and Taylor, among others. Though these authors offer very different suggestions about the form 'post-cognitive' psychology should take, they share the conviction that Bruner's insights expose conceptual confusions at the very heart of cognitive science as it is usually conceived.

So, Bruner's attempts at reconciliation threaten to satisfy no one. While some see him as wielding a priori arguments to restrain empirical enquiry, others accuse him of not taking those arguments far enough to initiate a really radical alternative to the entrenched orthodoxies.

Style and substance in Bruner's thought

Is this a fair assessment? And if it is, where does that leave our claim that Bruner's work contains a subtle and sophisticated interplay of conceptual and empirical strategies? There is no doubt that in Bruner's hands the division between causal-explanatory and interpretative-hermeneutical forms of thought threatens to belie his aspiration to reconcile cultural psychology and cognitive science. For if there is a basic distinction between how we explain physical goings-on and how we interpret human behaviour, psychology will always be internally divided. The explanation of the causal processes that underlie human mentality will proceed in ways that are fundamentally incommensurable with our interpretative strategies for the explanation of intelligent behaviour.

Does this set Bruner irreconcilably at odds with contemporary natural-ism? Certainly, Bruner's position conflicts with the idea that all that is natural can be explained by appeal to causal laws. He must advance a broader conception of the natural which encompasses the 'second nature' we acquire through the appropriation of culture, and which can only be understood by interpretative means (cf. McDowell, 1994: chs 4–5). But this, it seems to us, is a strength of his position rather than a weakness.

However, what is wrong with the objection developed in the last section is that it implies that Bruner's vision of cultural psychology rests on dogmatic a priorism. It is vital to appreciate that Bruner's distinction between modes of thought does not figure as an a priori truth established antecedent to empirical enquiry, but as a conceptual commitment that emerges precisely in confrontation with the facts.

This is best illustrated not by the letter of Bruner's psychology, but by its style. Consider his contribution to a symposium on 'theory of mind' which appeared in the journal *Human Development* (Bruner, 1995 (reprinted in Bruner, 1996: ch. 5)). In the lead paper, Janet Astington and

David Olson (the latter a contributor to this volume) argue that research on children's developing theories of mind offers the opportunity to integrate causal and hermeneutical approaches in a single naturalistic account. They grant that the ability to describe and explain behaviour in psychological terms involves hermeneutical skills of interpretation. That ability, however, is premissed upon the possession of concepts and other cognitive resources, the development of which proceeds through identifiable stages which can be traced by empirical enquiry and explained causally. Hence, 'theory of mind' promises to capture the acquisition and elaboration of meaning making in the causal-explanatory net (Astington and Olson, 1995).

It is instructive to consider Bruner's response to this argument. Rather than trying to undermine Astington and Olson's ambitions on the grounds, say, that they misconstrue the conceptual distinction between explanation and interpretation, he adopts a distinctly particularist approach. He concedes that the circumstances in which children learn to deploy mentalistic notions are open to empirical scrutiny in which testable hypotheses can be subjected to experimental verification. But, he argues, this hardly constitutes a synthesis of causal and interpretative approaches. First, it is not clear that the explanation of the development of the child's theory of mind is straightforwardly causal, for the subjectivity of others figures as a crucial precondition of that development. Development is possible precisely because the infant is treated by others as a minded, self-conscious being, even when she lacks a conception of mind in the full sense. Even if this process exhibits regularities that can be codified, it is unlikely that we can see the efficacy of the subjectivity of others in causal terms. Moreover, to give a causal explanation of the origin of a capacity is not to give a causal account of the capacity itself. A causal explanation of what must be in place for a child to 'mind read' is not a causal account of what constitutes 'mind reading'. It is one thing to have an explanation of the enabling conditions of a certain capacity, another to have a constitutive account of the capacity itself. The hermeneutical character of the latter remains undiminished by the availability of a causal account of the former. Finally, Bruner remarks that we should not be too confident that we really know what 'thought' is. We speak as if our 'folk psychology' was a theory designed to get at discrete, yet unobservable, mental entities that exist independently of our modes of description and understanding. But, in fact, the terms of this folk theory refer to entities that cannot be understood without essential reference to the character of our psychological discourse as a whole, to the cultural context of its use and the perspective of those who use it. That is to say, the very terms in which we propose to base this putatively causal account have a life only within our practices of interpretation and meta-interpretation.

Such considerations bring Bruner to the familiar point that the causal-explanatory and the interpretative-hermeneutical are two incommensurable modes of knowledge. It is crucial, however, that the distinction emerges as the *conclusion* of sustained reflection upon empirical considerations and conceptual connections. It sometimes happens that, when we examine the facts (in light of our best conceptions), we feel that we have no option but to embrace certain deep truths, that there is simply *nothing else to think*. The distinction between Bruner's two modes of thought issues from a judgement of this kind. It is dictated by the object of enquiry, though Bruner recognizes, of course, that our conception of the object is influenced by our present culture of enquiry and that even our entrenched conceptual distinctions are mutable, for circumstances we do not now envisage may change our perspective in unanticipated ways. Bruner, to his credit, remains an out and out fallibilist.

Thus, Bruner's cultural psychology is not premissed on an 'in principle' distinction between the two modes of thought. The force of the distinction is not metaphysical. Of course, Bruner has always been a conceptually oriented psychologist. What captures his imagination most are compelling representations of the mind, or, perhaps better, of the human condition. He evidently enjoys speculative reflection in the best sense of the term, and this attracts him to philosophy, literary theory, cultural criticism and other fields. And, as time has gone on, his interest in empirical research has been largely for the theoretical pictures that it yields. But Bruner has never ceased to recognize that all theoretical pictures of the mind must have empirical content. After all, mind is a real presence in the world. There is a way things are for minded beings which we can only find out by *encountering* minds. Matters are complicated, of course, by the essential reflexivity of psychological enquiry. We engage with minds in a way in which we do not engage with other objects. Moreover, the nature of mind is a consequence, at least in part, of how mind is conceptualized. For Bruner, mind is not a substantial presence, but an artefact of our self-understanding, and for the theoretical pictures we paint in psychology to carry conviction, we must be able to recognize ourselves in them. In psychology, the mind seeks to understand itself. It is this, rather than some reactionary conception of a priori 'analysis', that gives speculative, conceptual enquiry a vital role in any genuine psychology.

Conclusion: Bruner the pragmatist

We have argued that in the manner of his psychological thinking, Bruner provides a model of the harmonious interplay of conceptual and empirical strategies of enquiry. Bruner is all too aware that conceptual reflection cannot yield an ordnance survey map of platonic heaven, just as empirical research does not read the book of nature. No scientific theory can render itself immune from conceptual refutation and no conceptual speculation can avoid the threat of changing intuitions. We are left to tack back and forth, as judiciously as we can, between sensitive empirical observation and careful reflection on the concepts we deploy in making sense of what we observe.

This feature of Bruner's style situates him centrally within the tradition of American pragmatism, the pragmatism of Peirce, James, and especially Dewey. And like his predecessors, Bruner's guiding light is *practice*. What keeps Bruner's psychology down-to-earth is not so much the promise of testing his theories by experimental means, but the intention that his views will inspire creative educational policies, more refined self-awareness and better ways of living. This is the ultimate court in which theoretical conceptions, whether they issue from empirical generalization or armchair speculation, face the tribunal of experience. This erudite, practice-oriented fallibilism, combined with infectious enthusiasm for learning and unflagging epistemological optimism is very much Bruner's way with ideas. It is the core of his engagingly humanistic approach to psychology, an approach which is, at the same time, ebullient, fun and profoundly moral. It is a towering example to all who study the life of the mind.

Notes

1 A *Festschrift* for Bruner already exists: Olson, 1980.
2 According to this argument, the empiricist contention that children learn linguistic structure from their caregivers is belied by the fact that the language to which a child is exposed is full of grammatically incorrect sentences, slips of the tongue, incomplete sentences, slang, metaphors and homonyms.
3 For example, every human race has language, every human being (except those with brain damage) who has a normal exposure to language acquires language regardless of IQ or other variables, and all languages are putatively built upon the same principles (e.g., 'structure-dependence').

References

Amsterdam, A. and Bruner, J.S. (2000) *Minding the Law*. Cambridge, MA: Harvard University Press.

Astington, J.W. (1993) *The Child's Discovery of the World*. Cambridge, MA: Harvard University Press.

Astington, J.W. and Olson, D.R. (1995) 'The cognitive revolution in children's understanding of mind', *Human Development*, 38: 179–89.

Bermudez, J.L., Marcel, A. and Eilan, N. (eds) (1995) *The Body and the Self*. Cambridge, MA: MIT Press.

Bruner, J.S. (1960) *The Process of Education*. Cambridge, MA: Harvard University Press.

Bruner, J.S. (1966) *Toward a Theory of Instruction*. Cambridge, MA: Harvard University Press.

Bruner, J.S. (1979) *On Knowing: Essays for the Left Hand*. Expanded edition. Cambridge, MA: Harvard University Press.

Bruner, J.S. (1983a) *Child's Talk: Learning to Use Language*. Oxford: Oxford University Press.

Bruner, J.S. (1983b) *In Search of Mind: Essays in Autobiography*. New York: Harper & Row.

Bruner, J.S. (1986) *Actual Minds, Possible Worlds*. Cambridge, MA: Harvard University Press.

Bruner, J.S. (1990) *Acts of Meaning*. Cambridge, MA: Harvard University Press.

Bruner, J.S. (1995) 'Commentary' (on Astington and Olson's 'The cognitive revolution in children's understanding of mind'), *Human Development*, 38: 203–13.

Bruner, J.S. (1996) *The Culture of Education*. Cambridge, MA: Harvard University Press.

Churchland, Patricia (1986) *Neurophilosophy: Toward a Unified Science of the Mind–Brain*. Cambridge, MA: MIT Press.

Churchland, Paul (1989) *A Neurocomputational Perspective: The Nature of Mind and the Structure of Science*. Cambridge, MA: MIT Press.

Cole, M. (1996) *Cultural Psychology: A Once and Future Discipline*. Cambridge, MA: Harvard University Press.

Damasio, A. (1994) *Descartes' Error: Emotion, Reason, and the Human Brain*. New York: Putnam.

Damasio, A. (1999) *The Feeling of What Happens: Body and Emotion in the Making of Consciousness*. New York: Harcourt Brace & Company.

Dennett, D. (1991) *Consciousness Explained*. Boston, MA: Little, Brown.

Donald, M. (1991) *Origins of the Modern Mind: Three Stages in the Evolution of Culture and Cognition*. Cambridge, MA: Harvard University Press.

Edwards, D. and Potter, J. (1992) *Discursive Psychology*. London: Sage.

Eilan, N., McCarthy, R. and Brewer, B. (eds) (1993) *Spatial Representation: Problems in Philosophy and Psychology*. Oxford: Blackwell.

Fancher, R. (1979) *Pioneers of Psychology*. New York: Norton.

Gardner, H. (1985) *The Mind's New Science: A History of the Cognitive Revolution*. New York: Basic Books.

Gergen, K. (1999) *An Invitation to Social Construction*. London: Sage.

Gopnik, A. and Meltzoff, A.N. (1997) *Words, Thoughts, and Theories*. Cambridge, MA: MIT Press.

Harré, R. and Gillett, G. (1994) *The Discursive Mind*. London: Sage.

Locke, J. (1979 [1689]) *An Essay Concerning Human Understanding*, ed. P.H. Nidditch. Oxford: Clarendon Press.

McDowell, J. (1994) *Mind and World*. Cambridge, MA: Harvard University Press.

Olson, D. (ed.) (1980) *The Social Foundations of Language and Thought: Essays in Honor of Jerome S. Bruner*. New York: Norton.

Piaget, J. (1965) *Insights and Illusions*. W. Mays (trans.), London: Routledge & Kegan Paul.

Pinker, S. (1994) *The Language Instinct: The New Science of Language and Mind*. London: Allen Lane, Penguin.

Quine, W.V.O. (1953) 'Two dogmas of empiricism', in his *From a Logical Point of View*. Cambridge, MA: Harvard University Press.

Quine, W.V.O. (1969) 'Epistemology naturalized', in his *Ontological Relativity and Other Essays*. New York: Columbia University Press.

Shweder, R.A. (1990) 'Cultural psychology – what is it?', in J.W. Stigler, R.A. Shweder and G. Herdt (eds), *Cultural Psychology: Essays on Comparative Human Development*. Cambridge: Cambridge University Press.

Stich, S.P. (1983) *From Folk Psychology to Cognitive Science*. Cambridge, MA: MIT Press.

1

IMBALANCING ACT: JEROME BRUNER'S CULTURAL PSYCHOLOGY

Clifford Geertz

Rethinking the cognitive revolution

What does one say when one says 'psychology'? James, Wundt, Binet or Pavlov? Freud, Lashley, Skinner or Vygotsky? Kohler, Lewin, Lévy-Bruhl, Bateson? Chomsky or Piaget? Daniel Dennett or Oliver Sacks? Herbert Simon? Since it was truly launched as a discipline and a profession in the last half of the nineteenth century, mainly by Germans, the self-proclaimed 'science of the mind' has not just been troubled with a proliferation of theories, methods, arguments and techniques. That was only to be expected. It has also been driven in wildly different directions by wildly different notions as to what it is, as we say, 'about' – what sort of knowledge, of what sort of reality, to what sort of end it is supposed to produce. From the outside, at least, it does not look like a single field, divided into schools and specialities in the usual way. It looks like an assortment of disparate and disconnected enquiries classed together because they all make reference in some way or other to something or other called 'mental functioning'. Dozens of characters in search of a play.

From inside it doubtless looks a bit more ordered, if only because of the byzantine academic structure that has grown up around it (the American Psychological Association has 49 divisions), but surely no less miscellaneous. The wide swings between behaviourist, psychometric, cognitivist, depth-psychological, topological, developmentalist, neurological, evolutionist and culturalist conceptions of the subject have made being a psychologist an unsettled occupation, subject not only to fashion, as are all the human sciences, but to sudden and frequent reversals of course. Paradigms, wholly new ways of going about things, come along not by the century, but by the decade; sometimes, it almost seems, by the month. It takes either a preternaturally focused, dogmatic individual, who can shut out any ideas but his or her own, or a mercurial, hopelessly inquisitive one, who can keep dozens of them in play at once, to remain upright amidst this tumble of programmes, promises and proclamations.

There are, in psychology, a great many more of the resolved and implacable, *esprit de système* types (Pavlov, Freud, Skinner, Piaget, Chomsky), than there are of the agile and adaptable, *esprit de finesse* ones (James, Bateson, Sacks). But it is among the latter that Jerome Bruner clearly belongs. In a breathless, lurching, yet somehow deeply consecutive career spanning nearly 60 years, Bruner has brushed against almost every line of thought in psychology and transformed a number of them.

That career began at Harvard in the 1940s, during the heyday of behaviourism, rat-running, the repetition of nonsense syllables, the discrimination of sensory differences, and the measurement of galvanic responses. But, dissatisfied with the piling up of experimental 'findings' on peripheral matters (his first professional study involved conditioning 'helplessness' in a rat imprisoned on an electrified grill), he quickly joined a growing band of equally restless colleagues, within psychology and without, to become one of the leaders of the so-called 'cognitive revolution'.

By the late 1950s, this revolution was underway, and 'bringing the mind back in' became the battle cry for a whole generation of psychologists, linguists, brain modellers, ethnologists and computer scientists, as well as a few empirically minded philosophers. For them, the primary objects of study were not stimulus strengths and response patterns, but mental actions – attending, thinking, understanding, imagining, remembering, feeling, knowing. With a like-minded colleague, Leo Postman, Bruner launched a famous series of 'New Look' perception experiments to demonstrate the power of mental selectivity in seeing, hearing and recognizing something. Poorer children see the same coin as larger than richer ones do; college students are either very much slower ('defensive') or very much quicker ('vigilant') to recognize threatening words than they are to recognize unthreatening ones. With two of his students, he carried out a landmark study of abstract reasoning. How do people, in fact rather than in logic, test their hypotheses? How do they decide what is relevant to explanation and what is not? And in 1960, he and the psycholinguist George Miller, another restless soul, founded Harvard's interdisciplinary Center for Cognitive Studies, through which virtually all of the leading figures in the field, established or in the making, passed and which set off an explosion of similar centres and similar work both in the US and abroad. 'We certainly generated a point of view, even a fad or two', Bruner wrote of his and his colleagues' work during this period in his (as it turns out, premature) autobiography, *In Search of Mind*. 'About ideas, how can one tell?' (1983: 126).

After a while, Bruner himself became disenchanted with the cognitive revolution, or at least with what it had become. At the beginning of his 'goodbye to all that' proclamation of a new direction, *Acts of Meaning*, Bruner writes:

That revolution was intended to bring 'mind' back into the human sciences after a long cold winter of objectivism.... [But it] has now been diverted into issues that are marginal to the impulse that brought it into being. Indeed, it has been technicalized in a manner that even undermines that original impulse. This is not to say that it has failed: far from it, for cognitive science must surely be among the leading growth shares on the academic bourse. It may rather be that it has become diverted by success, a success whose technological virtuosity has cost dear. Some critics ... even argue that the new cognitive science, the child of the revolution, has gained its technical successes at the price of dehumanizing the very concept of mind it had sought to reestablish in psychology, and that it has thereby estranged much of psychology from the other human sciences and the humanities. (1990: 1)

In saving the cognitive revolution from itself, distancing it from high-tech reductionism (brain is hardware, mind is software, thinking is the software processing information on the hardware), Bruner has raised, over the past decade or so, yet another banner heralding yet another dispensation: 'cultural psychology'. What now comes to the centre of attention is the individual's engagement with established systems of shared meaning, with the beliefs, the values, and the understandings of those already in place in society as he or she is thrown in amongst them. For Bruner, the critical 'test frame' for this point of view is education – the field of practices within which such engagement is, in the first instance, effected. Rather than a psychology that sees the mind as a programmable mechanism, we need one that sees it as a social achievement. Education

is not simply a technical business of well-managed information processing, nor even simply a matter of applying 'learning theories' to the classroom or using the results of subject-centered 'achievement testing'. It is a complex pursuit of fitting a culture to the needs of its members and their ways of knowing to the needs of the culture. (Bruner, 1996: 43)

Bringing the mind into focus

Bruner's concern with education and educational policy dates from the studies of mental development in infants and very young children that, in his growing resistance to machine cognitivism, he began to carry out in the mid-1960s, just – such are the workings of the *Zeitgeist* – as the Head Start programme was coming grandly into being. These studies led him to an 'outside-in' view of such development, one which concerns itself with 'the kind of world needed to make it possible to use mind (or heart!) effectively – what kinds of symbol systems, what kinds of accounts of the past, what arts and sciences ...' (Bruner, 1996: 9). The unfolding of the critical features of human thinking, joint attention with others to objects and actions, attribution of beliefs, desires and emotions to others, grasping the general significance of situations, a sense of selfhood – what Bruner calls 'the entry into meaning' – begins very early in the development process, prior not just to formal schooling but to walking and the acquisition of language:

Infants, it turned out, were much smarter, more cognitively proactive rather than reactive, more attentive to the immediate social world around them, than had been previously suspected. They emphatically did not inhabit a world of 'buzzing, blooming confusion': they seemed to be in search of predictive stability from the very start. (Bruner, 1996: 71–2)

The Head Start programme began with a rather different – in some ways complementary, in others contrastive – view of early development based on a rather different set of scientific investigations: those showing that laboratory animals raised in 'impoverished environments', ones with few challenges and reduced stimulation, did less well than 'normals' on such standard learning and problem-solving tasks as maze-running and food-finding. Transferred, more metaphorically than experimentally, to schooling and to schoolchildren, this led to the so-called 'cultural deprivation hypothesis'. Children raised in an 'impoverished' cultural environment, in the ghetto or wherever, would, for that reason, do less well in school. Hence the need for corrective action to enrich their environment early on, before the damage was done. Hence Head Start.

Aside from the fact that correcting for 'cultural deprivation' depends on knowing what such deprivation consists of (what it has most often been taken to consist of is departure from the standards of an idealized, middle-class, 'Ozzie and Harriet' American culture), such an approach seems to assume that 'cultural enrichment' is a good to be provided to the deprived child by the wider society, like a hot lunch or a smallpox injection. The child is seen to be lacking something, not seeking something; regarded as receiving culture from elsewhere, not as constructing it *in situ* out of the materials and interactions immediately to hand. Bruner was a sometime adviser to Head Start, and he is still a defender of its very real successes and its possibilities for extension and reform (it is, after all, an 'outside-in' programme). But he argues that the results of his sort of research into the mental development of children – grown by now into a field in itself, turning up more and more evidence of the conceptual powers of children – renders the 'deprivation' approach obsolete. Seeing even the infant and the preschooler as active agents bent on mastery of a particular form of life, on developing a workable way of being in the world, demands a rethinking of the entire educational process. It is not so much a matter of providing something the child lacks, as enabling something the child already has: the desire to make sense of self and others, the drive to understand what the devil is going on.

For Bruner, the critical enabling factor, the thing that brings the mind to focus, is culture – 'the way of life and thought that we construct, negotiate, institutionalize, and finally (after it is all settled) end up calling "reality" to comfort ourselves' (1996: 87). Any theory of education that hopes to reform it, and there hardly is any other kind, needs to train its attention on the social production of meaning. The terms upon which society and child – the 'reality' already there and the scuttling intellect thrust bodily into it – engage one another are in good part worked out in the classroom, or at least they are in our school-conscious society. It is there that mentality is most deliberately fashioned, subjectivity most systematically produced, and intersubjectivity – the ability to 'read other minds' – most carefully nurtured. In the favourable case, not perhaps entirely common, the child, 'seen as an epistemologist as well as a learner', moves into an ongoing community of discoursing adults and chattering children where 'she ... gradually comes to appreciate that she is acting not directly *on* "the world" but on beliefs she holds *about* that world' (1996: 57, 49).

This turn towards concern with the ways in which the understandings abroad in the larger society are used by the schoolchild to find her feet, to build up an inner sense of who she is, what others are up to, what is likely to happen, what can be done about things, opens Bruner's 'cultural psychology' to a host of issues normally addressed by other disciplines – history, literature, law, philosophy, linguistics, and especially that other hopelessly miscellaneous and inconstant science, anthropology. Such a psychology, rather like anthropology, has an eclectic perspective and a vast ambition built directly into it. It seems to take all experience for its object, to draw on all scholarship for its means. With so many doors to open, and so many keys with which to open them, it would be folly to try to open all of them at once – that way lies knowing less and less about more and more. Sensitive as always to the practicalities of research, the door Bruner wants to open (not altogether surprisingly, given recent developments in 'discourse theory', 'speech-act analysis', 'the interpretation of cultures', and 'the hermeneutics of everyday life') is *narrative*.

Telling stories, about ourselves and about others, to ourselves and to others, is 'the most natural and the earliest way in which we organize our experience and our knowledge' (Bruner, 1996: 121). But you would hardly know it from standard educational theory, trained as it is upon tests and recipes:

> It has been the convention of most schools to treat the art of narrative – song, drama, fiction, theater, whatever – as more 'decoration' than necessity, as something with which to grace leisure, sometimes even as something morally exemplary. Despite that, we frame the accounts of our cultural origins and our most cherished beliefs in story form, and it is not just the 'content' of these stories that grip us, but their narrative artifice. Our immediate experience, what happened yesterday or the day before, is framed in the same storied way. Even more striking, we represent our lives (to ourselves as well as to others) in the form of narrative. It is not surprising that psychoanalysts now recognize that personhood implicates narrative, 'neurosis' being a reflection of either an insufficient, incomplete, or inappropriate story about oneself. Recall that when Peter Pan asks Wendy to return to Never Never Land with him, he gives as his reason that she could teach the Lost Boys there how to tell stories. If they knew how to tell them, the Lost Boys might be able to grow up. (Bruner, 1996: 40)

Growing up among narratives – one's own, those of teachers, schoolmates, parents, janitors, and various other sorts of what Saul Bellow once mordantly referred to as 'reality instructors' – is the essential scene of education. 'We live in a sea of stories', as Bruner puts it (1996: 147). Learning how to swim in such a sea, how to construct, understand, classify, check out, see through and use stories to find out how things work or what they come to, is what the school, and beyond the school the whole 'culture of education', is, at base, all about. The heart of the matter, what the learner learns whatever the teacher teaches, is 'that human beings make sense of the world by telling stories about it – by using the narrative mode for construing reality' (Bruner, 1996: 130). Tales are tools, 'instrument[s] of mind on behalf of meaning making' (1996: 41).

Constructing a cultural psychology

Bruner's most recent work is, then, dedicated to tracing the implications of this view of narrative as 'both a mode of thought and an expression of a culture's world view' (Bruner, 1996: xiv). He has launched enquiries into the teaching of science, into 'folk pedagogy', into the collaborative nature of learning, and into the child's construction of 'a theory of mind' to explain and understand other minds. Autism as the inability to develop such a theory of mind, the formal features of narrative, culture as praxis, and the respective approaches to education of Vygotsky, Piaget and Pierre Bourdieu (all related to Bruner's own, but also in tension with it), have all been discussed, at least in passing. So have recent developments in primatology, cross-cultural studies of education, IQ testing, 'metacognition' ('thinking about one's thinking'), relativism and the uses of neurology. It is all rather on the wing; a wondrous lot goes by wondrously fast.

This is not so serious a fault, if it is a fault at all, in what is still a series of forays designed to open up a territory rather than to chart and settle it. But it does leave even the sympathetic critic at a bit of a loss as to where it is all going, what 'cultural psychology' amounts to as a field among fields, a continuing enterprise with a budget of issues and an agenda for confronting them. One can, of course, get something of a sense of this by consulting Bruner's dozens upon dozens of technical investigations or by hunting down his even more numerous citations to studies by colleagues.

But since most of this 'literature', wrapped in statistics and enfolded in protocols, is scattered through professional journals and disciplinary symposia, few besides specialists are likely to find the patience for such a task. Genuine treatises, more summary, and thus more accessible, synthesizing works, authored by students, co-workers and followers of Bruner, are beginning to appear in increasing numbers, from which one can get a somewhat clearer picture of where the whole enterprise is at the moment and what progress it is making.[1] And in the final section of his most recent book, a section called, with uncertain surety, 'Psychology's Next Chapter', Bruner himself undertakes to lay out the directions in which cultural psychology should move and to describe how it should relate itself to other approaches to 'the study of mind'. As usual, his attitude is conciliatory, eclectic, energetic, upbeat:

Can a cultural psychology ... simply stand apart from the kind of biologically rooted, individually oriented, laboratory dominated psychology that we have known in the past? Must the more situated study of mind-in-culture, more interpretively anthropological in spirit, jettison all that we have learned before? Some writers ... propose that our past was a mistake, a misunderstanding of what psychology is about.... [But] I would like to urge an end to [an] 'either-or' approach to the question of what psychology should be in the future, whether it should be entirely biological, exclusively computational, or monopolistically cultural. (Bruner, 1996: 160)

He wants to show how

psychology can, by devoting its attention to certain critical topics ... illustrate the interaction of biological, evolutionary, individual psychological, and cultural insights in helping us grasp the nature of human mental functioning. [The] 'next chapter' in psychology [will be] about 'intersubjectivity' – how people come to know what others have in mind and how they adjust accordingly ... a set of topics ... central to any viable conception of a cultural psychology. But it cannot be understood without reference to primate evolution, to neural functioning, and to the processing capacities of minds. (Bruner, 1996: 161)

This is all very well, the sort of balanced and reasonable approach that softens contrasts, disarms enemies, skirts difficulties and finesses hard decisions. But there remains the sense that Bruner is underestimating the explosiveness of his own ideas. To argue that culture is socially and historically constructed, that narrative is a primary (in humans perhaps *the* primary) mode of knowing, that we assemble our 'selves' out of materials lying about in the society around us and develop 'a theory of mind' to comprehend the selves of others, that we act not directly on the world but on beliefs we hold about the world, that from birth on we are all active, impassioned 'meaning makers' in search of plausible stories, and that 'mind cannot in any sense be regarded as "natural" or naked, with culture thought of as an add-on' – such a view amounts to rather more than a mid-course correction (Bruner, 1996: 171). Taken all in all, it amounts to adopting a position that can fairly be called radical, not to say subversive. It seems very doubtful that such views and others connected with them – perspectivism, instrumentalism, contextualism, anti-reductionism – can be absorbed into the ongoing traditions of psychological research (or indeed into the human sciences generally) without causing a fair amount of noise and upheaval. If 'cultural psychology' does gain ascendancy, or even serious market share, it will disturb a lot more than pedagogy.

For it is in fact the case that not only is cultural psychology evolving rapidly, gathering force and amassing evidence, but so as well are its two most important rivals, or anyway alternatives – information processing cognitivism and neurobiological reductionism. The introduction into cognitivism of distributive parallel processing (which Bruner dismisses at one point as but a 'veiled version' of behaviourist associationism) and computer-mediated experimentalism has given it something of a second wind. A technology-driven spurt in brain research, the extension of evolutionary theory to everything from morality to consciousness, the emergence of a whole range of post-Cartesian philosophies of mind, and, perhaps most important, the dawning of the age of the absolute gene, have done the same for biologism. In the face of all this, and of the moral and practical issues at stake, courteous, to-each-his-own dividing up of the territory does not look to be on the cards.

'Psychology's Next Chapter' is more likely to be tumultuous than irenic as computational, biological and cultural approaches grow in power and sophistication sufficiently to assure that they will have transformative impacts upon one another. The simple assertion that biology provides 'constraints' upon culture, as it does, and that computationally based cognitive science is incompetent to deal with 'the messiness of meaning making', as it is, will hardly suffice to resolve the deep issues that, by its very presence, cultural psychology is going to make unavoidable. Bringing so large and misshapen a camel as anthropology into psychology's tent is going to do more to toss things around than to arrange them in order. At the climax of what is surely one of the most extraordinary and productive careers in the human sciences, a career of continuous originality and tireless exploration, Bruner seems to be in the midst of producing a more revolutionary revolution than he altogether appreciates.

Navigating difference

Within anthropology, the clarity, the relevance, the analytic power, even the moral status of the concept of culture have been much discussed in recent years, to no very certain conclusion save that if it is not to be discarded as an imperialist relic, an ideological manoeuvre, or a popular catchword, as its various critics variously suggest, it must be seriously rethought. Giving it a central role in 'psychology's next chapter', as Bruner suggests, should do much to encourage such rethinking, as well as to extend similar questionings to the no less embattled concept of mind he wishes to conjoin with it. But it will hardly simplify things. To the abiding puzzles afflicting psychology – nature and nurture, top down and bottom up, reason and passion, conscious and unconscious, competence and performance, privacy and intersubjectivity, experience and behaviour, learning and forgetting – will be added a host of new ones: meaning and action, social causality and personal intention, relativism and universalism, and, perhaps most fundamentally, difference and commonality. If anthropology is obsessed with anything, it is with how much difference difference makes.

There is no simple answer to this question so far as cultural differences are concerned (though simple answers are often enough given, usually extreme). In anthropology, there is merely the question itself, asked and re-asked in every instance. To throw so singularizing a science in amongst such determinedly generalizing ones as genetics, information processing, developmental psychology, generative grammar, neurology, decision theory, and neo-Darwinism is to court terminal confusion in a realm – the study of mental activity – already well-enough obscured by imperial programmes, inimical world-views and a proliferation of procedures. What, in the days of Sartre, we would have called Bruner's 'project', implies a good deal more than adding 'culture' (or 'meaning', or 'narrative') to the mix. It implies, as he himself has said, confronting the world as a field of differences, 'adjudicating the different construals of reality that are inevitable in any diverse society' (Bruner, 1990: 95).

Trying to bring together, or (perhaps more carefully) to relate in a productive manner, everything from 'psychic universals' and 'story telling' to 'neural models' and 'encultured chimpanzees', from Vygotsky, Goodman and Bartlett to Edelman, Simon and Premack (not to speak of Geertz and Lévi-Strauss!) obviously involves as much mobilizing differences as it does dissolving them, 'adjudicating' contrasts (not, perhaps, altogether the best word), rather than overriding them or forcing them into some pallid, feel-good ecumenical whole. It may just be that it is not the reconciliation of diverse approaches to the study of mind that is most immediately needed, a calming eclecticism, but the effective playing of them off against one another. If that miraculous cabbage, the brain itself, now appears to be more adequately understood in terms of separated processes simultaneously active, then the same may be true of the mind with which biologizers so often confuse it. History, culture, the body and the workings of the physical world indeed fix the character of anyone's mental life – shape it, stabilize it, fill it with content. But they do so independently, partitively, concurrently and differentially. They do not just disappear into a resultant like so many component vectors, or come together in some nicely equilibrated frictionless concord.

Such a view – that a useful understanding of how we manage to think must be one in which symbolic forms, historical traditions, cultural artefacts, neural circuits, environmental pressures, genetic inscriptions and the like operate coactively, often enough even agonistically – seems to be struggling towards more exact expression in recent work, at least in part stimulated by Bruner's own. Andy Clark's *Being There* (1997) is dedicated to nothing less than 'putting brain, body and world together again'. William Frawley's *Vygotsky and Cognitive Science* (1997) seeks 'to show that the human mind is both a social construct and a computational device as opposed to one or the other'. So far as culture – 'the symbolic systems that individuals [use] in constructing meaning' (Bruner, 1990: 11) – is concerned, what Clark calls 'the image of mind as inextricably interwoven with body, world and action' (1997: xvii), and Frawley, 'the mind in the world [and] the world ... in the mind' (1997: 295), makes it impossible to regard it any longer as external and supplementary to the resident powers of the human intellect, a tool or a prosthesis. It is ingredient in those powers.[2]

The course of our understanding of mind does not, therefore, consist of a determined march towards an omega point where everything finally falls happily together; it consists of the repeated deployment of distinct enquiries in such a way that, again and again, apparently without end, they force deep-going reconsiderations upon one another. Constructing a powerful 'cultural psychology' (or a powerful psychological anthropology – not altogether the same thing) is less a matter of hybridizing disciplines, putting hyphens between them, than it is of reciprocally disequilibrating them. At a time when monomaniac, theory-of-everything conceptions of mental functioning, stimulated by local developments in neurology, genetics, primatology, literary theory, semiotics, systems theory, robotics or whatever, have come increasingly into fashion, what seems to be needed is the development of strategies for enabling Bruner's 'different construals of [mental] reality' to confront, discompose, energize and deprovincialize one another, and thus drive the enterprise erratically onward. Everything that rises need not converge: it has only to make the most of its incorrigible diversity.

The ways of doing this, of making disparate, even conflicting, views of what the mind is, how it works and how it is most profitably studied into useful correctives to one another's assurances, are, of course, themselves multiple – extremely difficult to devise, difficult to put in place once they are devised, and extremely susceptible, once they are put in place, to bringing on an academic version of a Hobbesean war. Again, so far as anthropology is concerned, what most positions it to contribute to such a task, and to avoid its pathological outcomes, is not its particular findings about African witchcraft or Melanesian exchange, and certainly not any theories it may have developed about universal necessities and the ingenerate logic of social life, but its long and intimate engagement with cultural difference and with the concrete workings of such difference in social life. Surveying contrasts, tracing their implications and enabling them somehow to speak to general issues is, after all, its *métier*.

Managing difference, or if that sounds too manipulative, navigating it, is the heart of the matter. As with all such enterprises, there are a good many more ways of getting it wrong than there are of getting it right, and one of the most common ways of getting it wrong is through convincing ourselves that we have got it right – consciousness explained, how the mind works, the engine of reason, the last word. Whitehead once remarked that we must build our systems and keep them open; but, given his own passion for completeness, certainty and holistic synthesis, he neglected to add that the former is a great deal easier to accomplish than the latter. The hedgehog's disease and the fox's – premature closure and the obsessive fear of it, tying it all up and letting it all dangle – may be equally obstructive of movement in the human sciences. But, 'in nature', as the positivists used to say, the one is encountered far more frequently than the other, especially in these days of high-tech tunnel vision.

One thing that is certain (if anything is certain when one comes to talk of such things as meaning, consciousness, thought and feeling) is that neither psychology's nor anthropology's 'next chapter' is going to be an orderly, well-formed sort of discourse, with beginning and middle neatly connected to end. Neither isolating rival approaches to understanding mind and culture in fenced communities ('evolutionary psychology', 'symbolic anthropology') nor fusing them into an inclusive whole ('cognitive science', 'semiotics'), is, in the long run, or even the medium, really workable – the one because it reifies difference and exalts it, the other because it underestimates its ubiquity, its ineradicability and its force.

The reason that the legalism 'adjudication' may not be the best term to signal the alternative to these ways of avoiding issues is that it suggests an 'adjudicator', something (or someone) that sorts things out, that reconciles approaches, ranks them, or chooses among them. But whatever order emerges in either mind or culture, it is not produced by some regnant central process or directive structure; it is produced by the play of ... well, whatever it is that is, in the case, in play. The future of cultural psychology depends on the ability of its practitioners to capitalize on so turbulent and inelegant a situation – a situation in which the openness, responsiveness, adaptability, inventiveness and intellectual restlessness, to say nothing of the optimism, that have characterized Bruner's work since its beginnings are peculiarly well-suited. His outlook and his example seem likely to flourish, whoever it is who continues the narrative, and whatever it is that it turns out to say.

Notes

The bulk of this essay originally appeared, in a somewhat different form, in *The New York Review of Books*, 10 April 1997, pp. 22–4.

1   Two such works are Cole (1996) and Shore (1996). Cole, a developmental psychologist moving towards social anthropology, traces the history of cross-cultural research in psychology, in which he has himself played a major role, and develops a conceptual framework for the integration of anthropological and psychological enquiry based on 'the romantic science' ('the dream of a novelist and a scientist combined') of the Russian psychologists Alexander Luria, Alexei Leontiev and Lev Vygotsky. Shore, a social anthropologist moving towards cognitive psychology, reviews some classical ethnographic studies, including his own on Samoa, as well as various contemporary cultural forms – baseball, interior decorating, air travel – in an effort to relate what he calls 'personal' (that is, 'cognitive') and 'conventional' (that is, 'cultural') mental models to one another and thus transcend the long and unfortunate separation of anthropology and psychology.

Both these books bite off a good deal more than they can chew and do not come together very well; but they offer valuable accounts of the present state of play. For other such summary works, equally useful for getting a hands-on sense of the field and its prospects, see Shweder (1991), Stigler, Shweder and Herdt (1990), and Shweder and Levine (1984).

2   For a constitutive, as opposed to an add-on, view of the role of culture in human evolution, see Geertz, 1973: chs 2 and 3.

References

Bruner, J. (1983) *In Search of Mind: Essays in Autobiography*. New York: Harper & Row.

Bruner, J.S. (1990) *Acts of Meaning*. Cambridge, MA: Harvard University Press.

Bruner, J.S. (1996) *The Culture of Education*. Cambridge, MA: Harvard University Press.

Clark, A. (1997) *Being There: Putting Brain, Body, and World Together Again*. Cambridge, MA: MIT Press.

Cole, M. (1996) *Cultural Psychology: A Once and Future Discipline*. Cambridge, MA: Harvard University Press.

Frawley, W. (1997) *Vygotsky and Cognitive Science: Language and the Unification of the Social and Computational Mind*. Cambridge, MA: Harvard University Press.

Geertz, C. (1973) *The Interpretation of Cultures*. New York: Basic Books.

Shore, B. (1996) *Culture in Mind: Cognition, Culture, and the Problem of Meaning*. Oxford: Oxford University Press.

Shweder, R.A. (1991) *Thinking through Cultures: Expeditions in Cultural Psychology*. Cambridge, MA: Harvard University Press.

Shweder, R.A. and Levine, R.A. (eds) (1984) *Culture Theory: Essays on Mind, Self and Emotion*. Cambridge: Cambridge University Press.

Stigler, J., Shweder, R.A. and Herdt, G. (eds) (1990) *Cultural Psychology: Essays on Comparative Human Development*. Cambridge: Cambridge University Press.

2

BRUNER ON LANGUAGE ACQUISITION

Michael Tomasello

> Like a deck of cards ... You don't want a card because you want the card, but because in a perfectly arbitrary system of rules and values and in a special combination of which you already hold a part the card has meaning. But suppose you aren't sitting in a game. Then, even if you know the rules, a card doesn't mean a thing. They all look alike.
>
> Robert Penn Warren, *All the King's Men*

By his own account, Jerome Bruner did not begin an intensive study of language and language acquisition until he arrived at Oxford University in 1972 (Bruner, 1983a, 1983b). In the two decades prior to his well-known voyage across the Atlantic, Bruner concerned himself primarily with processes of perception and cognition (e.g., Bruner, Goodnow and Austin, 1956; Bruner, Greenfield and Olver, 1966), while also maintaining an active interest in education, culture and human ontogeny (e.g., Bruner, 1965, 1966). But in those early years of the cognitive revolution he viewed language only as a window on cognition – perhaps as a tool of cognition – not as an interesting cognitive and cultural phenomenon in its own right.

Bruner's studies of language acquisition during his decade at Oxford were truly ground breaking. They opened up for developmental psychologists an entirely new dimension in the study of language acquisition: the pragmatics of linguistic communication between children and adults. In addition, pragmatics raised the question of how children understand the minds of their communicative partners and the cultural contexts within which communication takes place, which in turn paved the way for studies of children's theories of mind and the role of culture in shaping them. Bruner's investigations in recent years have gone beyond the microcosm where infant meets culture to the consideration of culture writ large in such things as narratives and cultural institutions. Together, these micro- and macro-level studies have helped to shape – indeed to define – the emerging discipline of cultural psychology.

In this essay I attempt to explicate Bruner's approach to the process of language acquisition in early ontogeny. I focus mainly on his work on infants' early communication and language, carried out between 1972 and 1983. I first describe his approach to word learning, which spawned much subsequent research on pragmatics, joint attention and early language. I then turn to his view of grammar, which is much less well known and which, in my opinion, requires some modification if it is to achieve its aim. I conclude with a few words about Bruner's more recent investigations into narrative and culture and their significance for cultural psychology.

The nature and uses of immaturity

In 1972, Bruner published a remarkable paper entitled 'The nature and uses of immaturity'. The major topic of this wide-ranging paper was human ontogeny in evolutionary perspective, focusing on the question of how the human species could get away with having its young so vulnerable and so helpless for so long a period in ontogeny. Bruner's answer was that a longer period of immaturity creates more competencies based on learning, and that means more competencies that can be used flexibly and intentionally. In the case of human beings, much of this learning is social or cultural in nature, and so many of the resulting competencies benefit from the prior learning of conspecifics:

> The nature and uses of immaturity are themselves subject to evolution, and their variations are subject to natural selection, much as any morphological or behavioural variant would be. One of the major speculations about primate evolution is that it is based on the progressive selection of a distinctive pattern of immaturity. It is this pattern of progressive selection that has made possible the more flexible adaptation of our species.... Because our ultimate concern is with human adaptation, our first concern must be the most distinctive feature of that adaptation ... 'culture using' ... [providing] amplifiers and transformers for [human beings'] sense organs, muscles, and reckoning powers, as well as banks for [their] memory. (Bruner, 1972: 687)

Much of Bruner's paper was concerned to review observations of the cognition and social behaviour of nonhuman primates, observations that were then emerging from the field and the laboratory. He discerned that as one moves from monkeys to apes to human beings one sees more flexible interactions with both the physical and social environments – a 'loosening of the primate bond', as he put it. Monkeys seem to live in more tightly structured social groups, infused with issues of dominance, and to behave in a stereotyped fashion. Apes and humans, in contrast, live in much more loosely arranged social groups and seem freer to use their cognitive resources more creatively. This is evidenced by their greater tendencies towards combinatorial play, their use of tools to explore and transform the physical environment, and the emergence of social reciprocity, communicative symbols, and observational teaching and learning, all of which regulate their social interactions and learning experiences in flexible and cognitively powerful ways. All these tendencies are especially prominent in human beings, leading to the form of social organization known as culture.

Near the end of the paper Bruner tackles language specifically in a section entitled 'Using symbolic means: Language'. This brief discussion is important because it introduces the two central and complementary topics that dominate his later work on language acquisition: first, how children are able to learn the linguistic conventions of their culture; and, second, the role of language and other cultural conventions in introducing children to particular ways of thinking, acting and interacting.

With regard to the first topic, Bruner introduces, albeit sketchily, two key notions that underlie all of his subsequent work on this question. First, he suggests the communicative function of language 'in all probability ... determines many of its design features' (1972: 699). Language evolved for, and is learned in the context of, communication for purposes of coordinated action – responding to the 'need for help' in negotiating the social-technical way of life of the species (de Laguna, 1927). Second, Bruner argues that 'the initial use of language is probably in support of and closely linked to action' (Bruner, 1972: 700). That is, the structure of all languages revolves around syntagmatic relations such as agent, object, location, attribution and so forth – basic categories that, according to Piaget (1952) and others, also structure young children's nonlinguistic cognition and action in the world. Combining these two tenets, we arrive at the following position. Children learn to communicate linguistically in the context of coordinated activities with mature language users, and their talk is structured by their nonlinguistic cognition of actions, objects and properties.

Bruner then turns abruptly to the second topic, the influence of language on developing children. He writes:

> [But] with further growth, the major trend is a steadfast march *away* from the use of language as an adjunct of action.... [Language] frees the attention of the user from his immediate surroundings, directing attention to what is being said rather than to what is being done or seen. In the process, language becomes a powerful instrument in selectively directing attention to features of the environment represented by it ... and giving shape to a belief system.... Increasingly, then, language in its decontextualized form becomes among human beings the medium for passing on knowledge. (1972: 700–2)

Once children have reached a certain level of skill with the language, and with other symbolic artefacts of their culture, in concrete action-based situations, they are in a position to be influenced by the more complex, abstract and culturally specific values, attitudes and beliefs embodied in those artefacts. Although Bruner does not mention narrative specifically in this essay, he later addresses the same theme under the rubric of 'the narrative construction of reality'.

Bruner's research on language acquisition after the publication of this paper falls neatly into two chronological periods corresponding to the topics we have identified. First, during his decade in Oxford he studied how children acquire their native languages. Since his return to the

United States in the early 1980s, he has considered more broadly the linguistic and narrative construction of reality and other processes by which immature human beings become fully functioning members of their cultures. I deal here at length with the first topic; I will touch briefly on the second at the end of the chapter.

Child's talk: learning to use language

Bruner's research at Oxford concerned how children acquire their very earliest means of communication, both nonlinguistic and linguistic. The catalyst that took him beyond his views of 1972, as he explicitly acknowledges (Bruner, 1983a), was his introduction to Speech Act Theory. The originator of the theory, J.L. Austin, was an Oxford professor until his death in 1960. Austin left an active legacy embodied, for example, in the work of John Searle and Paul Grice, and his ideas influenced many Oxford philosophers, including Peter Strawson, Anthony Kenny and Rom Harré, all interested in different ways in the study of language and mind. The insight for Bruner, found nowhere in his earlier writings, is that linguistic communication does not just serve to coordinate action among persons, but is itself a form of social action. Speech Act Theory provided typologies of the social acts that language can be used to perform, such as indicating, requesting, promising, asking for information, threatening and persuading.

At this time, of course, British analytic philosophy was still grappling with the profound but cryptic writings of Ludwig Wittgenstein (1953) on the relation of language to understanding, practice and social life. Of particular interest to many psychologists was the notion of a 'language game', which Wittgenstein explicitly illustrated with examples from language acquisition. The basic point was that the symbols of language take their communicative significance from the social practices in which they are embedded. This is clear, for example, with a word like 'trump' as it is used prototypically in the game of bridge; it only has meaning in the context of this game in which other concepts and terms are known as well, for example, 'trick', 'suit', 'bid' and so forth. Wittgenstein's deeper point was that, in some sense, *all* language works this way. It is just that our forms of life (analogous to the game of bridge) are so taken for granted by mature human beings that they are invisible.

Further inspired by the preliminary work of Joanna Ryan (1974) on speech acts in early language acquisition, Bruner set out to observe prelinguistic and just-linguistic children. He wanted to look at language as social action as it was manifest in the language games played by mothers and infants in middle-class British culture. His initial attempts, influenced by his background as an experimental psychologist, occurred in what he describes as a very cold and artificial laboratory situation. However, following the lead of his ethologist friend and colleague, Niko Tinbergen, he soon began to study children in their natural ecological setting: their homes.

Perhaps the best representative of this research is a study by Ratner and Bruner (1978). The problem they addressed was Wittgensteinian: how can a child learn a word when no procedures, ostensive or otherwise, can unambiguously illustrate its reference? Their answer was also Wittgensteinian: the child acquires the conventional use of a word by learning to participate in a form of life she understands first nonlinguistically, so that the mother's language is grounded in shared experiences the social significance of which the child already appreciates.

The evidence for this claim came from case studies of two children learning to play one or another form of a hiding–finding game. In one, Jonathan learned to play a game with his mother involving a clown on a stick that could be withdrawn inside a cloth cone and then made to reappear. Jonathan was observed every three weeks from 5 to 14 months of age. During each session he and his mother engaged in numerous rounds of the game, each of which consisted, prototypically, of (1) Preparation ('Jonathan, look what I've got here!'); (2) Disappearance ('Gone! He's all gone!'); (3) Reappearance ('Peek-a-boo! Hello, Jonathan!'); and (4) Subsequence (e.g., using the clown to tickle Jonathan). Across the 74 rounds observed over this nine-month period, the game was predictable and routinized both in its physical structure and in how the mother used language, with the variations consisting of a relatively small set occurring at several predictable junctures. Jonathan's participation in the game during these months became more active, so that by the end he took over the mother's role of operating the toy on many rounds. With regard to Jonathan's language, it was found that he picked up a number of his mother's locutions in the context of this game, most notably at the disappearance phase 'All gone!' and at the reappearance phase 'Boo!'

In a number of publications Bruner reflected on the process of language acquisition illustrated by this and similar studies (e.g., Bruner, 1975, 1981, 1983a). He called forms of life such as the clown game 'formats' for language learning, and claimed that young children acquire almost all of their earliest language in the context of formats. On this view, a social interaction between adult and child is a format for language learning if it has: (1) a delimited number of significant elements (objects and actions); (2) a clearly repetitive structure allowing for the anticipation of elements, but with some possibilities for substitution of elements across rounds; (3) salient temporal positions for appropriate vocalizations; and (4) reversible role relationships between adult and child. In essence, the claim is that social interactions of this type are the forms of culture – among all the other forms of culture the child may experience – in which the child's cognitive and social cognitive skills can make enough sense of things to acquire a linguistic convention.

Making sense of things in a social interaction of this type depends both on children's ability to understand the game and on their ability to understand the adult's communicative intentions within it. Children express their understanding of the game by various signs of anticipation, and even active intervention, as a particular round unfolds. They express their understanding of what the adult is trying to do most clearly when they take on the adult's role, for example, when Jonathan begins to hide the clown from his mother as she had hidden it from him on previous occasions. And indeed Jonathan's use of the words 'All gone!', at precisely the juncture in the game that his mother had used it, is another form of this role-taking ability since he speaks to her as she has previously spoken to him – what other researchers have dubbed 'role reversal imitation' (to distinguish it from straightforward imitation in which the child duplicates the adult's behaviour with no role reversal, e.g., they both kick the same ball) (Tomasello, 1995a, in press). Realizing that children's ability to reverse roles in this way was inconsistent with Piaget's (1954) picture of the infant as radically egocentric – unable to take the perspective of others – Scaife and Bruner (1975) investigated the ability of young infants to enter into joint visual attention with adults by following their line of regard. The emergence of joint attention skills in the months prior to the onset of language demonstrated that 1-year-old infants have all of the social cognitive skills they need to discern adult communicative intentions in the context of language-learning formats.

The upshot of all this was a theory of language acquisition in explicit opposition to Noam Chomsky's nativism (e.g., 1968). Chomsky proposed that human beings are innately endowed with a universal grammar and a Language Acquisition Device, or LAD. In opposition, Bruner posited that human beings come into a world that is already structured culturally and linguistically, and their long period of immaturity is designed precisely for them to acquire the particular cultural and linguistic conventions into which they are born. Thus, in all cultures, adults and children engage in routine interactions involving nursing and eating, bathing and sleeping, dressing and undressing, and other activities, in which adults address them with at least some language. This may be called the Language Acquisition Support System, or LASS. Human children are not innately equipped with a universal grammar applicable to all of the languages of the world equally (see Tomasello, 1995b). They are adapted to enter into joint attentional interactions with adults and to understand adult intentions and attention, and eventually to adopt adult roles in these interactions, including their use of particular linguistic conventions.

Subsequent research on word learning

Bruner's influence on the study of infants' early social interaction and language acquisition is undisputed. Trevarthen's (1979) work on primary intersubjectivity (infant in face-to-face interaction with adult) and secondary intersubjectivity (infant in triadic interaction with adult and object) were clearly inspired by Bruner's analyses, as was the work of Bakeman and Adamson on the early development of joint attention in infants' interactions with different kinds of social partners (Bakeman and

Adamson, 1984; Adamson and Bakeman, 1985). Butterworth's research on pointing (summarized in 1991) was also inspired by Bruner, as was the work of Corkum and Moore (1995) on infant gaze following.

Perhaps of most direct relevance for the study of language acquisition is the research my colleagues and I have conducted over the last decade on the relation between joint attention and early word learning. First, Tomasello and Todd (1983) followed six infants longitudinally from 12 to 18 months of age. At monthly intervals we videotaped the infants' natural interactions with their mothers and also obtained estimates of their vocabulary size (based on maternal diaries). Consistent with Bruner's hypotheses, we found a strong correlation between the amount of time an infant–mother pair spent in joint attention in the taped interactions and the size of that infant's vocabulary at 18 months, especially with regard to object labels (since these represent the objects of joint attention). Of special importance were those joint attentional episodes in which the infant and mother both made active contributions to the initiation and maintenance of the triadic interaction. Tomasello and Farrar (1986) replicated this result with a larger sample of children, and provided both observational and experimental evidence that the way mothers used language in joint attentional episodes was related to children's vocabularies; that is, mothers who used language that followed into their child's already established focus of attention ('That's a nice ball'), rather than trying to direct it anew, had children with larger subsequent vocabularies. Tomasello, Mannle and Kruger (1986) provided further confirmation for these results in a sample of twins, who engaged in joint attention with adults much less than singletons (due to the extra demands on adults in situations with two infants) and whose language development was slow off the mark as a result (see Tomasello, 1988, 1992a, for reviews).

This research basically provided support for one component of Bruner's theory: the important role of joint attentional formats and adults' use of language in attentionally sensitive ways in children's early language development. But Bruner also emphasized that infants must have certain cognitive skills to enter into joint attentional interactions with adults and to learn their language. Crucially, they must be able to understand adult communicative intentions. Recent research has confirmed this proposal, and has shown that as the second year of life progresses infants rapidly become skilled at determining adult communicative intentions in all kinds of novel social situations that bear little resemblance to the highly structured and repetitive formats of mother–infant interaction that scaffolded their very earliest productive language. In other words, infants' skills at establishing joint attention with adults gradually become much more flexible and general.

First, Baldwin (1991, 1993) showed that 19-month-old infants – while they are assisted in their word learning by adults following on to their attention – are capable of using the adult gaze direction as a cue to determine the adult's intended referent even when this differs from their own current focus of attention. Gaze direction, as first studied by Scaife and Bruner (1975), is of course a cue that can be used across a number of different types of language-learning formats and social interactions. Second, my colleagues and I found further support for infants' rapidly growing social cognitive skills in the context of word learning. We exposed children from 18 to 24 months of age to novel words in a variety of types of social interactions where the children had to do significant cognitive work to determine adult communicative intentions – and without the aid of adult gaze cues. In all cases the majority of children learned the novel words in either comprehension or production. For example:

- In the context of a finding game, an adult announced her intentions to 'find the toma' and then searched in a row of buckets all containing novel objects (rejecting some by scowling and replacing them) until she found the one she wanted (indicated by a smile and the termination of search). Children learned the new word for the object that the adult's smile indicated was the one intended no matter how many rejected objects intervened in the search process (Tomasello and Barton, 1994).
- An adult announced her intention to 'dax Mickey Mouse' and then proceeded to perform one action accidentally and another intentionally (sometimes reversing the order). Children always learned the word for the intentional, not the accidental action irrespective of whether it came first or second in the sequence (Tomasello and Barton, 1994).
- An adult set up a script with the child in which a novel action was performed always and only with a particular toy character (e.g., Big Bird on a merry-go-round, with other character–action pairings demonstrated as well). She then picked up Big Bird and announced 'Let's meek Big Bird', but the merry-go-round was nowhere to be found – so the action was not performed. Later, using a different character, children demonstrated their understanding of the new verb even though they had never seen the referent action performed after the novel verb was introduced (Akhtar and Tomasello, 1996).
- A child, her mother and an experimenter played together with three novel objects. The mother then left the room. A fourth object was brought out and the child and experimenter played with it, noting the mother's absence. When the mother returned to the room, she looked at the four objects together and exclaimed 'Oh look! A modi! A modi!' Understanding that the mother would not be excited about the objects she had already played with previously, but that she very well might be excited about the object she was seeing for the first time, children learned the new word for the object the mother had not seen previously (Akhtar, Carpenter and Tomasello, 1996).

Together, these experimental studies of word learning demonstrate dramatically the scaffolding process as Bruner envisioned it. Initially, at one year of age, children require highly repetitive and predictable formats for language acquisition in which the adult is sensitive to the child's attentional focus. But as children become more skilful at determining adult communicative intentions in a wider variety of interactive situations, highly structured formats with very sensitive adults become less crucial to the process and may be discarded, just as real scaffolding is discarded once the building is built. Joint attention is essential throughout the process of language acquisition, but it manifests itself in different ways at different developmental periods.

The acquisition of grammatical competence

Word learning was not and is not the main battleground for nativist and more culturally based theories of language acquisition. The principal conflict between Chomsky's LAD and Bruner's LASS, for example, concerns the acquisition of grammatical competence. Chomsky has never considered the words of a language, or any other aspects of semantics or pragmatics, as a part of the innate linguistic endowment. What is innate is the computational structure of language, its syntax (e.g., Chomsky, 1986). Bruner, on the other hand, would like to believe that the syntactic conventions of a language are learned in ways similar to the learning of lexical conventions. Over the years, however, Bruner has changed his mind on how this might work – and indeed whether it is a viable approach at all.

In his earlier writings Bruner clearly throws down the gauntlet:

> What may be innate about language acquisition is not *linguistic* innateness, but some special features of human action and human attention that permit language to be decoded by the uses to which it is put.... Our argument relates to the grammatical level more generally, particularly to a 'natural' semantic or pragmatic base for initial grammatical rules. The argument has been that the structures of action and attention provide bench-marks for interpreting the order-rules in initial grammar: that a concept of agent-action-object-recipient at the prelinguistic level aids the child in grasping the linguistic meaning of appropriately ordered utterances involving such case categories as agentive, action, object, indirect object, and so forth. And by the same token, a grasp of the topic-feature structure of shared experience aids the child in grasping the linguistic relation inherent in topic-comment and subject-object. (1975: 2, 17)

There could scarcely be a clearer statement of the position that the structure of language comes directly from the structure of phylogenetically and ontogenetically prior psychological processes involving action, social interaction and shared attention.

In his later reflections, however, Bruner is not so sure. At some point he recognized that his 1975 account was simplistic, but he was not certain what should replace it. In 1983, Bruner traced the history of his thinking in this way:

> Grammar is what it is, I argued, because it 'emerges' from a prior appreciation of the structures or 'arguments' of action: agent, action, object, instrument, location,

etc. As one *acts*, one picks up 'protolinguistic' knowledge about these arguments. In time, this knowledge is abstracted and converted into a 'case grammar' that reflects the very same arguments. I even urged that the easy acquisition of Subject-Verb-Object order in sentences must be an outgrowth of the child's natural perception of the order of action in life.... The truth of the matter is of course, that grammars are extraordinarily arbitrary or 'artificial'.... Cause and effect may be a natural way of interpreting events in the world, but some languages will note this natural pattern 'ergatively' by marking the subject of the sentence as a 'causer', some will add something to the verb to indicate its 'causativeness', some will mark the *effect* of the cause by making the object of the sentence accusative.... Grammar, in short, constitutes its own problem space. Knowing about causation in the real world gives no clue about how it is represented in the grammar of a particular language. (1983b: 169)

In the midst of his uncertainty about how to deal with this new insight, and in a book published in the very same year (Bruner, 1983a), Bruner was downright conciliatory towards Chomsky and the idea of innate predispositions that are specifically linguistic. In two different places, one near the beginning and one near the end of this book, he outlines some of the prelinguistic skills that children must have to learn to use language involving action, social interaction, joint attention, the ability to abstract and so forth. But in both places he suggests that this may not be enough:

But [the child] could not achieve the prodigies of language acquisition without, at the same time, possessing a unique and predisposing set of language learning capacities – something akin to what Chomsky has called a Language Acquisition Device, LAD.... In a word, it is the interaction between LAD and LASS that makes it possible for the infant to enter the linguistic community. (Bruner, 1983a: 18–19)

No doubt the aspirant speaker of a language requires far more mental machinery than this at the outset to 'get into' the formal, abstract rules that govern his local language.... It may include innate knowledge of a universal grammar, as Chomsky suggested, or it may be in the form of initial sensitivities to distinctions in both language and the real world. (1983a: 119)

Although Bruner does not say specifically what caused the turnaround in his thinking, the late 1970s and early 1980s was a time when many new discoveries were made about languages differing in structure from English in fundamental ways, for example, the ergative languages to which Bruner alludes in the discussion of the arbitrariness of syntax quoted above (1983b: 169). What these discoveries meant was that no simple formula will take us from action to grammar. Indeed, there are even a small minority of languages where direct objects come consistently before subjects in utterances (Givón, 1995), which would seem to be temporally 'backward' with respect to the natural order of action in experience. The discovery that there is great diversity and arbitrariness in the grammars of the world, combined with Bruner's primary desire to establish pragmatics as an important topic in its own right, led him to leave the question of grammar open, so that he could focus on the dimensions of language that were unarguably pragmatic.

Bruner came to at least a partial resolution to the problem of grammar in the context of his later work on narrative. Here he proposes an analogy that shifts the emphasis away from the grammatical structure of language per se to the communicative motivation for grammatically structured language:

> Phonemes are mastered not for themselves but because they constitute the building blocks of the language's lexemes: they are mastered in the process of mastering lexical elements. I should like to make the comparable argument that grammatical forms and distinctions are not mastered either for their own sake or merely in the interest of 'more efficient communication'. Sentences as grammatical entities, while the fetish of formal grammarians, are not the 'natural' units of communication. The natural forms are *discourse units* that fulfill either a 'pragmatic' or a 'methetic' discourse function.... [O]ne of the most ubiquitous and powerful discourse forms in human communication is *narrative*. (Bruner, 1990: 76–7)

Despite the fact that particular syntactic forms are only arbitrarily related to their communicative functions, it is still the case that discourse/communicative functions drive the process of grammatical development.

In support of this view Bruner points out that the content of children's early utterances reflects a deep concern with narrative: their 'principal linguistic interest centres on *human action and its outcomes*, particularly *human interaction*' (1990: 78). Consequently, it is events concerning human action and interaction whose linguistic formulation children first strive to master. These are events that contain certain kinds of roles concerning agents, instruments, recipients and the like. What is new in this account is that the *structure* of nonlinguistic experience is no longer seen as determining the structure of children's grammatical competence; rather, the *content* of nonlinguistic experience, especially the narrative dimensions of experience, is taken to contain the experiential elements that must be encoded by any grammatical system – since this is what children wish to talk about. This newer claim is in many ways a weaker one, for it proffers no explanation of why the syntactic conventions of a language are as they are.

Thus, over time, Bruner went from positing a fairly direct grounding of syntax in human action to recognizing the arbitrariness of syntactic form. In this latter view, pragmatics – in the form of a concern with human intentional action and narrative – mainly serves to motivate syntax in that it determines many of the experiential elements that syntax serves to structure.

New views of grammar and its acquisition

Bruner's ideas about the acquisition of grammar have not played as important a role in subsequent research and theorizing as have his ideas on joint attention and word learning. But there are intriguing insights here that deserve further scrutiny. Indeed, I believe there is considerable merit to Bruner's original idea that the structure of the language that the child is acquiring is a reflection of: (1) the structure of action in the guise of the participant roles of agent, recipient, patient, instrument and so on; and

(2) the structure of attention in the guise of topic-focus structure. The mistake was to look for the structuring role of these cognitive processes in language acquisition. The structuring of language takes place not during acquisition, but between mature language users during human history. And the structure of action and attention determine powerful linguistic universals in the way human beings communicate with one another. But a variety of other factors conspire to make for relatively rapid historical changes in particular languages – most especially information processing factors (e.g., erosion of phonological content at the ends of words, making less salient such things as inflectional endings) and cultural choices about how to highlight or background certain kinds of information for inter-locutors (e.g., ergative versus accusative syntax as a reflection of the perspective from which an event is viewed).

To explicate this view, we need first to reconsider the nature of grammar. Of particular importance are recent approaches to language structure called either Cognitive or Functional Linguistics (e.g., Langacker, 1987, 1991; Talmy, 1988; Givón, 1995; Goldberg, 1995). These approaches differ from Chomskian Generative Grammar (which Bruner accepted too readily) in their basic assumptions about the nature of language. Generative Grammar takes as its model of natural language formal languages such as mathematics and propositional logic, in which the distinction between syntax and semantics is absolute and rigorously maintained. In Cognitive and Functional Linguistics, on the other hand, natural languages, like biological organisms, are composed most fundamentally of structures with functions (symbol and meaning, signifier and signified). Linguistic structures vary from relatively simple entities such as words and gram-matical morphemes to more complex entities such as phrases and whole linguistic constructions. *All of these have communicative functions.* There is no such thing as syntactic structure devoid of meaning.

The grammar of a language is nothing more or less than the inventory of its morphemes, words, phrases and constructions, along with their func-tions and categorical generalizations of these. These constructions vary independently in both their complexity and their abstractness. Thus, the utterance 'Fore!' in the game of golf is both simple and concrete; it is one word, with a particular intonation contour, that is used in one particular communicative circumstance. Other constructions are more complex because they are designed to indicate whole scenes of experience with multiple participants related to one another in complex ways. Some of these complex constructions are concrete in that they are based on particular words, such as many idioms like 'Nothing ventured, nothing gained', but some are abstract and categorical. For example, the passive construction in English does not concern any particular words but has the abstract form X + be + Verb-en (+ by + Y) and the function to report a transitive event from the perspective of the patient of the action. It is this schematization of grammatical patterns, into which novel linguistic items and construc-tions can be fitted, that gives language its creative power.

The constructions of a language arise historically through processes of grammaticization that take place in various forms of discourse among mature language speakers (Givón, 1979, 1995; Bybee, 1985). They emerge from communicative interactions in which the speaker is concerned with such things as economy of effort and the listener is concerned with such things as unambiguousness of expression (Slobin, 1997). The world the speaker and listener share is composed most importantly of events and states of affairs that are worthy of talk, and these contain the kind of event-participant structure (agents, instruments, recipients, etc.) that Bruner highlighted – what might be called the semantics of the construction.

The pragmatics of the construction has two aspects, one concerning the speaker's communicative intentions and the other concerning the speaker's adaptations to the listener's perspective. First, the speaker has a communicative goal in the sense that she is trying to manipulate or influence the listener's attention to something in the world. This prompts the need for ways to indicate requests, questions, comments and so forth. But second, the speaker must always take account of the listener's knowledge and expectations, so that the talk about the event is structured differently in different communicative circumstances. This is the topic-focus structure that Bruner highlighted. And while there are many variations to the pragmatic structuring of utterances in different languages, there are also universals that depend on human attentional processes (e.g., new information that needs to be highlighted is never inserted with low volume and stress into the middle of utterances).

To illustrate the semantics and pragmatics of constructions, let us examine a single event involving Fred, a window, a rock, and breaking. In the English language we may say such things as:

Fred broke the window with a rock.	Did Fred break the window?
The rock broke the window.	Did the rock break the window?
The window broke.	Did the window break?
The window was broken by Fred.	Break the window!
It was Fred that broke the window.	Was it Fred that broke the window?
It was the window that Fred broke.	Was it the window that Fred broke?
What happened was Fred broke the window.	

The semantics of these varied constructions all concern a single event. They all involve as pragmatics the combination of a speech act construction such as a question, an indicative, or an imperative (the speaker's communicative goal) and a perspectival construction such as a simple transitive, a simple intransitive, a passive and/or a cleft (adaptations for the listener's knowledge and expectations). These different constructions are used in different discourse circumstances, depending on what the interlocutor knows and expects. For example, if an interlocutor states 'Mary broke the window', the speaker might affirm that the window was indeed broken but at the same time highlight a disagreement over the person who did it by using a cleft construction: 'No, it was Fred that did it.' Or if an interlocutor asks 'What happened to the window?' the speaker will naturally want to make the shared information the topic of the reply, and the new information the focus, by using a passive construction: 'It got broken.'

Precisely how each of these constructions was grammaticized in the hundreds of years of the history of English (and before) is not known, but there are various theoretical accounts of how language becomes structured as adults communicate with one another, first, in a loosely pragmatic mode of discourse with much repetition and redundancy and little structure (as in current-day pidgins), and then over time in a more highly coded, tightly organized, less redundant, more automatized syntactic mode (Givón, 1979, 1995). In all cases, a particular sentence-level construction, such as a cleft or a passive, arises as a single semantic-pragmatic package for talking about a particular type of scene or event in a particular type of pragmatic-discourse context. As might be expected, semantic-pragmatic contexts that are both recurrent and general tend to give rise to the most abstract and general constructions (e.g., the situations of giving encoded by the ditransitive construction as in 'He gave/threw/sent her an X'). In all cases, the process of grammaticization is a complex mix of: (1) semantics, in terms of such things as number of participants (e.g., laughing only requires one participant whereas giving requires three); (2) pragmatics, in terms of speech act intention (e.g., question, request) and perspectival adjustment (e.g., cleft, passive); and (3) processing requirements involving the cognitive and attentional capacities and tendencies of speaker and listener in the process of communication.

Given these considerations, a Brunerian approach to children's acquisition of grammatical competence during ontogeny might go as follows. Languages are structured through various processes of grammaticization historically, based on the semantics of events, the pragmatics of communication, and various processing considerations. The resulting constructions do not reflect in any transparent way (either iconically or indexically) their communicative function. The child's task is simply to learn to use the constructions that speakers of her native language have so constructed. Although there are some iconic aspects to complex constructions, they are ultimately, like simpler linguistic forms such as morphemes and words, only arbitrarily connected to the scenes they depict. The child must therefore learn them just as she learns words: in a social situation in which she understands something of the speaker's communicative intentions in using the construction. Thus, the English child learns that word order most often signals who-did-what-to-whom in a particular way, whereas the Russian child learns that this function is signalled by small markers on the participants, by observing their use in meaningful communicative contexts.

Although the learning process is more cognitively complex – since learning constructions requires some mapping between multiple elements of experience and multiple elements of language – it is, in essence, just like word learning. The child must learn to read the adult's communicative intention connected with a linguistic structure, including the aspects of the referential event she wishes to indicate (semantics) as well as her speech act intentions and the perspectival adjustments she is making for the listener (pragmatics). One theory for English claims that this initially occurs on a very concrete level in which syntactic constructions are defined by specific verbs (e.g., kicker-kicks-kickee is one construction and kisser-kisses-kissee is another structurally unrelated construction), and only over time does the child come to abstract out a verb-general construction that can generate novel sentences with the same abstract structure (e.g., agent-action-patient or subject-verb-object) (Tomasello, 1992b; Tomasello and Brooks (1999)).

The essence of this analysis, then, is to redefine syntax in terms of linguistic constructions – of various levels of complexity and abstractness, but always with meaningful communicative functions – and then to apply Bruner's more general acquisition theory to syntax as well. The child is thus learning linguistic structures on several levels of complexity simultaneously (morphemes, words, phrases, constructions) all in basically the same way, and in some cases is discerning patterns that lead to the creation of abstract categories or schemas. The components of complex constructions can undergo elaboration independently as the child learns, for example, more elaborate ways to indicate objects for listeners through the use of such devices as articles and relative clauses (noun phrases), and more elaborate ways to indicate for listeners the time-sensitive dimensions of the utterance such as tense and aspect by, typically, markers close to the main predicate (Langacker, 1991). And of course children can also combine smaller constructions into larger constructions creatively, as when a prepositional phrase is added onto a transitive construction.

Notwithstanding the many details that need to be worked out in such an approach, the key point is this. If the syntax of language is seen not as disembodied and meaningless structure, but rather as a collection of meaningful and more or less generalized linguistic constructions, we can preserve many elements of Bruner's theory of the acquisition of grammatical competence. The key is to recognize that languages, like biological organisms, are structured over time through processes of organism–environment interaction. Many of the processes that Bruner posited as key for the child in learning grammar are indeed operative in structuring language, but only during the historical process. The child's learning of complex constructions is not reliably aided by such things as iconicity with the order of action and attention (as it is not in the acquisition of lexical items), but of course the talk is about action and its participants, and the managing of the attention of the other is in some sense the whole point of the use of language. So children must learn some way – whatever way their culture has created within the constraints provided by human-cognitive and social-cognitive abilities – to symbolize events, participants, communicative goals and discourse perspectives. In this view, human language is the way it is because adults create language structure, and children then re-create, relatively faithfully, what the adults have created. Language thus represents a prototypical case of the dialectic of adult cultural creation and child cultural learning that leads to cumulative cultural evolution in the form of artefacts with a 'history' (Tomasello, Kruger and Ratner, 1993).

Conclusion

Bruner's main concern since the mid-1980s has been narrative, that is, the canonical stories and myths, but also the reasons and excuses, that comprise a culture's way of symbolically representing reality, especially social reality. 'Narrative deals with the vicissitudes of human intentions', as Bruner puts it (1986: 16). For the most part narratives are made up of language, but at this level of analysis language is only material and thus not of primary interest in and of itself. Bruner's primary interest in narrative, as alluded to above, concerns the way in which coming to use language and other symbolic artefacts and institutions influences those who use them. Indeed, in some formulations, persons are actually constituted through their interactions with others within this cultural nexus. Of special importance in Bruner's most recent work are cultural artefacts at the most general level of organization, including everything from historical narratives to legal statutes to institutions of higher learning (Bruner, 1996).

But I would argue, and Bruner would likely agree, that all of these more complex and elaborated forms of culture derive ultimately from the human adaptation for a special form of social life (Tomasello, 1999). This form of life is made possible, as Bruner stressed over a quarter of a century ago, by the long period of immaturity during which children are given time to master the particular cultural practices and traditions of the particular persons around them. Among the most important of these cultural artefacts is language, and Bruner has contributed as much as anyone to our understanding of how it may be acquired in the context of social interactions with others. His ideas and empirical research in the areas of joint attention, word learning and narrative are all substantial and will continue to influence scientists investigating these phenomena for many years to come.

Bruner's ideas on the grammatical aspects of language and language acquisition should provide scientists with many interesting directions for future research as well. In this case, however, after some initial insights of great power and depth, he turned his attention to other matters and neglected to follow through and fully 'deconstruct' the grammatical aspects of language into their constituent psychological processes – including whole grammatical constructions. This radical move might have enabled him to recognize the structuring role of historical processes of grammaticization, as now described by a number of functional linguists, thus relieving young children of the burden of structuring language themselves. Children do not have to create language, only acquire it. In addition, as I hope I have demonstrated at least to some degree, this theoretical move also makes possible an approach to language acquisition in which the processes by which children acquire the lexical and syntactic conventions of their language are essentially identical.

In its grandest perspective, therefore, Jerome Bruner's legacy in the study of language acquisition is his attempt to identify and specify the ways in which the process of acquiring linguistic conventions is fundamentally similar to the process of acquiring cultural and communicative skills in general. This is consistent with his vision of a cultural psychology in which the less mechanical and more organic and humane aspects of human experience are highlighted, and in which human linguistic competence is accorded a key role as both a consequence of and a contributor to human cultural life.

References

Adamson, L. and Bakeman, R. (1985) 'Affect and attention: infants observed with mothers and peers', *Child Development*, 56: 582–93.

Akhtar, N., Carpenter, M. and Tomasello, M. (1996) 'The role of discourse novelty in children's early word learning', *Child Development*, 67: 635–45.

Akhtar, N. and Tomasello, M. (1996) 'Twenty-four-month-old children learn words for absent objects and actions', *British Journal of Developmental Psychology*, 14: 79–93.

Bakeman, R. and Adamson, L. (1984) 'Coordinating attention to people and objects in mother–infant and peer–infant interactions', *Child Development*, 55: 1278–89.

Baldwin, D. (1991) 'Infants' contributions to the achievement of joint reference', *Child Development*, 62: 875–90.

Baldwin, D. (1993) 'Infants' ability to consult the speaker for clues to word reference', *Journal of Child Language*, 20: 395–418.

Bruner, J.S. (1965) 'The growth of mind', *American Psychologist*, 20: 1007–17.

Bruner, J.S. (1966) *Toward a Theory of Instruction*. Cambridge, MA: Harvard University Press.

Bruner, J.S. (1972) 'The nature and uses of immaturity', *American Psychologist*, 27: 687–706.

Bruner, J.S. (1975) 'The ontogenesis of speech acts', *Journal of Child Language*, 2: 1–19.

Bruner, J.S. (1981) 'The pragmatics of acquisition', in W. Deutsch (ed.), *The Child's Construction of Language*. New York: Academic Press.

Bruner, J.S. (1983a) *Child's Talk: Learning to Use Language*. New York: Norton.

Bruner, J.S. (1983b) *In Search of Mind: Essays in Autobiography*. New York: Harper & Row.

Bruner, J.S. (1986) *Actual Minds, Possible Worlds*. Cambridge, MA: Harvard University Press.

Bruner, J.S. (1990) *Acts of Meaning*. Cambridge, MA: Harvard University Press.

Bruner, J.S. (1996) *The Culture of Education*. Cambridge, MA: Harvard University Press.

Bruner, J.S., Goodnow, J. and Austin, G. (1956) *A Study of Thinking*. New York: Wiley.

Bruner, J.S., Greenfield, P. and Olver, R. (1966) *Studies in Cognitive Growth*. New York: Wiley.

Butterworth, G. (1991) 'The ontogeny and phylogeny of joint visual attention', in A. Whiten (ed.), *Natural Theories of Mind*. Oxford: Basil Blackwell.

Bybee, J. (1985) *Morphology*. Amsterdam: John Benjamins.

Chomsky, N. (1968) *Language and Mind*. New York: Harcourt Brace.

Chomsky, N. (1986) *Knowledge of Language*. Berlin: Praeger.

Corkum, V. and Moore, C. (1995) 'Joint visual attention', in C. Moore and P. Dunham (eds), *Joint Attention: Its Origins and Role in Development*. Hillsdale, NJ: Lawrence Erlbaum.

de Laguna, G. (1927) *Speech: Its Function and Development*. Bloomington: University of Indiana Press.

Givón, T. (1979) *On Understanding Grammar*. New York: Academic Press.

Givón, T. (1995) *Functionalism and Grammar*. Amsterdam: John Benjamins.

Goldberg, A. (1995) *Constructions: A Construction Grammar Approach to Argument Structure*. Chicago, IL: University of Chicago Press.

Langacker, R. (1987) *Foundations of Cognitive Grammar*, Vol. 1. Stanford, CA: Stanford University Press.

Langacker, R. (1991) *Foundations of Cognitive Grammar*, Vol. 2. Stanford, CA: Stanford University Press.

Piaget, J. (1952) *The Origins of Intelligence in Children*. New York: Norton.

Piaget, J. (1954) *The Construction of Reality in the Child*. New York: Norton.

Ratner, N. and Bruner, J. (1978) 'Games, social exchange, and the acquisition of language', *Journal of Child Language*, 5: 391–402.

Ryan, J. (1974) 'Early language development', in M. Richards (ed.), *The Integration of the Child into a Social World*. Cambridge: Cambridge University Press.

Scaife, M. and Bruner, J. (1975) 'The capacity for joint visual attention in the infant', *Nature*, 253: 265–66.

Slobin, D. (1997) 'Crosslinguistic evidence for the language-making capacity', in D.I. Slobin (ed.), *The Crosslinguistic Study of Language Acquisition*. Vol. 5. *Expanding the Contexts*. Hillsdale, NJ: Lawrence Erlbaum.

Talmy, L. (1988) 'The relation of grammar to cognition', in B. Rudzka-Ostyn (ed.), *Topics in Cognitive Linguistics*. Amsterdam: John Benjamins.

Tomasello, M. (1988) 'The role of joint attention in early language development', *Language Sciences*, 10: 69–88.

Tomasello, M. (1992a) 'The social bases of language acquisition', *Social Development*, 1(1): 67–87.

Tomasello, M. (1992b) *First Verbs: A Case Study of Early Grammatical Development*. Cambridge: Cambridge University Press.

Tomasello, M. (1995a) 'Joint attention as social cognition', in C. Moore and P. Dunham (eds), *Joint Attention: Its Origins and Role in Development*. Hillsdale, NJ: Lawrence Erlbaum.

Tomasello, M. (1995b) 'Language is not an instinct', *Cognitive Development*, 10: 131–56.

Tomasello, M. (1999) *The Cultural Origins of Human Cognition*. Cambridge, MA: Harvard University Press.

Tomasello, M. (in press) 'Perceiving intentions and learning words in the second year of life', in M. Bowerman and S. Levinson (eds), *Language Acquisition and Conceptual Development*. Cambridge: Cambridge University Press.

Tomasello, M. and Barton, M. (1994) 'Learning words in non-ostensive contexts', *Developmental Psychology*, 30: 639–50.

Tomasello, M. and Brooks, P. (1999) 'Early syntactic development', in M. Barrett (ed.), *The Development of Language*. London: UCL Press.

Tomasello, M. and Farrar, J. (1986) 'Joint attention and early language', *Child Development*, 57: 1454–63.

Tomasello, M., Kruger, A. and Ratner, H. (1993) 'Cultural learning', *Behavioral and Brain Sciences*, 16: 495–511.

Tomasello, M., Mannle, S. and Kruger, A. (1986) 'The linguistic environment of one to two year old twins', *Developmental Psychology*, 22: 169–76.

Tomasello, M. and Todd, J. (1983) 'Joint attention and lexical acquisition style', *First Language*, 4: 197–212.

Trevarthen, C. (1979) 'Instincts for human understanding and for cultural cooperation: development in infancy', in M. von Cranach, K. Foppa, W. Lepenies and D. Ploog (eds), *Human Ethology: Claims and Limits of a New Discipline*. Cambridge: Cambridge University Press.

Wittgenstein, L. (1953) *Philosophical Investigations*. New York: Macmillan.

3

THE HOUSE THAT BRUNER BUILT

Stuart G. Shanker and Talbot J. Taylor

Removing the scaffolding

La maison est une machine à habiter.

Le Corbusier, Vers une Architecture

No house should ever be *on* any hill or on anything. It should be *of* the hill, belonging to it, so hill and house could live together each the happier for the other.

Frank Lloyd Wright, An Autobiography

Those of us, who, like Bruner, were in Oxford in the late 1970s, can understand why the scaffolding metaphor so appealed to him when he wrote *Child's Talk* (1983a). Thanks to the ravages of time, Oxford's 'dreaming spires' had become a nightmare of boards and trestles. Typical was Magdalen Tower, which seemed to be crumbling before one's eyes. Years of renovation went by with little discernible progress and anxiety mounted that it was too late to save the magnificent structure. It is difficult to convey the emotion the entire town felt when the scaffolding finally came down and Magdalen Tower emerged with its ancient glory restored. Certainly, that emotion was in marked contrast to the outrage expressed in Paris when the Pompidou Centre was completed. Parisians complained that their new monument to culture appeared to be layer upon layer of scaffolding with no building at its core. It is worth considering, however, whether it is the scaffolding of the Pompidou Centre, rather than that of Magdalen Tower, that is the more apt metaphor for the view of language development presented in *Child's Talk*.

Scaffolding theory holds that caregivers monitor and adjust the amount of support received by the child as she begins to master language. The scaffolding metaphor had an immediate impact on the study of language acquisition, and became one of the major ideas in psycholinguistics. Since the publication of *Child's Talk*, Bruner's somewhat sketchy picture of the 'behavioural formats' involved in scaffolding has been supplemented with detailed explanations of the socioaffective, communicative and neurobiological mechanisms of dyadic interaction.

Today the consensus among developmentalists who adopt a social interactionist perspective is that development involves an ongoing, complex interplay between biological and environmental factors, and hence it is difficult to draw hard-and-fast distinctions between social, emotional, cognitive, communicative and linguistic elements in development. Accordingly, any attempt to explain some aspect of a child's development must consider such diverse factors as:

1 the child's ability to regulate her states and activities, and to perceive and respond to the world (primarily a function of the child's responsiveness to stimuli and facility with bodily movement);

2 the biological constraints on dyadic interaction that result from secondary altriciality;[1]

3 the child's propensity to engage in relationships with others;

4 the importance of shared affect for the child's developing awareness of self and other;

5 the significance of shared and directed gaze for the child's socioaffective and communicative development;

6 the importance of the caregiver's behaviour (e.g., smiling, facial animation, body posture, gaze) during 'critical periods' of the child's brain growth for her cortico-cortical and neurohormonal development;

7 the stimulatory and communicative significance of gestures and declarative pointing;

8 the child's growing ability to signal her intentions and desires, to describe and express her ideas and feelings, and to engage in complex communicational acts with caregivers;

9 the facilitating role which Child Directed Speech (Motherese) plays in the child's acquisition of language, as the caregiver regulates her prosody according to the child's signals of (non)comprehension, and employs, for example, expansions, extensions, recasts, reflective questions, clarification questions and repetitions to sustain and enhance communication;

10 the significance of make-believe play for virtually all aspects of a child's development.

The idea that early infant–caregiver interactions can be described in dialogic terms pre-dated *Child's Talk* (see Trevarthen, 1979). But what made Bruner's position revolutionary was its emphasis on a Vygotskian view of language socialization. One of the book's central messages is that language and culture cannot be disentangled. Thus, in addition to the above themes, *Child's Talk* stresses:

11 the presence in primates of a 'drive' to conform with the norms that define their society;

12 the significance of rule-following in the child's socioaffective and communicative development;

13   the primacy of 'learning how to do things with words' (Bruner, 1983a: 7, 8, 46, 115).

Thus scaffolding theory integrates interactionist and cultural views of child development, presenting the child as *trying* to become a member of her linguistic community (see Shatz, 1994: 8, 9). Scaffolding theory therefore seemed to be a radical alternative to the generativist view of language acquisition as automatic, spontaneous and nonconscious. But although Bruner dismisses generativism as 'implausible' and 'miraculous' (1983a: 17, 34), he treated scaffolding merely as a precursor to language acquisition conceived as generativism recommends. Bruner simply supplemented the Language Acquisition Device (LAD) with a Language Acquisition Support System (LASS). As a result, scaffolding theory is commonly seen merely as a propaedeutic to language acquisition: a preliminary structure that enables language, like Magdalen Tower, to emerge fully formed in all its architectural splendour.

But what if we were to excise LAD entirely from the picture? Would the social interactionist explanation of the child's burgeoning linguistic skills collapse, or do the roots of language actually lie in such primal activities as sharing, requesting, imitating and playing? Do the 'universal stages' that have been documented in (normal) language acquisition (see Brown, 1973) compel us to assume that the 'abstract structure of language' must somehow be represented in the brain (see Pinker, 1994) or is an alternative picture possible, one which stresses the essentially cultural character of the child's learning 'how to do things with words'?

In our view, the rejection of LAD enables us to appreciate the real contribution that *Child's Talk* can make to our understanding of, not just linguistic development, but language per se. By formally distinguishing between competence and performance, the generativist proposes a neat division of labour between linguist and psychologist. But this should be resisted, for continued allegiance to LAD serves only to undermine social interactionism. In what follows, we do our best to reveal the potential of an interactionist approach liberated from the generativist orthodoxy.

Born to talk

> The baby has the all-important first task of learning the nonverbal basis of social interaction upon which language will later be built.
>
> Daniel Stern, *Diary of a Baby*

It is frequently claimed in psychological writings that the human infant is 'born social'. Often, no more is meant than the truism that infants depend on caregivers to survive and develop. If the claim is to be a substantive one, it must be shown that children are born with certain biological traits that dispose them, in appropriate contexts, to become social agents. Read in this way, the claim sets the daunting task of explaining how a child's senses, 'processing mechanisms', reflexes, and/or needs somehow dictate that she will become someone who, as Shatz puts it, 'understands and uses social means to interact with others in mutually comprehensible ways' (1994: 6).

The emergence of the 'ethological view' in psychology over the past generation has helped developmentalists address this issue by identifying innate 'social mechanisms' which human infants share with other primates (Bowlby, 1969).[2] Newborns are perceptually attuned to the human face, voice, odour, touch, taste and movement (with marked preference shown in each case to the primary caregiver). In addition, infants are predisposed to engage in behaviours, such as crying, smiling, gazing, cooing and imitation, which evoke caregiver responses (Messer, 1994). Likewise, caregivers exhibit behaviours which reveal that they are themselves preadapted to nurture and protect their infants. For example, mothers can hear their infants crying in the noisiest of environments, can reliably distinguish their own infant's cry and smell. And caregivers have an extraordinary ability to fine-tune their behaviours to help their infants master all kinds of social and problem-solving skills, including, of course, language (Gallaway and Richards, 1994).

The above social behaviours seem closely tied to the emergence of secondary altriciality in hominid evolution (King and Shanker, 1997). For, as Noble and Davidson put it, 'the conditions of increased altriciality of hominids led to increased occasions for joint attention with caregivers, and increased opportunities for observational learning' (1996: 200). Yet, as important as joint attention is in the emergence of language, secondary altriciality may have a still deeper impact on the infant's neurobiological development. For far from following a fixed maturational design, a child's cortical development is fundamentally bound up with the nature and quality of its interactions with primary caregivers.

One striking difference between *Homo sapiens* and nonhuman primates is that human beings have a significantly larger prefrontal cortex. And yet five-sixths of the development of the human prefrontal cortex occurs postnatally, before the child is two. Moreover, the infant's socioaffective environment has a crucial influence on its cortico-cortical and neuro-hormonal development. Processes responsible for postnatal brain growth are 'significantly influenced by the stimulation embedded in the infant's socioaffective transactions with the primary caregiver' (Schore, 1994: 13). It seems that early interactions with primary caregivers supply the higher-order regulatory controls that are as yet undeveloped in the child's prefrontal cortex. Mothers not only nurture and protect their infants in the first year of life; they act as something of an external central nervous system, significantly influencing the child's cortical development (Trevarthen, 1979).

The primary mechanism whereby this is accomplished is the affectively charged exchange of shared gaze (and/or touch). From virtually the first days after its birth, an infant and her caregiver are engaged in an 'interactive system of reciprocal stimulation' (Schore, 1994: 71). Caregivers of newborns pay far more attention to their infant's eyes than any other body part. Infants are attuned to focus on objects 20–25 cm away, which is the distance mothers tend to hold them both during breast-feeding, or when the child is held up *'en face'*. An infant's gaze can reliably evoke a mother's gaze, and, beginning around the age of 2 months, the infant starts to focus on eyes. The gleam in a mother's eyes – which may be literally a flash of light reflected off her fovea caused by excitatory activity in her limbic system – triggers pupil dilation in the infant (Schore, 1994: 72ff.).

Significantly, an infant smiles more when the mother's pupils are dilated, and vice versa. The mother's facial expression stimulates positive affect in the infant, which is communicated back to the mother via the infant's facial expression, so that both are in a symbiotic state of heightened arousal. In contrast, a non-affectively expressive maternal face, with no brightness in the eyes, triggers negative affect in the infant. Similarly, a non-responsive infant, or one who constantly averts her gaze, can produce profound negative affect in the mother. In other words, shared gaze (or touch[3]) triggers positive hedonic arousal in mother and infant, and the absence or disruption of such interaction can cause anxiety and depression in both (Cohn, Matias and Tronick, 1990; Greenspan, 1997).

Schore speaks of these gaze exchanges as inducing an 'affect-amplifying', 'symbiotic' state shared between mother and child. Here may lie one of the reasons why, as the child matures and makes its first movements away from its mother, it constantly monitors her expression for signs of safety or danger (Oatley and Jenkins, 1992). It was Bowlby who first explained how the mother's face, and the emotional responses it displays, provide the child with a secure base from which to launch explorative sorties into the world, but to which it may always return in the event of need or danger (Bowlby, 1988). But it may also be that, at the neurobiological level, the affectivity expressed in the mother's face serves to amplify the child's positive arousal and thereby provide the child with the necessary stimulation to motivate further exploration of its environment (Schore, 1994: 102).

The important point here for the child's socioaffective development is that the infant finds stimulation that excites it pleasurable and hence comes to seek it out. In some primitive sense, the child smiles in order to evoke the mother's smile. Conversely, the infant finds too much arousal unpleasant and will avert its gaze, whereupon the psychologically attuned mother responds by reducing the stimulation (Schore, 1994: 82ff.). Although one should not exaggerate the intentional nature of these early behaviours, it is certainly tempting to see them as forming the interactional template for the genuinely communicational behaviours that emerge between 5 and 9 months of age. There has been considerable debate over the past decade about whether young infants are active participants in shared gaze and vocalization exchanges or whether it is the caregiver who shapes the infant's behaviour (Schaffer, 1984). But if Schore is right, 'long before the infant either comprehends or speaks a single word, it possesses an extensive repertoire of signals to communicate its internal states' (Schore, 1994: 88).

In other words, the communication of affective states is *bi-directional* from a remarkably young age. This is why Schore, following Bateson (1975), refers to the early stages of dyadic interaction as 'conversation'. What Bateson had in mind was that exchanges between an infant and the caregiver serve to cement emotional ties between them (Bateson, 1975). Schore adds the idea that the members of a dyad are involved from the outset in shared gaze 'dialogues' which maximize the optimal levels of arousal for the infant and minimize the infant's negative affects.[4]

The metaphor of conversation crops up time and time again in inter-actionist writings, as does the idea of 'turn taking' (Trevarthen, 1993).[5] In this idealized format of alternating sequential roles, little overlap or conflict is envisaged between infant and caregiver communications. As Savage-Rumbaugh and her colleagues put it, both members of the dyad are involved in

> something like a delicate dance with many different scores, the selection of which is being constantly negotiated while the dance is in progress, rather than in advance. Experienced partners know what turns the dance may take, and, more important, they have developed subroutines for negotiating what to do when one or both partners falter in the routine. (Savage-Rumbaugh, Murphy, Sevcik, Brakke, Williams and Rumbaugh, 1993: 27)

The use of these metaphors reflects an intriguing attempt to trace the origins of language to the child's earliest social interactions and, moreover, to read the child's earliest interactional patterns forward into language; that is, to treat language as essentially interactive. Thus, social inter-actionism suggests a fascinating response to the nativist thesis that the human being is 'born to talk' (Hulit and Howard, 1997). In a sense, the baby is born 'talking', at least insofar as the 'visual dialog between the mother and child, the most intense form of interpersonal communication, acts as a crucible for the forging of preverbal affective ties' (Schore, 1994: 80). And, we might add, the affective nature of early social interaction acts in turn as a crucible for the forging of language skills.

Architectural discord

> The world is a quiet place for Piaget's growing child. He is virtually alone in it, a world of objects that he must array in space, time and causal relationships. He begins his journey egocentrically and must impose properties on the world that will eventually be shared with others. But others give him little help. The social reciprocity of infant and mother plays a very small role in Piaget's account of development. And language gives neither hints nor even a means of unravelling the puzzles of the world to which language applies. Piaget's

child has one overwhelming problem: to bring the inner representations of mind into equilibrium with the structures of experience. Piaget's children are little intellectuals, detached from the hurly-burly of the human condition.

Jerome Bruner, *In Search of Mind*

Since the appearance of *Child's Talk* we have acquired a much better understanding of the importance of social relations for a child's emotional development. Infants have intense emotional reactions to people, but only relatively mild emotional responses to objects. (Indeed, it is a reliable sign of a developmental disorder if a child responds with the same sort of intensity to objects as to people (Greenspan, 1997).) Dyadic interaction is essential for both cognitive and communicative development (Berk, 1994; Owens, 1996). And, of course, as far as language development is concerned, it is well known that if a child's only exposure to language is from television or radio, she will invariably grow up with a severe language deficit.

Generativists have sought to minimize the significance of this last point by arguing, first, that a child deprived of normal social interaction suffers such severe emotional and cognitive deficits that its language abilities will naturally be impaired; and second, that if a child is to acquire language, it must be exposed to a normal linguistic environment within some sort of 'critical period' (e.g., the first seven years of life) (Lenneberg, 1967; Curtis, 1977). But it has never been made entirely clear why the 'language faculty', which is supposedly isolated from cognitive and emotional factors in such cases as Williams syndrome (Pinker, 1994) or linguistic savants (Yamada, 1990; Smith and Tsimpli, 1995), is none the less so severely impaired by social deprivation. Moreover, recent research on second-language acquisition casts doubt on the 'critical period' hypothesis (Bialystok and Hakuta, 1994). And when one looks at the so-called 'anomalous' cases of high language proficiency/low IQ that have been highlighted in the generativist literature, one finds virtually no discussion of the various psychological reasons why savants may have overdeveloped skills in one particular domain (Howe, 1989); moreover, it transpires that the IQs of the subjects involved places them at a mental age of at least 5 years: that is, they are well beyond the point of normal language acquisition *vis-à-vis* IQ (Tomasello, 1995). But perhaps the most important point to make against generativism is this: it is not just that social interaction is a vital ingredient in a child's development; rather every aspect of that development fundamentally involves a process of socialization.

Take the emotions. Psychologists of emotion distinguish between basic (e.g., interest, enjoyment, surprise, anger, fear) and higher emotions (e.g., empathy, altruism, pride, compassion, love). The basic emotions are said to be innate because they have derived through evolutionary-biological processes and serve adaptive functions, they are universally accompanied by distinct facial expressions (which even blind infants demonstrate at birth), and they are associated with specific neural substrates (Izard, 1991).

The higher emotions – such as what in Spanish are called *'pundonor'* and *'gracia'* – are enculturated; that is, the child learns, not just how to behave, or what to feel, but further, that acting in this way in such-and-such circumstances counts as acting with honour or grace. But even the 'basic emotions' become socialized, for every culture insists that the child develop control over them and learns what its community regards as their proper expression (see Briggs, 1970, on the Inuit).

The same point applies to children's play-acting, their problem-solving and thinking (Vygotsky, 1962; Rogoff, 1990). Thus interactionists have concluded that 'the child should be seen as more of a socioaffective than a sensorimotor being' (Stechler and Carpenter, 1967, quoted in Schore, 1994: 71). That is, social interaction is not just essential for a child's emotional and cognitive development, for that development is essentially social. And the same is true of the child's linguistic development. Indeed, in many respects language constitutes not just the paradigm, but the primary vehicle for the child's socialization (Shatz, 1994).

Language socialization begins long before the child utters or even understands its first word. Over its first seven months of life (and possibly earlier; see Locke, 1993) the child becomes attuned to the characteristic speech sounds of its community. Recent research on monkeys (Kuhl, 1991), as well as Savage-Rumbaugh's work on bonobos (Savage-Rumbaugh, Shanker and Taylor, 1998), suggests that this phenomenon is common to all primate infants, and not just human infants. But categorical perception, as it is often called, only develops in social interaction. It does not occur if the subject is simply exposed to a mechanical language source.

Child Directed Speech (CDS) represents an even more important aspect of language socialization. One of the most striking discoveries about CDS is that mothers are most effective in facilitating their child's language development when they 'do not talk at children, but with them' (Snow, 1986: 80). Children acquire language more quickly when their caregivers engage with them in joint activities. This is as true for language-delayed children as it is for normal children; for the former improve markedly in their language skills if their caregivers switch from directive to interactive styles of communication (Snow, 1994). Indeed, between 20 per cent and 50 per cent of children diagnosed with Specific Language Impairment can recover fully, provided their therapy is interactive and not directive (Leonard, 1997).

As we saw, on the classical view of scaffolding theory, social interaction simply takes over the role that the generativist theory assigns to innate processing mechanisms. On this reading, if the child is not born with the 'heuristics' required to process the 'complex information' that is being 'accessed', then those 'constraints' must be supplied by the child's primary caregivers. Hence social interaction is seen as a support system – a set of socially imposed constraints and guidelines – which enables the child to acquire the cognitive or linguistic 'structures' an isolated organism could not acquire inductively (according to such arguments as 'the poverty of the stimulus').

Thus the original debate over CDS was conceived in terms of the processing role of social interaction. This was partly as a result of Gold's proof that since only finite-state languages are learnable from Text Presentation, for a computer program to 'learn' an open-ended language it must be presented with both positive and negative information (Gold, 1967). This way of viewing the issue, however, accepts *ab initio* the suitability of the computational metaphor for framing psychological questions about language acquisition. But the real moral of recognizing the essentially social character of a child's linguistic development is that it is simply inappropriate to compare a child learning how to interact with others linguistically to a device that mechanically processes information. It is not simply the computational metaphor which is to blame here, but the underlying epistemological picture which invites it (and other reductionist metaphors that mechanists have deployed over the past two centuries): the picture of an isolated mind confronted with an array of complex information on which it seeks to impose order (Shanker, 1998). It is precisely this picture which Bruner challenges when he emphasizes the 'social reciprocity of infant and mother' in virtually every aspect of a child's development (Bruner, 1983b: 138).

Thus there is far more to the interactionist story than the role of 'proto-conversations' in regulating attention and sustaining positive hedonic states. For it is in the context of these affect-intensified interchanges that the child's first 'socializing' experiences occur: the very experiences that provide the necessary foundations for language acquisition. Starting around 11 months, the mother typically begins to break shared gaze and to display various negative facial expressions (e.g., conveying anger or disgust) in response to, and in order to alter, her child's behaviour. These sudden affective shifts, which the mother often makes unconsciously, have a startling effect: in an instant the child stops moving, her head hangs limply, her smile disappears, and she averts her eyes. Schore writes: 'The infant is thus propelled into an intensified low arousal state which he cannot yet autoregulate. Shame represents this rapid transition from a pre-existing high arousal positive hedonic state to a low arousal negative hedonic state' (1994: 203). This so-called 'shame' response, Schore argues, is 'the essential affect that mediates [the] socializing function' (1994: 200). The mother's 'frequent attempts to change the child's behaviour against his will and the child's attempts to have his way despite knowing what his parent wants' set the stage for 'a dramatic shift [in the parent's role] from primarily a caretaker to primarily a socialization agent' (Hoffman, 1975, quoted in Schore, 1994: 200). The child learns, through these episodes of 'dyadic dissonance', that he must control certain impulse behaviours which elicit the 'disgust face' from his caregiver. The most obvious example of this is toilet training, which introduces the child to the need for 'voluntary control over an involuntary process' (Schore, 1994: 228). Interestingly, this latter achievement, which plays such an important role in the socialization process, occurs at roughly the same time as the child's 'linguistic explosion'. However, the use of socialization techniques is hardly restricted to particular types of interactional events; they are part of the flow of daily interaction (Schaffer, 1984).

The generativist literature on language development places little emphasis on the occurrence and function of socialization in the child's acquisition of linguistic skills. This is hardly surprising as the generativist sees language acquisition in purely epistemological terms: that is, as a matter of the child (or rather, a particular module of the child's mind) working out the formal properties of a language system or 'grammar'. These formal properties are conceived as the facts of language, those which, with the necessary assistance from its innate knowledge of linguistic principles and parameters, the child must discover. In contrast, Bruner has always regarded language acquisition less as a matter of discovering pre-existent facts and more as a matter of the child's socialization into culture-specific forms of communicative behaviour (e.g., Bruner, 1975). This perspective comes through clearly in *Child's Talk*, with its emphasis on the role of behavioural routines, games and formats in language development. These are the nursery stages of the long process that is the child's enculturation into language.

Yet it is essential that linguistic enculturation should not be thought of simply in terms of the child's developing awareness of certain regular patterns of behaviour. It is true, as Bruner says, that there is 'a surprisingly high degree of order and "systematicity"' (1983a: 28) in the child's communicational environment and that this greatly facilitates her linguistic development. However, we must be wary of representing those routines and formats as 'scaffolding' for the epistemologically conceived task of mapping linguistic regularities and hypothesizing their underlying rules – that is, of mastering the facts of 'the linguistic code' (cf. Bruner, 1983a: 11). For a crucial conclusion of recent research is that the child does not simply notice or expect concomitant events in its interactions with its caregiver. Rather, the child learns how it and its co-interactants are supposed to behave. Language, as a form of social interaction, has a fundamentally normative character. The child's acquisition of formats and interactional routines is thus a matter of her gradual socialization into the normative techniques of cultural life. Thus, recent research within the social interactionist perspective leads us to see how the child's linguistic development is inseparable from her socioaffective development; and this realization provides the study of linguistic development with one of the means to liberate it from the epistemological model which underpins generativism, and, equally, the classical view of scaffolding theory which holds that 'it is the interaction between LAD and LASS that makes it possible for the infant to enter the linguistic community' (Bruner, 1983a: 19; cf. Savage-Rumbaugh, Shanker and Taylor, 1998). For as Bruner emphasized in *Child's Talk*, and even more explicitly in *Acts of Meaning* (1990), the child's socialization into language demands its transformation into a cultural agent.

Languacultural development

> To imagine a language means to imagine a form of life.
>
> Ludwig Wittgenstein, *Philosophical Investigations*

Child's Talk argues that to understand how a child acquires language we have to view language from the child's own perspective. This requires us to see the child not as a computing device, but as a human agent (Harris, 1996). Accordingly, the acquisition of language emerges, not as an epistemological problem the child's brain must solve (through innate knowledge or experiential learning), but as the gradual development of practical techniques whereby the child engages with her social environment.

The child initially learns that her interactional ends may be realized by means of her own behaviours and vocalizations: shifts of gaze, turns of the head, crying, pointing, facial expressions, etc. Gradually the child develops these proto-communicative behaviours into more and more 'adultlike' forms of interaction and, at the same time, more effective means of securing her ends. As *Child's Talk* illustrates, the child's mother typically demands increasingly sophisticated behaviour if those ends are to be realized. Thus the child's development of more sophisticated techniques emerges partly in response to the increasing demands of her environment, and partly as a result of her seemingly natural fascination with language itself (Karmiloff-Smith, 1992).

If, as Bruner argues, the child develops language as a means of 'doing things with words', then what are these 'things' that the child is learning to do? What are the young child's interactional intentions and goals? *Child's Talk* presents the child as learning to perform such classic speech acts as referring, requesting, ordering, commenting, telling stories and so on. Yet when the book raises the question of the origin of such speech acts, Bruner falls back on the assumption that they must be innate. Children apparently have a natural drive to refer to things, to request things, to tell stories and so on (see the discussion in Taylor, this volume).

Bruner is surely right to insist that the child acquires ways of performing particular kinds of communicational acts. However, it is crucial that communicational acts must not be treated as if they were separable – or as if they could be studied independently – from their conceptualization within a particular cultural form of life. The child's acquisition of particular speech acts is no less an integral part of her emerging competence in that form of life than is the acquisition of other culturally defined activities. Such acts and their cultural conceptualization are, to use Saussure's analogy, like two sides of the same sheet of paper: if you cut one, you inevitably cut the other. 'Referring to something', for example, cannot be something the child can do except as a feature of the child's reflexive integration into the forms of life of her cultural environment.

The following three related points clarify this claim and examine its implications. First, what the child acquires is not 'raw' behaviour, but cultural techniques. That is, she learns ways of behaving that count, within her environment, as the performance of particular culturally conceived acts. For instance, the child does not simply learn to produce certain vocal sounds or gestural patterns in the presence of particular objects: she learns how to do what we call 'talking about' objects. Similarly, she doesn't just learn to utter particular sounds when she desires some action from her mother; she learns how to 'ask for it', as 'asking for something' is conceived of in her cultural environment, her 'languaculture', as Michael Agar (1994) terms it. Producing certain sounds or gestures amounts to, for example, asking for something only as conceptualized within the reflexive practices of a particular languaculture. Analogously, moving two pieces of carved wood in a certain way across a checkerboard's two-dimensional surface is not 'castling' except as conceptualized within the game of chess.

What children acquiring, for example, English learn are not 'nameless' (i.e., unconceptualized) vocal and gestural patterns. They learn how to:

'say you're sorry'
'thank somebody'
'say what your name is' ('say what you are called')
'answer me'
'tell me what happened'
'tell the truth' (and how to 'lie')
'tell me where it is'
'say bye-bye'
'tease someone'
'say what you want'
'describe what it looks like'
'tell me what you're thinking'
'say where it hurts'
'ask what it means'
and so on ...

Children brought up in other speech communities learn how to perform other, culturally conceived communicational acts: other things that may be done with words within their cultural forms of life. They learn, for example: how to 'se plaindre' (French), 'govorit' (Russian), 'aanstoken' (Dutch), 'tatoti' (Futunan), 'tohutohu' (Maori), 'amo' (Mangaian), 'isani' (Blackfoot), 'gwaadmawaad' (Ojibwa), how to 'pahsoy' (Yurok), and so on (Verschueren, 1989: 20–4).

The point is that language development is indeed, as Bruner says, a matter of learning 'how to do things with words'. However, what those 'things' consist of – and what behaviour counts as an instance of any one of them – are matters determined by the reflexive practices of the cultural environment in which the child is raised. Analogously, the child learning how to play chess is not learning, for example, how to move her hand to grasp and manoeuvre wooden shapes, she is learning how to do something that in a chess environment is called 'castling'.

Second, the child should not be conceived as merely learning how to produce the behaviour that in her cultural environment counts as performing certain speech acts. For an integral component of learning how to do things with words is learning what 'things' she will be taken to have 'done' when she utters those words, that is, what speech acts she will be taken to have performed.

For example, a child cannot truly be said to have learned to say what her name is if, when she says 'Charlotte', she does not know that what she is doing is 'saying what her name is'. Likewise, she cannot be said to have learned how to apologize if she does not yet know that saying 'I'm sorry' in the appropriate circumstances is (what we call) 'apologizing'. Imagine a little girl who utters the sounds [aim sari] ('I'm sorry') at apparently random points in the day, yet her behaviour indicates that she does not understand what it is to apologize. She does not act as one typically does before or after apologizing, she doesn't address her remarks to anyone in particular, she does not say 'I'm sorry' at the contextually appropriate moments (i.e., when she has something to apologize for). It is no more justified to say of her that she has learned to apologize than it is to say that a parrot which can squawk, 'A parrot's life is hell', has learned to complain about his lot in life.

There is, in other words, an essentially *reflexive* character to what a child acquires in acquiring language. Learning a culture's reflexive conceptualization of the acts one can perform with language is, we would like to say, part and parcel of learning to perform those speech acts. The child learning English learns, for instance, that saying particular words in particular sorts of circumstances is 'Saying what you want' and that saying other words in other sorts of circumstances is 'Saying what your name is'. Acquiring the English-speaking culture's reflexive conceptualization of these 'things you can do with words' is an ineliminable component of learning how to do those 'things'.

Third, learning, for example, how to apologize involves even more than learning when and how to say [aim sari] and that doing so in the right circumstances is (what we call) 'apologizing'. For it also includes learning, for instance, that merely saying [aim sari] is not enough to succeed in apologizing. If you have learned how to apologize, then you know that you have to address this vocalization not just to anybody but to the right person. And this means that you need to be able to determine who 'the right person' is. (What sense would it make to say that Charlotte had learned to apologize if she could never work out to whom her utterance of 'I'm sorry' should be addressed?) Saying sorry to the right person is not sufficient if you don't mean it. And this means that learning how to apologize involves learning what in our culture counts as 'meaning it'. Furthermore, you also have to learn that you can only apologize for certain things. You can't apologize for something for which you were not responsible. So learning how to apologize involves learning to determine what you can be held responsible for according to the norms of our languaculture.

Nor can you succeed in apologizing for something for which you are responsible but which is not perceived as 'bad', 'unfortunate', or otherwise inappropriate. So, if you are to learn to apologize, you have to learn what, within our languaculture, counts as 'bad' or 'unfortunate'. Finally, what *you* have to do to succeed in apologizing is only half the story. For it is equally important that you learn to tell when someone else has apologized. How could a child be accurately described as having learned to apologize if she never understood when someone else had apologized to her?

Let us return to the example of learning 'to say what your name is'. To do this, the child must learn more than that she should pronounce 'Charlotte' when asked 'What's your name?' For it makes little sense to say that Charlotte has learned

(1) to say what her name is

if she does not know that

(2) 'Charlotte' is her name

and, therefore, that when she says 'Charlotte' in reply to 'What's your name?', she is saying what her name is. However, this in turn entails that she must know what a name is. For how can she have learned that

(2) 'Charlotte' is her name

if she does not yet know

(3) what a name is?

Learning how to say what your name is requires the development of reflexive knowledge of what it is for a vocalization/word to be a name. The parrot who squawks 'Eliza' when asked 'What's your name?' does not know that 'Eliza' is its name, for it does not know what a name is.

And this is not all. Knowing what a name is also involves – at least in our culture – knowing such things as that every person has a name, that names often have parts, that your name belongs to you (although it is possible that someone else may have it as well), that a name cannot be easily changed, that (usually) when someone calls out your name, they are seeking your attention, that putting your name on things is usually to identify them as your own, and so on. In other cultures it may be that knowing what a name is involves knowing that saying an adult's name in public is impolite, or that you are not supposed to utter the name of a dead person, or that a person's name tells something about them (e.g., indicates who their parents are), and so on.[6] In other words, to know

(3) what a name is

is to know

(4) what a name is for us.

To know what a name is is to know how, in our languaculture, we use names, what function they have, and how we value, choose, change and generally treat them. 'Name' is neither a cultural universal nor some sort of acultural (autonomously linguistic) concept. If one is to learn a name, as Wittgenstein put it, one must already know what 'post' names occupy in our culture's language games (Wittgenstein, 1953: §257). The same point applies, we would argue, to learning how 'to talk about' something, how to 'ask for something', how to 'say what you mean', and how to perform all of those speech acts for which those in our (or any other) languaculture use words.

Consider one notable criticism that has been addressed to some attempts to facilitate the development of language by nonhuman primates. Some critics objected to the claim that the chimpanzee Lana had learned the symbol for 'please' (Rumbaugh, 1977) on the grounds that although Lana had learned to push the button marked 'please' at the beginning of a request sequence, she did not really understand what 'please' means because she had no awareness of the cultural function of saying 'please'. That is, she did not understand the difference between 'asking nicely' and 'not asking nicely', or how 'please' functions in creating and signalling that difference. To her, it was argued, 'please' is just a button that must be pushed to attain a desired object, much as one has to push the button marked 'Coke' to get a Coke from a soda machine. In contrast, when a child learns 'to ask nicely', she is not just learning to make the vocalization [pliz] before she says something. Rather, she is learning how to do what in her family's culture counts as 'asking nicely'. (It is irrelevant that in many cases this is not a precisely defined category or that the criteria for inclusion are indeterminate, context-relative, etc.) Moreover, learning how to 'ask nicely' involves learning a great deal more than just which words or sentences 'please' should be combined with. It involves learning what, in our culture, it is to ask nicely, the connections between asking nicely and various 'character traits' recognized within our culture: for example, 'being rude', 'being polite', 'being good', 'being well behaved', 'being respectful', and so on.

In other words, the linguistic world into which the child is entering is a *reflexively enculturated* world (Taylor, 1997: ch. 1). It is a world that we make and remake every day by talking about it, commenting on it, evaluating it and trying discursively to fashion it according to our likes and needs. Its structure and properties do not exist independently of reflexively constructive activities of the speakers and hearers themselves. What this means is that there is a reflexive character to knowing how to do things with words – in this case, knowing how to use words as names, as apologies, as requests, and so on. And there is also an enculturated character to that knowledge. That is, knowing how to do things with words is knowing the kinds of 'things' *we* do with words – the ways we conceive that words may be made use of in the cultural techniques that make up our form of life. (And this is not to imply that what counts as 'us' is anything but a socially contested, and reflexive, matter.) In learning how to use words to 'do things', the child is learning a reflexively enculturated form of knowledge. If we do not keep this clearly in view in the study of language acquisition, we will inevitably misunderstand how that knowledge is acquired.

At the same time it is crucial to see that the general point being made here is not limited to the acquisition of speech acts such as 'saying your name', 'apologizing', 'requesting', 'asking nicely', and so on. The reflexive enculturation of what the child learns extends right into the structural and semiotic 'core' of language. Consider: could a word – say, 'eyebrow' – have a meaning, the *particular* meaning that we say it has in English, if we had no reflexive means of saying what its meaning is, of explaining its meaning, or of distinguishing between its meaning and that of, say, 'eyelash' or 'eyelid'? What if we had no way of talking about its meaning, or about 'what the word for *this* is' (said by someone pointing at his eyebrow)? How, then, could its 'having a meaning' be anything like 'eyebrow' having the meaning that it has in modern English? And how would the property of 'having a meaning' (a *particular* meaning) be anything like we take it to be if there were no reflexive practices for talking about and thereby individuating 'meanings'? To become competent in language – including learning what particular words mean – the child must also become competent in those reflexive practices (cf. Taylor, 1997, 2000).

Speaking about the object of linguistic enquiry, the so-called 'founder of modern linguistics', Ferdinand de Saussure, said: 'The object is not given in advance of the viewpoint: far from it. Rather, one might say that it is the viewpoint adopted which creates the object' (Saussure, 1916: 8). We create names by speaking of certain vocalizations as names and by embedding those vocalizations in certain reflexive practices. We make words have the meanings they do, at least in part, by speaking of them as having those meanings. Human vocalizations, gestures and visible marks are not names and do not have meanings 'in advance of the viewpoint', as Saussure would say. The viewpoint creates the (languacultural) object. If we accept the implications of Saussure's point (which Saussure himself did not realize), then we must conclude that the child's development of language depends as much on the development of that reflexive viewpoint as it does on vocalizations, gestures and marks.

We do not wish to be misunderstood. Of course it is the case that children produce a great deal of verbal behaviour, and are typically (charitably) interpreted as performing many different kinds of speech act, long before they manifest any reflexive linguistic awareness of what the speech acts are that they are being taken to perform: in other words, long before they can participate competently in the reflexive practices. This is true whether we are talking about the speech acts of 'apologizing', 'saying your name' and 'describing' – or even 'talking about', 'requesting', 'answering' and 'meaning'. A child may well be saying 'Charlotte' at more or less appropriate moments but not yet manifest reflexive linguistic awareness that doing so counts as saying her name or what it means to have a name in our culture. But to become a competent member of our languaculture – truly to learn to do the things that we do with words – she must do more than act in ways that (at a superficial level) are indistinguishable from our 'primary' verbal behaviour. She must develop a competence in the reflexive languacultural practices that manifest her awareness of what she is doing when she speaks. Naturally this competence does not come all at once. The child will learn gradually what it means in her culture for 'Charlotte' to be her name, what it is for the word X to have the 'meaning' Y, what it is to 'ask for something', or to 'talk about something', or to 'say where it hurts', or to 'apologize'. There is no a priori reason to assume that this learning ever attains a 'steady state'. If this means that we must abandon the 'commonsense' notion of a child moving from not knowing 'what X means' yesterday to knowing 'what X means' today, then so be it. Surely this 'commonsense' notion is another of those legacies of the codebook conception of language whose abandonment is long overdue.

   To summarize: the language learner is not just an agent, but a cultural agent learning to do the sorts of culturally significant things that make up our form of life. To learn how to do things with words is to learn our culture's reflexive conceptualization of what can be done with language and how language matters in the living of our common lives. What a child learns in learning about language is inextricably woven together with the other things the child learns about our culture. In other words, in learning a language, a child is learning a necessarily enculturated phenomenon. To the extent that developmentalists 'abstract' the child's acquisition of linguistic ability from its acquisition of other cultural abilities, they render the former both incomprehensible and inexplicable (except by a *deus ex machina* such as LAD).

Conclusion: the house the child builds

> Let us imagine a language for which the description given by Augustine is right. The language is meant to serve for communication between a builder A and an assistant B. A is building with building-stones: there are blocks, pillars, slabs and beams. B has to pass the stones, and that in the order in which A needs them. For this purpose they use a language consisting of the words 'block', 'pillar', 'slab', 'beam'. A calls them out; – B brings the stone which he has learnt to bring at such-and-such a call. – Conceive this as a complete primitive language.
>
> Ludwig Wittgenstein, *Philosophical Investigations*

There is something appealing about comparing a child learning language to an apprentice learning how to build a house. For language is something that we ourselves construct and inhabit, something that shapes us as much as we shape it. What Bruner showed is that, while the child may be ideally suited to become a language-builder, this can happen only if she has a caregiver-mentor to assist her in acquiring the many skills required to be proficient in the craft. For not only are the functions of words as diverse as the functions of the various tools that one finds in any particular culture's toolbox (Wittgenstein, 1953: §11), but the tools themselves are constantly changing according to a culture's ever-changing tastes in housing styles. If language is like a building, it is one that can never be finished.

Like so many of the fundamental properties of language and its development, this open-ended, constructive character of language acquisition is obscured on the generativist account. Language acquisition is given the form of a logico-mechanical problem. How must a neuro-machine be designed so that when it receives the input of a language (as this is conceived by the generativist model), it will deduce the language's 'structure'? Generativism renders invisible agency, normativity and reflexivity, and portrays culture as something peripheral to language. The language-user's agency becomes a matter of 'performance', the characteristics of which depend entirely on the theoretically more interesting 'competence' which it merely enacts. The normative character of language is reduced to a matter of internal, mechanical rules. And the things done with language, together with 'words', 'names', 'meanings' are rendered as species of *realia*: autonomously linguistic universal entities and acts that exist and have distinct properties independently of the language-user's reflexive conception of them.

In this light, Bruner's breakthrough has been to nudge the essentially agential, normative, reflexive and enculturated nature of language back into view. Seen from the perspective of the social interactionist revolution that his work has stimulated, these are the ingredients that make language acquisition possible. But to complete the aspect-shift begun by Bruner we now need to abandon the generativist picture of what the child acquires: that free-standing, reflexivity-less, normative-less, agency-less, culture-less entity that language supposedly is once the scaffold is pulled away. Instead we need to explore the implications of the idea that the 'scaffold', which assists the child in developing language, remains a no less essential part of the 'product' of that development. That is, we need to recognize that, like the Pompidou Centre, what was initially thought to be the constructor's external scaffolding is actually part of the edifice itself.

Notes

1   The term 'secondary altriciality' was coined by Adolf Portmann in the 1940s, but made famous by Stephen Jay Gould's 'Human babies as embryos' (1977). Portmann describes mammals that have large litters of undeveloped, helpless offspring as 'altricial' in contrast to 'precocial' mammals, which give birth to a few well-developed offspring capable of taking care of themselves at birth. In many respects, humans have characteristics associated with precocial mammals, e.g., long life spans, large brains and complex social behaviour. But by precocial standards the human infant is born approximately nine months prematurely (a longer gestation period would be incompatible with bipedality in the mother), and is helpless at birth. Thus Portmann describes human babies as 'secondarily altricial'.

2   We use the term 'innate' with trepidation, for the term is often used simple-mindedly. Sometimes when a behaviour is described as innate, it is meant that the behaviour is produced by a specific, identifiable set of genes. Few behaviours of any complexity can be innate in this sense. It is more plausible to take

the term to refer to our genetic endowment per se, but then its use is often empty, since there are so many factors involved in how that endowment is realized (Elman, Bates, Johnson, Karmiloff-Smith, Parisi and Plunkett, 1996: 357).

3   For a discussion of the obstacles confronting caregivers of blind infants, see Fraiberg, 1977.

4   The same point no doubt applies to the mother's vocalizations. The very fact that – in Western cultures at any rate – primary caregivers direct so much speech at the infant from birth, and that caregivers' speech patterns are so closely attuned to the baby's states of arousal, suggests that speech, as much as gaze, is vital for a child's neurobiological and physical development (see Monnot, 1999).

5   Kaye (1982) even refers to the 'dialogue-like' pattern of the infant's burst–pause sucking, with the mother quiet during the bursts and active during the pauses.

6   Amongst the Inuit, a child receives the name of some individual, either living or dead, of either sex, and this defines that child's kinship relations with the rest of his or her community. Thus, if a boy is named after his paternal grandmother, he will call his father *irniq* ('son'), and his father will call him *anaana* ('mother'). These kinship names are taken very seriously; so much so that, whenever possible, one addresses people by kinship terms rather than by their personal names. Thus name-learning involves mastering the complex social matrix of one's community (Dorais, 1997).

References

Agar, M. (1994) *Language Shock: Understanding the Culture of Conversation*. New York: William Morrow & Company.

Bateson, M.C. (1975) 'Mother–infant exchanges: the epigenesis of conversation interaction', *Annals of the New York Academy of Science*, 263: 101–13.

Berk, L. (1994) *Child Development*, 4th edn. Needham Heights, MA: Allyn & Bacon.

Bialystok, E. and Hakuta, K. (1994) *In Other Words: The Science and Psychology of Second-Language Acquisition*. New York: Basic Books.

Bowlby, J. (1969) *Attachment and Loss*. Vol. 1: *Attachment*. New York: Basic Books.

Bowlby, J. (1988) *A Secure Base*. New York: Basic Books.

Briggs, J. (1970) *Never in Anger: Portrait of an Eskimo Family*. Cambridge, MA: Harvard University Press.

Brown, R. (1973) *A First Language*. Cambridge, MA: Harvard University Press.

Bruner, J.S. (1975) 'From communication to language – a psychological perspective', *Cognition*, 3: 255–87.

Bruner, J.S. (1983a) *Child's Talk: Learning How to Use Language*. Oxford: Oxford University Press.

Bruner, J.S. (1983b) *In Search of Mind: Essays in Autobiography*. New York: Harper & Row.

Bruner, J.S. (1990) *Acts of Meaning*. Cambridge, MA: Harvard University Press.

Cohn, J., Matias, R. and Tronick, E. (1990) 'Face-to-face interactions of depressed mothers and their infants', in E. Tronick and T. Field (eds), *New Directions for Child Development*, Vol. 34. San Francisco: Jossey-Bass.

Curtis, S. (1977) *Genie: A Psycholinguistic Study of a Modern-day 'Wild Child'*. London: Academic Press.

Dorais, L.-J. (1997) *Quaqtaq: Modernity and Identity in an Inuit Community*. Toronto: University of Toronto Press.

Elman, J., Bates, E., Johnson, M., Karmiloff-Smith, A., Parisi, D. and Plunkett, K. (1996) *Rethinking Innateness: A Connectionist Perspective on Development*. Cambridge, MA: MIT Press.

Fraiberg, S. (1977) *Insights from the Blind: Comparative Studies of Blind and Sighted Infants*. New York: Basic Books.

Gallaway, C. and Richards, B. (eds) (1994) *Input and Interaction in Language Acquisition*. Cambridge: Cambridge University Press.

Gold, E. (1967) 'Language identification in the limit', *Information and Control*, 16: 447–74.

Gould, S.J. (1977) 'Human babies as embryos', in his *Ever Since Darwin: Reflections in Natural History*. New York: W.W. Norton.

Greenspan, S. (1997) *The Growth of the Mind and the Endangered Origins of Intelligence*. Reading, MA: Addison-Wesley.

Harris, R. (1996) *Signs, Language, and Communication*. London: Routledge.

Hoffman, M. (1975) 'Moral internalization, parental power, and the nature of parent–child interaction', *Developmental Psychology*, 11: 228–39.

Howe, M. (1989) *Fragments of Genius*. London: Routledge.

Hulit, L. and Howard, M. (1997) *Born to Talk: An Introduction to Speech and Language Development*. Boston: Allyn & Bacon.

Izard, C. (1991) *The Psychology of Emotions*. New York: Plenum Press.

Karmiloff-Smith, A. (1992) *Beyond Modularity: A Developmental Perspective on Cognitive Science*. Cambridge, MA: MIT Press.

Kaye, K. (1982) *The Mental and Social Life of Babies*. Chicago, IL: University of Chicago Press.

King, B. and Shanker, S. (1997) 'The expulsion of primates from the garden of language', *Evolution of Communication*, 1: 59–99.

Kuhl, P. (1991) 'Perception, cognition, and the ontogenetic and phylogenetic emergence of human speech', in S.E. Brauth, W.S. Hall and R.J. Dooling (eds), *Plasticity of Development*. Cambridge, MA: MIT Press.

Lenneberg, E. (1967) *Biological Foundations of Language*. New York: Wiley.

Leonard, L. (1997) *Children with Specific Language Impairment*. Cambridge, MA: MIT Press.

Locke, J. (1993) *The Child's Path to Spoken Language*. Cambridge, MA: Harvard University Press.

Messer, D. (1994) *The Development of Communication: From Social Interaction to Language*. New York: John Wiley & Sons.

Monnot, M. (1999) 'Function of infant-directed speech', *Human Nature*, 10 (4): 415–43.

Noble, W. and Davidson, I. (1996) *Human Evolution, Language and Mind*. Cambridge: Cambridge University Press.

Oatley, K. and Jenkins, J. (1992) 'Human emotions: function and dysfunction', *Annual Review of Psychology*, 43: 55–85.

Owens, R. (1996) *Language Development: An Introduction*. 4th edn. Boston: Allyn & Bacon.

Pinker, S. (1994) *The Language Instinct*. New York: William Morrow.

Rogoff, B. (1990) *Apprenticeship in Thinking: Cognitive Development in Social Context*. New York: Oxford University Press.

Rumbaugh, D.M. (ed.) (1977) *Language Learning by a Chimpanzee*. New York: Academic.

Saussure, F. de (1983 [1916]) *Course in General Linguistics*. R. Harris (trans.), London: Duckworth.

Savage-Rumbaugh, E.S., Murphy, J., Sevcik, R.A., Brakke, K.E., Williams, S. and Rumbaugh, D.M. (1993) *Language Comprehension in Ape and Child*. Monographs of the Society for Research in Child Development, Serial No. 233, Vol. 58, Nos. 3–4.

Savage-Rumbaugh, S., Shanker, S. and Taylor, T. (1998) *Apes, Language and the Human Mind*. New York: Oxford University Press.

Schaffer, H. (1984) *The Child's Entry into a Social World*. London: Academic Press.

Schore, A. (1994) *Affect Regulation and the Origin of the Self*. Hillsdale, NJ: Lawrence Erlbaum.

Shanker, S. (1998) *Wittgenstein's Remarks on the Foundations of AI*. London: Routledge.

Shatz, M. (1994) *A Toddler's Life*. Oxford: Oxford University Press.

Smith, N. and Tsimpli, I.-M. (1995) *The Mind of a Savant*. Oxford: Basil Blackwell.

Snow, C. (1986) 'Conversations with children', in P. Fletcher and M. Garman (eds), *Language Acquisition: Studies in Second Language Development*. Cambridge: Cambridge University Press.

Snow, C. (1994) 'Beginning from baby talk: twenty years of research on input in interaction', in C. Gallaway and B. Richards (eds), *Input and Interaction in Language Acquisition*. Cambridge: Cambridge University Press.

Stechler, G. and Carpenter, G. (1967) 'A viewpoint on early affective development', in J. Hellmuth (ed.), *The Exceptional Infant*, Vol. 1. New York: Brunner/Mazel.

Taylor, T.J. (1997) *Theorizing Language: Analysis, Normativity, Rhetoric, History*. Oxford: Pergamon Press.

Taylor, T.J. (2000) 'Language constructing language: the implications of reflexivity for linguistic theory', *Language Sciences*, 22 (4): 483–99.

Tomasello, M. (1995) 'Language is not an instinct', *Cognitive Development*, 10: 131–56.

Trevarthen, C. (1979) 'Communication and cooperation in early infancy: a description of primary intersubjectivity', in M.M. Bullowa (ed.), *Before Speech: the Beginning of Interpersonal Communication*. New York: Cambridge University Press.

Trevarthen, C. (1993) 'The self born in intersubjectivity: the psychology of an infant communicating', in U. Neisser (ed.), *The Perceived Self*. Cambridge: Cambridge University Press.

Verschueren, J. (1980) *On Speech Act Verbs*. Amsterdam: John Benjamins.

Verschueren, J. (1989) *Language on Language: Toward Metapragmatic Universals*. Special issue of *Papers in Pragmatics*, Vol. III, No. 2, December.

Vygotsky, L. (1962) *Thought and Language*. Cambridge, MA: MIT Press.

Wittgenstein, L. (1953) *Philosophical Investigations*. Oxford: Basil Blackwell.

Yamada, J. (1990) *Laura*. Cambridge, MA: MIT Press.

4

BRUNER AND CONDILLAC ON LEARNING HOW TO TALK

Talbot J. Taylor

It is quite illusory to believe that where language is concerned the problem of origins is any different from the problem of permanent conditions. There is no way out of the circle.

Ferdinand de Saussure, *Course in General Linguistics*

In Book Three of his *Essay Concerning Human Understanding*, Locke poses a puzzle which has troubled scholars ever since. He suggests that language is not adequate to accomplish its principal task, which is to convey thoughts from the mind of the speaker to that of the hearer (Locke, 1978: III.i.2). Nevertheless, Locke maintains that the 'common use' of words regulates their meaning tolerably well for the purposes of ordinary discourse (III.ix.8). So what is it about the use of language in ordinary talk that mitigates or conceals its fundamental inadequacy?

For Locke, 'the imperfection of words' is that they can signify only thoughts in the speaker's mind. As the hearer cannot know the speaker's thoughts, he cannot be sure what the latter's words signify. The words you utter express your ideas, but when I hear those words, I can interpret them only as signs of my own. Thus language fails to provide an intersubjective conduit between our minds. It is therefore puzzling that Locke should feel that our ordinary use of language is successful. How, in spite of the privacy of our minds, do we manage to communicate with each other?

In the *Essay*, Locke passes over this issue with little comment. His aim is rather to repair the imperfections of language so that it may become a reliable tool in scientific discourse. The puzzle did, however, exercise the minds of his eighteenth-century followers, such as the abbé de Condillac. They struggled to show how language could be used as an effective vehicle of communication, despite the fact that 'the same words have in different mouths, and often in the same, very different meanings' (Condillac, 1947: 762).

Condillac hoped to find the solution to Locke's puzzle through speculation about the phylogenetic origins of language. If we could determine how men first came to use language, we could discover the intersubjective principle regulating ordinary discourse. For although language is primarily an artificial creation – a social institution – it arose from natural capacities with which every human individual is endowed. There is presumed to be an essential continuity between the human individual's natural gifts and the artificial, social practice of using language for communication. Thus, by discovering how human beings in their natural state might have learned to use language, we can identify its fundamental principle of intersubjectivity, thereby resolving Locke's communicational puzzle.

The question of the phylogenetic origins of language does not arouse the same interest today as it did in the Enlightenment, when it was perhaps the central mystery about language. It is not that contemporary linguists are indifferent to the topic; it is just that there is no way to approach it without relying heavily on speculation, a method few modern linguists find congenial. We have no 'hard' evidence about the phylogenesis of language, nor can we hope to discover any. Those baffled by Locke's puzzle today tend to turn rather to the ontogenesis of language, hoping that the explanation of the intersubjective success of ordinary linguistic practices resides in how children learn to use language.

The thesis to be argued here is that the investigations of the origins of language, whether phylogenetic or ontogenetic, are equally regressive enterprises. The assumptions they adopt and the reasoning they embody are strikingly similar. *The study of ontogeny recapitulates the study of phylogeny.* Yet while the 'bow-wow' and 'grunt-grunt' theories of phylogenesis provide readers of linguistic textbooks with comic relief, current models of linguistic ontogenesis are the height of theoretical respectability.

It is obvious that Locke's puzzle will only interest proponents of a mentalist view of language. It had no place among the behaviourist's concerns. Nor did it receive much attention after generativism transformed the psychological foundations of linguistics, for the extreme nativist position adopted by Chomsky and his followers also stifled interest in the issue. The epistemological worries behind Locke's puzzle take hold only once it is conceded that crucial aspects of language-use are learned.

In this regard, psycholinguistics is ripe for a revival, in some form or other, of Locke's puzzle. After the downfall of behaviourism, generativism dominated psycholinguistic investigations. Psycholinguists sought evidence of the mental representation of transformational rules, deep structures, lexical insertion, cyclical ordering of rules, and the like. This had a striking effect on studies of language acquisition. What had traditionally been the domain of psychology became a central topic of linguistics proper. Moreover, methods of study were significantly altered. It is a major tenet of generativism that the principles underlying language competence are innate. Consequently, there is no real point in studying how children learn language; in an important sense, they already know it. Instead, energy was devoted to characterizing that innate competence by discovering the principles universal to all languages. In this way, studies of language acquisition had no need to investigate children at all; they could search instead for the universal properties of fully developed grammars.

Recently, however, Chomsky's dominance has declined. Psychological and computational explorations of language processing have provoked increasing doubts that any features of the generativist model of language have psychological reality. Psychologists in turn have gradually reclaimed certain areas of child language studies. This has resulted in the re-emergence of a certain degree of empiricism. In this, the work of Jerome Bruner has had the greatest influence.

The ontogenesis of language use: mediating between genes and culture

In *Child's Talk: Learning to Use Language* (1983), Bruner situates his position somewhere between the extremes of empiricism and nativism. He adopts George Miller's characterization of a pure empiricist view of language acquisition as 'impossible' and pure nativism as 'miraculous', and professes to occupy a middle position incorporating only the best of each. In order to bridge the gap between empiricism and nativism, and, at the same time, to restore some part of language acquisition to psychology, Bruner splits language acquisition into two. Not only must the child somehow attain knowledge of language (i.e., linguistic competence), he must also acquire an ability to use that knowledge for communicational ends (i.e., pragmatic competence). It is the acquisition of the latter that forms the topic of the psychological investigation of child language. The linguist, we may assume, retains possession of the question of how linguistic knowledge is acquired. With this division, Bruner is able to achieve a (historic?) compromise with nativist generative linguistics. He concedes the nativist position on linguistic knowledge, yet maintains that it remains to be discovered how children learn to use that knowledge for the purposes of communication: that is, how they acquire the ability to refer, request, deny, warn, query and so on:

> In this view, entry into language is an entry into discourse that requires both members of a dialogue pair to interpret a communication and its intent. Learning a language, then, consists of learning not only the *grammar* of a particular language but also learning how to realize one's intentions by the appropriate use of that grammar. (Bruner, 1983: 38)

While Bruner accepts that the child's knowledge of language is largely the product of an innate 'set of language-learning capabilities, something akin to ... LAD' (1983: 18–19), he argues that the child's pragmatic competence is formed in the environment of socialization routines imposed by the mother. The child's formative communicational experiences are not random but are the result of constructive patterns of interactional training:

The development of language, then, involves two people negotiating. Language is not encountered willy-nilly by the child; it is shaped to make communicative interaction effective – fine-tuned. If there is a Language Acquisition Device (LAD), the input to it is not a shower of spoken language but a highly interactive affair shaped, as we have already noted, by some sort of Language Acquisition Support System (LASS). (Bruner, 1983: 39)

In other words, without the LASS there would be nothing for the little LAD to do. The acquisition of language is aided by the mother, who arranges early interaction with the child within routinized and familiar formats. These formats – the central vehicle of LASS – provide a controlled, competence-sensitive guide to the child's experience of the function of language, forming a continuous bridge between prelinguistic and linguistic interaction.

Thus, while Bruner accepts the nativists' claim that linguistic knowledge is biological in origin, he insists that this biological capacity necessarily requires cultural expression. And culture must to some degree be learned:

While the *capacity* for intelligible action has deep biological roots and a discernible evolutionary history, the *exercise* of that capacity depends upon man appropriating to himself modes of acting and thinking that exist not in his genes but in his culture. (Bruner, 1983: 23)

But, while culture is a social phenomenon, a biological capacity is the possession of an individual. So how does the child learn to exercise an individual capacity in a shared, social form? Bruner continues:

There is obviously something in mind or in 'human nature' that mediates between the genes and the culture that makes it possible for the latter to be a prosthetic device for the realization of the former. (1983: 23)

What mediates between genes and culture is the learned ability to use genetically encoded linguistic knowledge for the communicational ends of social interaction. Thus a (the?) central puzzle in the study of language acquisition must be how the individual child acquires the ability to perform the social activity of using language.

Perhaps the most significant feature of Bruner's theory is that, having split the notion of language acquisition into two, he insists that linguistic and pragmatic development are interdependent:

the infant's Language Acquisition Device could not function without the aid given by an adult who enters with him into a transactional format. That format, initially under the control of the adult, provides a Language Acquisition Support System, LASS. It frames or structures the input of language and interaction to the child's Language Acquisition Device in a manner to 'make the system function.' In a word, it is the interaction between LAD and LASS that makes it possible for the infant to enter the linguistic community. (Bruner, 1983: 19)

So, the development of the child's genetically endowed Language Acquisition Device depends upon her acquiring the mediating ability to use the fruits of that endowment in social intercourse. The origin and development of that mediating ability form the twin topics of *Child's Talk*.

The enlightenment: linguistic phylogenesis

In his *Essai sur l'origine des connoissances humaines*, Condillac's primary
concern, like Locke's, is to examine the foundations of human knowledge
and render them more secure. He argues that man is distinguished from
animals by the exercise of his innate powers of reflection. Had primitive
humans not learned to control the reflective powers with which they were
naturally endowed, they would have remained in an unenlightened state.
It is only by the use of language that man can control reflection. Consequently, if man had not learned to use language (specifically, how to use
arbitrary signs), his rational gift of reflection would have remained an
unfulfilled potential:

> The progress of the human mind depends entirely on our proficiency in the use
> of language. (Condillac, 1947: 366)

Thus, like Bruner, Condillac holds that man's rational and linguistic
development are fundamentally interdependent:

> It is the use of signs which enables the exercise of reflection; but, at the same
> time, this faculty serves to multiply the number of signs.... So signs and reflec-
> tion are causes which provide mutual assistance and which reciprocally
> contribute to their progress. (Condillac, 1947: 733)

Thus, from Condillac's point of view, this interdependence of reflection and
language poses a chicken-and-egg question for the epistemologist. How
could primitive man, in his natural state, have learned to use language,
given that the ability to use language presupposes a certain degree of
control over the reflective powers? As he puts it himself:

> It might appear that one would not know how to make use of conventional
> signs if one were not already capable of sufficient reflection to choose them and
> attach them to ideas: how then, it might be objected, can the exercise of reflection
> only be acquired by the use of signs? (Condillac, 1947: 226)

It is important to recognize that, as Aarsleff has shown (1982), Condillac's
work constituted a merger of post-Locke empiricism and the Port-Royal
tradition of *grammaire générale*. For Condillac, as for Arnauld and Lancelot,
language is an expression (or 'picture') of the mental operation of reflection.
But, as an empiricist, Condillac did not accept that the ability to control
reflection is innate. Condillac's originality was to add an historical, developmental perspective to universal grammar (much as Locke had added a
developmental perspective to the study of government in *The Second Treatise
on Government*). The rationality underlying language could not be understood from a purely synchronic perspective since its present form was
largely the result of man's improving ability to use language, an ability
acquired in part from experience. Consequently, the foundation of rationality lay in the origin of language-using; and so, Condillac argued, that origin
provided the key to the study of the principles of human understanding.

It is here that the influence of Locke's puzzle becomes clear. For who is
to say that I use language to control and express my thoughts in the same

way as you? If language-using is an ability learned through experience, then it is crucial that we all acquire the *same* ability. Not only must we share innate reflective powers; we must also somehow learn to control those powers through the use of language in the same way. Given the importance that Condillac attributes to language-using, Locke's puzzle poses a challenge to the epistemology presented in the *Essai*. Hence, Condillac's enquiries into the origin of language can be seen as an attempt to discover a shared source that guarantees intersubjective accord in the use of language and reflection.

Condillac believed that the use of conventional signs had originated in natural expressions of emotion. A cry of fear upon seeing a predator, for example, is a natural, context-determined response. For Condillac, however, even a complex 'vocabulary' of emotional responses would not constitute a 'true' language because the production of such responses is not under the speaker's control, but depends on the occurrence of appropriate stimuli. Possession of such a vocabulary, then, would not allow man to exercise control over his mind, for it would not even constitute control over the use of the vocalizations themselves.

Condillac argues that an important step was taken when man came to live in society with others. For he then heard similar vocalizations produced by those around him and recognized them as (natural) signs of the producer's emotions. At this stage, then, the emotional cry is not simply a response to felt emotion; it also acquires a use, albeit an as yet uncontrolled and unintentional one. It now also serves as an intersubjective link informing others of the speaker's emotions. But the most crucial stage is when man comes to use such natural signs with an intention to communicate. For instance, suppose from a high tree I see a predator creeping up on you and I use the 'fear vocalization' to warn you of the danger, even though I do not myself feel threatened by the predator. In this case, my production of the natural sign is an expression of my intention to warn you, rather than a simple uncontrolled reaction of fear. (Condillac describes a similar scene (1947: 61).)

This is crucial because, for the first time, the stimulus which triggers the fear-vocalization is, in a sense, self-generated by the intention to warn. (Condillac makes no mention of the origins of such intentions; we can only assume them to be a natural endowment.) Heretofore, fear-vocalization had been the natural response to an emotion which itself was stimulated by the environment. Man exercised no control over the natural stimulus–response chain which resulted in his fear-vocalization. However, when man produces the same fear-vocalization as the result of his intention to warn, it is man who generates the stimulus (the intention) which leads to the vocalization response. In other words, the intention to warn, like the intention to refer which is crucial in the next stage of the language-learning process, is not context-determined, but originates in the speaker.

It is noteworthy that Condillac speaks of the connection between the intention to warn and the fear-vocalization as an 'imitation' of the uncontrolled connection between genuine fear and its expression. For the essential feature of true language-use for Condillac is that it is an artificial invention; its artificiality and conventionality provide man with the means to exercise control over his natural powers of reflection. The key to Condillac's argument, however, lies in his 'demonstration' that the source of the artificiality of true language-using lies in its originally being an imitation of a natural behaviour pattern, namely, the natural behavioural response to emotional stimuli. Thus, the guarantee that we all use language in the same way inheres in the fact that the ability to use language is based on a more primitive, shared, natural stimulus–response system. Language-using may be an artificial, social phenomenon, but it is grounded in the natural endowment common to every individual.

Once man has reached this stage, Condillac argues, it is a simple step to begin supplementing the vocabulary of natural emotive signs with arbitrary conventional signs. The crucial skill has already been mastered: that is, the ability to control the source and means of expression. For this ability allows man to control his reflective powers and thereby to bring into play his innate rationality. Once this is achieved, the invention of arbitrary signs presents no problems:

> Natural cries served men as a model on which to form a new language. They articulated new sounds, and by repeating them a number of times while accompanying them with gestures indicating the objects to which they wanted to draw attention, they became accustomed to giving names to things. (Condillac, 1947: 61)

From this point, the development of languages, and the growth of the ability to use them, progress slowly but steadily, receiving support from and, at the same time, giving assistance to, the developing mastery of reflection.

Condillac's theory of the origin of language-using thus rests on three crucial factors:

1 a natural stimulus–response system;
2 intentionality;
3 a social, cooperative environment.

Once, within (3), man has somehow discovered that he may make imitative use of (1) for the purposes of (2), he has crossed the threshold into true language-using. For he now has the means to control his innate power of reflection and this, in turn, enables him to develop more sophisticated methods of using language.

The germination of competence

There are likewise three components to Bruner's picture of how a child learns to talk. Two are 'natural endowments', the third is cultural.

First, there is the innate Language Acquisition Device. Bruner refrains from speculating about the specific characteristics of LAD, being more concerned with how the child acquires the ability to use the linguistic knowledge LAD provides. To learn to communicate verbally, the child requires a second set of innate capacities – in this case nonlinguistic endowments. Particular attention is paid to four such 'enabling conditions', but at least five more are identified and play an important role. The first four 'original mental capabilities' are:

1   means–end readiness;
2   a sensitivity to transactional enterprises;
3   systematicity in organizing experience; and
4   abstractness in rule formation. (Bruner, 1983: 119)

Of the first, Bruner describes the child as 'active in seeking out regularities in the world about him' and in 'converting experience into species-typical means–end structures' (Bruner, 1983: 24–5). The child is pictured as naturally endowed with a desire to discover (or, perhaps, create) what we might call paradigmatic regularities (viz., repetitions of the same thing) and syntagmatic regularities (viz., patterns of temporal sequence). This search for regularities is goal-oriented. The child has natural desires and is naturally able to recognize patterns connecting her desires with their satisfaction.

By the child's innate 'sensitivity to transactional enterprises', Bruner seems to mean that the child is naturally social. 'Social interaction is both self-propelled and self-rewarding' (Bruner, 1983: 27). In one sense this is undeniable, for if the child were naturally asocial, she would have difficulty (to say the least) entering the world of verbal interaction. On the other hand, this 'innate sensitivity to transactional enterprises' appears simply to be a consequence of the child's innate means–end readiness. If the child naturally seeks out patterns to help her attain specific goals, would this not naturally include employing the people around for those purposes? A similar criticism can be made of the third endowment: innate 'systematicity in organizing experience'. Is this not equally an instance of the child's purportedly innate drive to seek out regularities?

If the second and third natural capacities seem to be consequences of the first, the fourth endowment – 'abstractness in rule formation' – seems equally redundant. In its support, Bruner writes:

> Infants during their first year appear to have rules for dealing with space, time, and even causation. A moving object that is transformed in appearance while it is moving behind a screen produces surprise when it reappears in a new guise…. The infant's perceptual world, far from being a blooming, buzzing confusion, is rather orderly and organized by what seem like highly abstract rules. (1983: 29–30)

But it is never explained why the child's surprise when an object disappears behind a screen is evidence for the innate organization of the child's perceptual world by 'highly abstract rules'. One must hold a rather odd notion of abstract rules to take as evidence for their existence the fact that a child manifests surprise if the world about him loses its spatio-temporal continuity! Nor is it explained why the only alternative to the child's perceptual world being 'a blooming, buzzing confusion' is its being organized by 'highly abstract rules'. Does not the innate tendency to seek out regularities, supposedly an aspect of the first natural endowment, offer a middle ground between these two equally implausible extremes?

In addition to these four 'original mental capacities' Bruner also attributes an innate ability to follow the mother's gaze and to follow a point. Furthermore, the child is said to be born with innate intentionality. She does not have to learn to demand, to deny, to seek mutual attention with a partner, or, indeed, to recognize certain intentions in the mother's behaviour (Bruner, 1983: 85, 92, 122–3). Were these abilities not innate, the child supposedly could not learn to master the complex cultural functions of language. In other words, what the child eventually learns to communicate to her mother must be innate to the child as well as to her mother and other future addressees, for otherwise the intersubjectivity which is presumed to be the essence of successful communication would be unattainable.

The third component required for language acquisition, LASS, is not biologically endowed, but a product of the cultural context of infancy. Even with innate possession of the aforementioned gifts, linguistic and non-linguistic, the child still needs to be made into a communicator. Without the appropriate 'training', she would not develop the ability to use language. Moreover, because the development of her linguistic knowledge depends on the concurrent development of her ability to use it, that 'training' is essential if she is to come to know language in the full sense.

The crucial feature of the child's environment, which enables her to learn to talk, is the routinized interactional behaviour pattern, what Bruner calls the 'format':

> A format is a standardized, initially microcosmic interaction pattern between an adult and an infant that contains demarcated roles that eventually become reversible. (Bruner, 1983: 120–1)

These 'familiar routines in the child's interaction with the social world' are primitive forms of adult speech acts. At first,

> they have a scriptlike quality that involves not only action but a place for communication that constitutes, directs, and completes that action. Given that play is the culture of childhood, it is not surprising that formats often have a playful, gamelike nature. (Bruner, 1983: 121)

Formats emerge in the mother's repeated activity patterns with the child. For instance, mother and child play 'peek-a-boo' or 'hide-and-seek' together, or they jointly examine the pages of a picture book:

> Such games provide a type case for the framing of early communication. For not only do they fill the bill as role-structured transactional microcosms in which words produce, direct and complete the action, but they have certain crucial language-like properties of their own. They are, within their bounds, language-like 'ways of life'. (Bruner, 1983: 121)

An essential feature of the format is that its behavioural components are fixed and ordered. Bruner gives the following instance of the 'book reading' format, involving a child of 13 months. Each of the mother's contributions is labelled by Bruner with its intentional category:

Mother: Look! (Attentional Vocative)
Child: (Touches picture)
Mother: What are those? (Query)
Child: (Vocalizes a babble string and smiles)
Mother: Yes, they are rabbits. (Feedback and Label)
Child: (Vocalizes, smiles, and looks up at mother)
Mother: (Laughs) Yes, rabbit. (Feedback and Label)
Child: (Vocalizes, smiles)
Mother: Yes. (Laughs) (Feedback). (Bruner, 1983: 78)

According to Bruner, the four intentional components of this format – Attentional Vocative, Query, Label, Feedback – account for 'virtually all of the mother's utterances' in examples of the reading format he studied. They constitute the mother's side of a routinized interactional 'game'. Places are left for the child's participation, which is encouraged and reinforced. Crucially, the format allows the child to participate without demanding more linguistic sophistication than she can manage. And it allows the mother to treat the child's vocalization as appropriate even if it is not a recognizable token of the required linguistic expression. In other words, the mother may 'over-interpret' what the child says in order to reinforce the child's attempt to participate communicatively. As the child reaches greater levels of linguistic sophistication the mother increases the required degree of approximation to an appropriate verbal token that she will accept.

So the formatting of mother–child interaction at the prelinguistic and early linguistic stages allows the child to practise communicating without yet possessing the linguistic skills required for 'true' linguistic communication. As the example shows, the child is treated as communicationally successful – as having produced the appropriate speech act at the appropriate moment – before she has uttered her first words. The format thus not only reinforces the child's attempts to play the communication game, but encourages the mother to think that the child is in fact catching on. In this way, the mother leads the child to make greater use of naturally endowed linguistic knowledge, and increased functional demand on that innate knowledge causes it to grow.

A further important feature of the format is that it establishes continuity between prelinguistic and linguistic interaction. The format allows the mother to exploit the child's nonlinguistic endowments in order to turn the child into a communicator. Once the child has mastered these primitive language games, all that remains is to demand more and more of her verbal contributions to them. She is thus forced to draw upon her innate linguistic knowledge and will, as a consequence, progress linguistically. In a sense, then, the child learns to 'talk' before she has the linguistic means to do so, by being placed in an interactional environment which exploits her natural, nonlinguistic skills and innate intentionality. Then, thanks to LAD, her 'talking' gradually becomes more and more linguistically appropriate. That is, like Condillac's original man, the child begins to do by truly linguistic means what she has already been doing nonlinguistically.

It is worth emphasizing here the parallel between Bruner and Condillac. In Condillac's picture, man is led by his social environment (as well as by sheer good luck) to develop his natural signing ability to a point where he can use it at will to communicate his intentions to others. By using signs, he is able to bring his reflective powers under control and, consequently, to use reflection to invent arbitrary signs, the hallmark of true language. Thus the intentional use of signs, whether natural or arbitrary, arises when man's natural endowments are called upon to fulfil a social function (like warning). For both Bruner and Condillac, this is the crucial step in learning to communicate verbally, and a step which guarantees escape from Locke's puzzle. In his *Projet d'éléments d'idéologie*, Destutt de Tracy, a leading exponent of Condillac's linguistic thought, gives a perfect summary of the position shared by Condillac and Bruner. He says that for language to be possible,

> prior to language we must have the means of reciprocally understanding each other ... and this means can only be the consequence of our being, a necessary effect of our organic being. (quoted in Aarsleff, 1982: 352)

An evaluation of Bruner's theory: the Krypton Factor

As a response to the nativist domination of child language study, Bruner's theory of the acquisition of language-using constituted a significant and encouraging development. *Child's Talk* showed that psychology does have a genuine contribution to make in this field. The book drew attention away from scholastic speculation about linguistic structure in the genetic code, and invited psychologists to apply their investigative energies to the study of how, within certain social contexts, children learn to use language for the complex purposes of communication.

Of course, Bruner was not the first to advocate the study of how children learn to use language. Since the first studies of 'motherese', psychologists have been interested in the interactional context of language acquisition. Bruner is only one of the leading figures in this trend. But his originality lies in merging this trend with related ideas from speech-act philosophy and psycholinguistics, specifically with the growing interest in intentionality and linguistic performance. Bruner argues that not only must the child become linguistically competent, she must acquire a pragmatic competence. 'Developmental pragmatics' and 'developmental linguistics' cannot be treated independently.

It remains open to doubt, however, whether *Child's Talk* provides a fruitful conception of the theoretical foundations of this project. Thus far, we have explored similarities between Bruner's account of linguistic ontogenesis and Condillac's theory of linguistic phylogenesis. The problems with the speculative nature of Condillac's ideas are well known. Less well known is that similar problems haunt Bruner's account of the ontogenesis of language-using.

The most conspicuous problem is the distinction between linguistic and pragmatic competence. Condillac made a related distinction. For primitive *Homo sapiens*, it was not enough to have innate reflective powers; they also had to acquire an ability to exercise their reflective powers through the use of signs. Similarly, it is not enough for Bruner's child to be born with innate LAD; she must also acquire an ability to use the knowledge which LAD provides.

Invoking LASS to explain how LAD can be put to use plugs one explanatory gap only to open another. For, in turn, the possession of pragmatic competence is presumably sterile unless the possessor knows how to put *that* to use. It cannot be maintained that the acquisition of this further (metapragmatic) competence is already assured by either LAD or LASS (which allegedly merely puts LAD to work). For systems of knowledge do not incorporate all the possible uses to which they might be put. If they did, the original problem would never have arisen, for postulating an innate LAD would have provided all the explanation required. But once we embark on the alternative explanatory route, there is nowhere to stop. If one system of knowledge, A, requires another system of knowledge, B, in order to apply it correctly, then B will require a third system, C, in order to apply it, and so on ad infinitum. If the relevant metapragmatic ability is said to be innate, no real explanatory gain has been achieved, granted that in the present state of linguistic studies any appeal to innate mechanisms is simply an appeal to the biologically unknown; if it is learned, then we have substituted one learning problem for another. The latter move might be counted an advantage if the second problem were more tractable than the first, but, on Bruner's account, that could hardly be so.

Furthermore, if the acquisition of pragmatic competence is postulated in order to explain how LAD is put to work, we need to know exactly what LAD lacks to assess whether LASS supplies what is missing. Otherwise, the explanation must fail, for the same reason that an engineer cannot hope to design the missing components to complete a circuit unless she is clear about what the equipment that is already available can do and how it falls short of what is required. Bruner's account is unsatisfactory, because he is deliberately vague about the nature of LAD. Consequently, he affords no grounds for assessing how well – or ill – LASS supplies what is missing. Just as there is no point in harnessing a horse to a Pullman coach if what is needed is a locomotive, there is no point in offering a pragmatic acquisition programme that is inadequate to make linguistic knowledge utilizable in communication. For example, it is far from clear that training in the picture-book format is able to supply what Junior needs to grasp the difference between success in a nursery 'gee-gee' game with his mother and success in achieving reference to a (or any) horse. Bruner seems to assume that it is intuitively obvious how the link is made. But is it? And what happens in those cultures where children are deprived both of picture books and picture-book-oriented mothers?

Furthermore, nothing in LASS guarantees that the results will be uniform over a whole community. From both Bruner's and Condillac's perspectives, uniformity is essential, or else the problem of communication is left unresolved. If, having grasped a rule, we must still acquire the ability to apply it in practice, it must be ensured that we all acquire the same ability. Otherwise we might apply the rule differently from one another in practice. Shared knowledge of the Highway Code does not guarantee safe driving. We must all apply its rules in the same way, otherwise accidents will occur. The analogue to an accident in language is communicational breakdown, a failure to transmit the message from sender to receiver. But unless the LASS programme is applied in essentially the same form to all individuals it is difficult to see how it inculcates the uniformity required. It is consequently obligatory for any theorist who takes Bruner's position to spell out what invariant core in LASS guarantees the required uniformity (or to explain the uniformity another way).

Ironically, Bruner ends up attributing many more innate endowments to the child than Chomsky does. While Chomsky simply assumes an innate LAD, Bruner also credits the newborn with the four 'original mental capacities' discussed above as well as innate intentions to refer, deny, request, seek mutual attention and query. Furthermore, Bruner's child has an innate ability to follow a point and the gaze of a co-interactant. For someone who seeks a compromise between 'miraculous' nativism and 'impossible' empiricism, Bruner seems much happier compromising with nativism. To see how, consider in outline what Bruner calls 'the growth of reference'.

To begin with, it is assumed that the child has an innate drive to seek mutual attention with her mother. This is first realized in the early establishment of eye-contact between mother and child. Then the mother begins to introduce an object, such as a doll, into their joint visual field for their shared attention. She develops a routinized way of preparing the child for the presentation of the object. This is normally done with what Bruner calls an 'attentional vocative' (e.g., 'Oh, look!'), which tells the child that there is something in the environment to attend to. With this, the seed of conventionalized reference is sown. Thus far, however, the child only plays a passive role. But during the latter half of the first year the child begins to reach for objects she desires. This may be accompanied by 'effortful' noises:

> The principal achievement during this active phase is that the child now becomes a *giver* of signals about objects desired and is not just involved in comprehending and decoding others' efforts to direct his attention. (Bruner, 1983: 75)

From this activity, 'pure pointing' develops by 13 months, a behavioural achievement that is genetically pre-programmed. Throughout this period, the mother will have been exploiting the child's growing natural abilities by incorporating their behavioural expression into routinized interactional formats, such as the 'book reading format' discussed above. The essential feature of such formats is that they exploit the child's natural abilities (1) to seek joint attention with the mother, (2) to appreciate the intention of a query, and (3) to recognize the intention to refer. By incorporating the behavioural expression of these natural abilities in a routinized format, the mother 'teaches' the child how reference is conventionalized in the culture. True reference begins 'with nominals placed appropriately in a dialog format where attention is jointly concentrated on a target' (Bruner, 1983: 123). Thus, learning how to use words to refer originates in a naturally endowed intention to refer (as well as to recognize another's intention to refer) and in the natural tendency to seek joint attention. Furthermore, intersubjectivity of adult reference is assured by its natural origins in shared intentionality and joint attention.

A similar account is given of how the child learns to request. By means of the format, the newborn's innate intention to demand, evident in the form of crying known as 'demand crying', is developed into the conventionalized form of the speech act Request. Negation also grows from its natural intentional seed, inherent in the newborn's 'denial crying'. Essentially, the child is born with certain innate intentions, shared with all other children, and these are guided and transformed by LASS so that they grow into their conventionalized forms. The intersubjectivity of conventional language-using arises from shared, innate intentional seeds, and Locke's puzzle about the privacy of minds and the intersubjectivity of discourse is thereby resolved. Our ability to understand each other is the result of the continuity of pragmatic intentions, from innate source, through formatting, to developed linguistic forms. It is easy to detect Bruner's agreement with Condillac that, were our reasons for using language not naturally endowed in the individual, and as a result socially shared, we would never be able to formulate conventional methods for securing the recognition of those reasons by others:

> Indeed, I rather assume that it is this continuity of function that makes it possible for an adult to 'understand' the more primitive forms by which a child realizes various communicative functions. In this sense, functional continuity provides a basis for adult fine tuning and for the operation of the Language Acquisition Support System. (Bruner, 1983: 127)

In other words, the child is always trying to do the same sorts of things with words, or with prelinguistic vocalizations. The mother's contribution is to assist its acquisition of the conventional (culture-specific) methods for realizing those intentions. And, indeed, were the child not born with innate intentions, there would be nothing for the mother to conventionalize. She needs, at the prelinguistic stage, to recognize the child's intentions as primitive versions of adult intentions, even though they are not yet conventionally formulated. So, she 'understands' that the child is demanding when it cries one way and denying when it cries another, and she 'understands' the child when it tries to draw her attention to an object. It is her ability to recognize these primitive expressions of intention that enables her to begin teaching pragmatic conventions.

Thus, although Bruner's assumption of innate intentions may serve to provide a shared, mental basis to language-using, it results in a picture of the newborn child as containing an innate homunculus, complete with a handful of adult, but as yet undeveloped, communicational intentions. While Bruner seems anxious to re-establish the respectability of 'learning' in an account of linguistic ontogenesis, he seems unable to settle for anything but a nativist account of the fundamentally intersubjective properties of language-using. The following makes evident his respect for Locke's puzzle:

> Some basis for referential intersubjectivity must exist before language proper appears. Logically, there would be no conceivable way for two human beings to achieve shared reference were there no initial disposition for it. (Bruner, 1983: 122)

Bruner may not overtly confront the puzzle, but there can be little doubt that his account, like Condillac's, is heavily influenced by its implications.

Let me summarize this critical evaluation of Bruner's theory of language acquisition. First, the concept of pragmatic competence, as an ability-to-use, mediating between linguistic competence and performance, leads to a regress and, as a result, presents the child learner with an impossibly infinite task. Second, Bruner's response to Locke's puzzle about communicational intersubjectivity consists in the postulation of innate sources for the intentional features of language-using. Consequently, the combination of these two implications of Bruner's theory results in the attribution of infinite natural powers to the child. For if there is an infinite number of mediating abilities required to use language, and if for each of those abilities to have an intersubjective ground we need to postulate a further set of innate endowments, then there will be no end to the innate endowments the child will need. On this view, only a baby Superman, infinitely provided with language-using abilities, could ever learn to talk.

Linguistic origins (reprise)

The question raised by Locke's puzzle is essentially that of the dialectic of the individual and the social in communicational interaction: how can individuals transfer their private mental content to other individuals? Bruner and Condillac (and, for that matter, Chomsky) give ample evidence that the only answer lies in some form of nativism: we can communicate because, to some extent, our minds have had the same (ontogenetic, phylogenetic or biogenetic) origin. But the question that ought to be asked, yet almost never is, is *why is Locke's puzzle taken seriously?* Why must we follow Locke in assuming that communication consists in the conveyance of thoughts from speaker to hearer? If that telementational picture of communication is dropped, Locke's puzzle collapses with it. At the same time, parts of Bruner's theory become salvageable, particularly the account of the socializing influence of routinized interactions, play, games and formats. For it is not mentally represented competence that the child must acquire in learning to use language. Instead he must learn to speak, to act and to use words in ways that adults will approve as communicatively competent. If he manages that, no one will deny his membership of the linguistic community, regardless of his subjective, private and/or original intentionality.

It is generally acknowledged that the origins of the Western tradition of linguistic thought lie in Plato's *Cratylus*, a three-cornered debate about how words mean. Nevertheless, the contents of the *Cratylus* have been more often the subject of ridicule in modern linguistic writings than of admiration or of serious study. After all, much of the debate consists of far-fetched speculation about the etymological origins of Greek words, intended as evidence for naturalist or conventionalist views on the connection between words and their referents.

What has often been overlooked in accounts of the *Cratylus* is the reason why its topic should have interested the ancient Greeks. Why did it matter to them, or at least to Plato, what sort of connection a word has to what it stands for? The answer to this question is to be found in Plato's critique of the Sophists, masters of the rhetoric of persuasive argument. Plato strove to distinguish between the laws of rhetoric, the object of which is persuasion, and the laws of logic (or dialectic), the object of which is truth. The laws of rhetoric, from this perspective, rely on the unstable nature of man's opinions and the effect that skilful discourse can have on them. The laws of logic, on the other hand, are determined by the representational correspondence between words and what they signify: that is, between language and reality. Consequently, the application of logical laws can lead speakers from truth to undeniable truth; while the use of rhetorical laws can, at best, only guarantee the inculcation of (always provisional) opinions which may in fact have little or no correspondence to the truth.

From this perspective, Plato's project depends on there being a representational connection between words and what they stand for. Consequently, the foundations of that connection must be assured. Do people call certain things 'boulders' and others 'pebbles' because of some natural, immutable connection between those words and their *nominata*? If so, the laws of logic originate in nature itself and are universal. Or does the source of their appellations lie in human convention? And, if logic does originate in social agreement, are its laws fundamentally no different from those of rhetoric? To discover a firm ground for reasoning, knowledge and communication, the ancient Greeks, like Condillac and Bruner, speculated about the origins of our words. In this speculation lies the source of linguistic thought.

In the end, Socrates proposes a compromise between the extreme naturalism of Cratylus and the extreme conventionalism of Hermogenes. He suggests that the origin of language is part conventional and part natural. Ever since, linguists have been dividing up the spoils.

Note

An earlier version of this chapter appeared as 'Linguistic orgins: Bruner and Condillac on learning how to talk' in *Language and Communication*, 4 (4): 209–24, © 1984. We are grateful to Elsevier Science Ltd for permission to republish.

References

Aarsleff, H. (1982) *From Locke to Saussure*. London: Athlone Press.

Bruner, J.S. (1983) *Child's Talk: Learning to Use Language*. Oxford: Oxford University Press.

Condillac (1947 [1746]) *Essai sur l'origine des connoissances humaines*. In *Oeuvres philosophiques de Condillac*, Vol. I. Georges le Roy (ed.), Paris: Presses Universitaires de France.

Locke, J. (1978 [1690]) *Essay Concerning Human Understanding*. P.H. Nidditch (ed.), Oxford: Oxford University Press.

Saussure, F. de (1983 [1916]) *Course in General Linguistics*. R. Harris (trans.), London: Duckworth.

5

EMOTION, PRAGMATICS AND SOCIAL UNDERSTANDING IN THE PRESCHOOL YEARS

Judy Dunn and Jane R. Brown

In Bruner's extraordinarily stimulating writings on the early development of communication and cultural understanding, two themes have been particularly important in bridging the gap between ideas on cognitive and social development. The first is that the impetus for children to learn to use a language is a pragmatic one: they acquire language, Bruner argues, to 'get what they want, to play games, to stay connected with those on whom they are dependent' (Bruner, 1983: 103). As he puts it, 'the engine that drives the enterprise is not language acquisition per se, but the need to get on with the demands of the culture' (1983: 102). He shows, moreover, that learning to 'get things done by language' (1983: 115) is in a key sense a matter of learning the culture – learning, for example, the canonical ways of requesting, signalling intentions and negotiating reference.

The second theme is the significance of certain familiar, regular routines in children's daily lives with their parents – the 'epiphanies of the ordinary' that form constrained, game-like formats, highly familiar to the child. These formats are said to play a crucial role in transmitting the culture, as well as its language. 'Ordinariness implies a shared culture', Bruner argues, and formats 'embed the child's communicative intentions in a cultural matrix' (1983: 134).

The examples on which Bruner based his argument in *Child's Talk* (1983) focused on mother–child conversations at the stage when babies are just beginning to talk. In our view, however, Bruner's arguments form the foundation for a revolution not only in conceptions of language development, but in views of children as social beings. In particular, his focus on pragmatics is of profound importance for conceptions of the development of children's social understanding. During the second, third and fourth years of life there are astonishing developments in children's understanding of mind and emotion – currently the focus of considerable attention among cognitive developmentalists (Wellman, 1990; Perner, 1991; Astington, 1994). The growth of these capacities is 'conventionally' viewed in terms of purely cognitive development. In contrast, we argue in this chapter that these developments cannot be understood without appreciating the significance of pragmatics. We will consider the conversations, interactions and growing social understanding of children over the period between two and five years, when children make such striking advances in their discovery of mind and emotion.

With this emphasis on children's developing psychological understanding, issues emerge that take us away from the focus on familiar 'formats' and games with adults that Bruner stresses in his account of early language development. The role of pragmatics continues to be central. But key developmental changes in communication and the appreciation of others' minds and feelings often, we argue, take place in interactive contexts that differ in two key respects from the familiar 'formats' of feeding, caretaking and greeting, or the well-orchestrated games with adults, emphasised in *Child's Talk*. The first is the significance of the *emotional context* of the interactions that are central to children's discovery of the mind. The second is the importance of children's *interactions with other children*, as well as their exchanges with adults. In this chapter, we explore these aspects of children's social experience, and the role they play in children's understanding of the social world, an understanding that grows so dramatically during their second, third and fourth years.

In what follows, we draw on findings from a longitudinal study of children followed from their second year through their early school years, to examine, first, the *significance of the emotional context* and, second, the *significance of social partners* for the development and use of social understanding in the preschool years (Dunn, Brown, Slomkowski, Tesla and Youngblade, 1991).[1] In our discussion of the *emotional context*, we argue that emotional interactions so frequent within the family setting both reveal and foster children's growing social understanding. This is illustrated with reference to three domains of interaction in early childhood: discourse about inner states, attempts at deception and early narratives. In the following section on *social partners*, attention focuses on the importance of child–child interaction in the development of the understanding of other minds. From evidence for links between child–child interaction and individual differences in children's ability to 'mind read', we move to consider two social processes which contribute to these connections – joint pretend play and discourse about inner states.

The significance of the emotional context

Bruner's emphasis on 'epiphanies of the ordinary' is surely insightful. It is important, however, that such everyday interactions frequently involve dramas imbued with negative emotion or intense desire, rather than the neutral routines of caretaking or the simple pleasures of games of peek-a-boo or hide-and-seek so vividly highlighted in *Child's Talk*. While the latter of course generate surprise and amusement, our study of children from the middle of their second year demonstrates that their social understanding is also frequently revealed – and probably also fostered – in 'ordinary' interactions suffused with negative emotions and in contexts where they act as agents, victims, victimizers or accomplices. These are the daily dramas engendered by the power politics of the family, and precipitated by children's urgent needs, desires and frustrations. The significance of children's feelings and desires is key, as we have argued elsewhere, to what they attempt to achieve, and what they understand and learn in these early exchanges (Dunn, 1988; Dunn and Brown, 1994).

Even in the earliest exchanges between parent and child emotions can play a central role. Bruner and others have highlighted the key place that mothers' attributions of intention to very young babies have in the development of communication. When such babies cry in distress they may have no intention to communicate, yet their parents treat such evidence of distress as intentional communication. It is within such situations that children begin to understand the meaning ('non-natural' in Grice's (1957) terms) of their crying for others. The proposal, plausible enough, is that children gradually acquire the ability to communicate intentionally within the conventions of the culture they share with their parents, through the interpretations offered by those adults. Our point is that such interactions are rarely emotionally neutral.

It is arguable, indeed, that we can only relate to very young infants by attributing intentions, feelings and desires to their grimaces, sounds and waving arms. In the early exchanges of the first year, parents set both sides of the conversation with explicit comments on what the baby wants or feels. 'Oh you *are* hungry, I know! You want your milk!', 'Yes, it is awful being so tired, poor Baby!', 'Yes, you like that, don't you!' Thus parents frame the beginnings of intentional communication for the child, attempting to make the world more intelligible to the baby, and the baby more intelligible to themselves. Their attributions are, by and large, benevolent. They are trying to make the world a more supportive place for the baby (not always, of course, but chiefly). And much of this attribution of intention in the early months is centred on, and precipitated by the baby's expression of emotion – distress, frustration, anger, and after a month or so, happiness or pleasure.

In the second and third year, emotions are often clearly implicated in the contexts in which children reveal early powers of understanding others (Dunn, 1988). The situations in which they demonstrate such powers all have a particular emotional valence; they are not emotionally neutral. For two-year-olds, contexts of threatened self-interest, for instance, are often situations in which children show an early grasp of others' intentions and expectations through their attempts to deflect blame, to obtain desired but competed-for resources and to avoid punishment.

Children's efforts to influence their own and others' emotions in these encounters is a notable feature of their relationships. And through their attempts to manipulate others' emotional states – the frequent, repeated, emotion-laden exchanges which characterize interactions among family members and between friends – children learn about and experiment with the cultural precepts of a folk psychology which gives meaning to shared experience. The evidence of this comes from the observation of children in their second year engaging in *teasing* which entails some comprehension of what another will find annoying or upsetting, *jokes* which anticipate a shared notion of what may violate the expected, and *comforting* which reflects a grasp of what will decrease someone else's distress. During children's third and fourth years, the connections between their emotional states and their increasingly sophisticated grasp of others' minds and feelings are especially clear in three types of interaction. These are first, children's participation in discourse about feelings and mental states, second, their attempts at deception, and third, their early narratives.

Discourse about inner states

It is crucial to note that, even among families in a particular culture – the USA, Canada, or the UK for instance – there are marked differences in the kinds of behaviour with which we are concerned. In our study, children differed a great deal in the frequency and range of emotions that they and their families discussed, in the subtlety of understanding revealed in their jokes and teasing, in their interest in influencing others' affective states, and in their pleasure in sharing positive emotions. They also varied greatly in their performance on tasks in which they were asked to explain emotional experience – explanations themselves constrained by cultural beliefs.

We know that children's participation in discourse about feelings, thoughts, beliefs and the world of the mind is associated with the development of individual differences in understanding others' inner states. Three separate studies, based on very different groups of children in the UK and the USA, have found positive associations between participation in such talk and later success on formal assessments of understanding inner states (Dunn, Brown and Beardsall, 1989; Dunn, Brown, Slomkowski, Tesla and Youngblade, 1991; Hughes and Dunn, 1998).

If we ask what precipitates such conversations about feelings, we cannot ignore children's expressions of affect. In our longitudinal study in Pennsylvania, mothers were more than twice as likely to talk about feelings with their children (aged 33 and 47 months old) when their children were expressing negative emotions than when they were expressing happiness or neutral feelings (Dunn and Brown, 1994). And the children at 33 months were more likely to engage in causal discussion of feelings (behaviour correlated with their later understanding of emotion assessed in standardized tasks) when they were angry or upset than they were when happy. Our analyses established three important general points pertaining to the links between emotional experience and children's growing understanding of the inner states of others.

The first concerns the relevance of the general level of emotional expression in the family. In families where a high frequency of negative affect was expressed, there was no association between the expression of emotion and talk about feelings. That is, while in general the expression of negative emotion presents an opportunity for talk about feelings, the opportunity is less likely to be taken up in these families.

Second, the significance of children's affective state varies for different aspects of their developing understanding. We found, for instance, that children's engagement in social pretend play, which often involves a sophisticated sharing of an imaginary framework, is unlikely to happen when children are upset or angry. Similarly, angry or upset children are unlikely to share jokes (which can involve a relatively advanced understanding of what a particular other will find funny).

The third point is that the intensity of children's emotions is important. Roberts and Strayer (1987) report an inverted U-shaped function in the relations between children's competence and parental responsiveness to negative affect, with a decline in children's competence at high levels of parental responsiveness. Do children in fact 'lose' their social competence when they are very upset or angry and operate at their most mature level when they are emotionally neutral? Or is it when they are emotionally engaged (albeit at a level that is not extreme) that they function at a particularly mature level? Our findings on the family discourse concerning feelings indicate that such conversations about emotions are precipitated by children's expressions of distress and mild frustration. However, the data gives a rather different picture of how children manage conflicts in which they are intensely angry or upset. Here we found that children who expressed extreme anger or distress when in dispute with mother or sibling were less likely than others to use reasoning that took account of the other person's point of view, and indeed were more likely to use no reasoning at all, but simply protest without offering any justification (Dunn and Brown, 1994). These examples illustrate Hoffman's observation that 'affect may initiate, terminate, accelerate, or disrupt information processing ... it may provide input for social cognition; and it may influence decision making' (Hoffman, 1986: 200). Hoffman's argument, however, stresses the intrapersonal regulative properties of emotional experience. Our observations, on the other hand, highlight the interpersonal aspects of emotion's influence on cognition.

This evidence on discourse about emotions and the emotional context of such conversations provides a counterbalance to accounts of the development of understanding couched solely in terms of cognitive and maturational processes. The following caveats should, however, be noted. First, it is of course likely that forms of talk other than the explicit reference to feelings may also be important in these developments, and second, that experiences other than those involving talk may well contribute to understanding feelings and inner states. Sharing emotional responses with children (laughing together), for instance, could well contribute to their growing sensitivity to others' feelings. Finally, it should be noted that the pattern of association between children's states of anger and their failure to reason could arise as a consequence of children becoming angry *because* they 'see' that reasoning will not help them attain their goals.

Attempts at deception

Deception is a key topic in the debates on children's early understanding of mind. The question of whether children aged three and four can deliberately attempt to mislead or to manipulate someone else's beliefs has provoked much controversy. Several studies using standardized tasks report young children are unable to do so (Strichartz and Burton, 1990; Sodian, 1991). In contrast, studies that focus on naturally occurring incidents of apparent deception by young children suggest the opposite (Newton, 1994; Newton and Reddy, 1996). First, three-year-olds do attempt to manipulate what is thought or expected by family members. In both Newton's work and our own (Dunn, 1988), such incidents often involve false excuses, attempts to blame others, to avoid blame, and to 'trick' other family members in a joking way. Here is a characteristic example of a 30-month-old who 'reported' to her mother a transgression by her sister Carol (an act which had not in fact taken place during the preceding two hours of our observations). The incident centred on a prohibited garden hose, which the children had been told by their mother not to touch.

Child:	Carol's – Carol's touching a sprayer.
Mother:	Is she? [*goes to look*]. She's not doing anything.
Child:	Carol's getting it [*water*] all over my hair. [*not true*]
	[*M goes to look again*]

Many of the two-year-olds in our family observations made such attempts to mislead their parents or siblings.

The attempts of three-year-olds in Newton's study to deceive others in their family are less frequent than those of the four-year-olds, but they do show as wide a range of types of deception as the older children. That is, the three-year-olds were already attempting to manipulate the thoughts and expectations of others in all the ways that the four-year-olds did. And – the key point for our argument here – the contexts in which such attempts were made were frequently those of family conflict 'in which the child is in an emotionally charged state of opposition to parental control' (Newton, 1994: 99). The circumstances in which the deceptions documented by Newton took place were clearly very different from those of the test situations in which deception has been experimentally studied; the significance of the emotional charge of these situations cannot be ignored. Neither can the sophistication of these attempts at deception in the family setting compared with the behaviour described in experiments on deceptive behaviour.

Early narratives

The third aspect of children's communicative interaction that reveals, and possibly fosters, their early understanding of the links between mind, emotion and human action is their production of narratives. Bruner has argued powerfully for the significance of narrative as a process through which the development of understanding of mind and emotion may be influenced (Bruner, 1990). Patterns of narrative, he has proposed, support or scaffold the kind of metacognition about intentions that lies at the core of the idea of 'theories of mind' (see also Feldman, 1992). It is especially interesting, in light of these arguments, that some experimental studies now provide parallel evidence for the significance of narrative experience in children's understanding of false belief. Lewis and his colleagues showed, for instance, that children faced by a false belief task succeeded when given the opportunity to link the events involved in the task in a coherent narrative (Lewis, Freeman, Kyriakidou, Maridaki-Kossotaki and Berridge, 1996).

In our longitudinal studies of the second, third and fourth years, the development of children's own unsolicited narratives parallels that of their comments on mental states and psychological issues more generally (Dunn, 1988). Children begin to relate the 'story of what happened' at very much the time that they first begin to talk about inner states and to ask questions about why others behave as they do. But these early narratives should not be seen as emotionally neutral examples of cognitive sophistication. Brown's examination of the early narratives in our Pennsylvanian children showed that these were chiefly focused on socioemotional incidents – and especially on negative events (Brown, 1993). Further, the children mustered their most sophisticated linguistic skills – referring to inner states, sequencing events temporally and causally – when they reported on events involving fear, anger, or distress, as in the following example of a child who runs back from the garden to the house to tell her sibling:

> *Child to sibling*: I came running back 'cause I saw two snakes and I was scared and runned back!

Mothers questioned, and/or provided support to, only a fraction of the accounts children proffered in the uninhibited give-and-take of family discourse we observed. At the same time, however, the younger children had diverse opportunities to learn how best to tell 'what happened' from listening to their more competent older siblings, who won arguments and provoked maternal intervention with their more sophisticated narrative accounts. We would do well to consider how these conversations scaffold children's cognitive abilities. In our observations, they clearly demonstrated the opportunities a child has in a multi-speaker world, and a multi-sibling family, to attend to and learn from more competent others – others whose interests may even be at odds with the child's own.

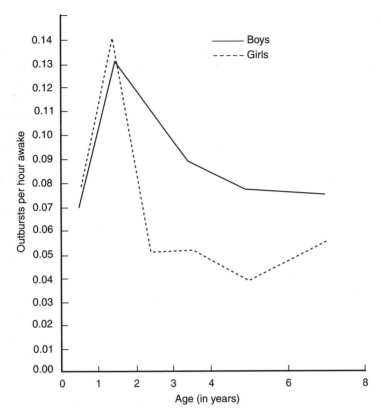

Figure 5.1 *Frequency of angry outbursts in the home (from Goodenough, 1931)*

Developmental changes in the significance of emotion

The argument that we must consider children's emotions and motivation if we are to clarify the links between pragmatic setting and children's social understanding is supported, as we have seen, by evidence concerning children's discourse about feelings, their engagement in deception, and their early narratives. But the dramatic developmental changes in children's expression (and presumably experience) of intense emotions over the early years raise the question of whether the significance of these emotions changes during the preschool period.

It is unquestionable that during the second year, and the first months of the third, children express their frustration, anger and distress in a very uninhibited fashion. Frances Goodenough's classic study from the 1930s demonstrated this very clearly, with the striking peak in children's outbursts of anger at home (Figure 5.1). Such expressions of negative emotions decrease in frequency during the third and fourth years. In our Pennsylvanian study, children's interactions with their siblings illustrated this most vividly. At 33 months, a notably high 21 per cent of interactions with the sibling were accompanied by the expression of marked anger or distress. By 47 months this had dropped to only 9 per cent, and by 69 months to 6 per cent of interactions (Dunn, Creps and Brown, 1996). Over this same period, of course, there are marked increases in children's communicative and metacognitive abilities. It is possible, then, that the significance of the immediate emotional context for the development and the use of children's social understanding diminishes as their powers of reflection and communication increase. There is evidence, for instance, that there are developmental changes in the significance of intense anger and distress in children's reasoning in disputes. As already noted, the 33-month-old children in our Pennsylvanian study appeared less able to draw on their reasoning ability when intensely angry or distressed than they were when less upset. But at 47 months these same children used reasoned argument in disputes equally often whether upset or not (Dunn et al., 1996). As children's metacognitive abilities increase, they are less at the mercy of their emotions than they were as two-year-olds, and more able to marshal their powers of argument even when angry or distressed.

The significance of the *pragmatic* context – and of children's interactive goals – remains clear in the development and use of children's understanding over these years. Consider our findings on the implications of mothers' talk about the causes of people's behaviour. We found in the Pennsylvanian study that there were associations over time between mothers' discussion of cause with their children, and the children's own later ability to understand emotions (Dunn and Brown, 1993). The pattern of these associations, however, depended crucially on the pragmatics of the earlier conversations in which mother and child referred to causes or sequelae of behaviour or inner states. Children whose mothers' causal talk was chiefly designed to control them, later did poorly on assessments of sociocognitive development, while those whose mothers causal talk was in the context of shared play, comforting or joking were particularly successful on the later assessments. Evidently it is not just the content of parent–child discourse to which we have to pay attention. Bruner's stricture in *Acts of Meaning* that we have to focus on the 'contexts of practice' is reinforced: 'it is always necessary to ask what people are *doing* or *trying* to do in that context' (1990: 118). A focus on children interacting with different social partners brings this clearly to the fore.

The significance of social partners

In most writing on the significance of social interaction for cognitive development within a Vygotskian framework the emphasis is upon child-as-apprentice to a competent adult (e.g., Rogoff, 1990). But children's social worlds include others as well as expert, didactic adults. Indeed, from early childhood they spend more time interacting with siblings and peers than they do with adults. And interacting with other children presents quite different challenges and rewards from those of communicating with sympathetic adults – mothers in particular. A close look at child–child interactions reveals some, perhaps surprising, evidence for their potential as influences on social understanding, implicating quite different aspects of social experience from those that figure centrally when adults influence children's communication.

Consider the following. Children with siblings are reported to do better on mind-reading tasks than those without siblings (Perner, Ruffman and Leekham, 1994). Moreover, the number of siblings children have, and the number of kin with whom they interact daily are both reported to be positively correlated with success on mind-reading tasks (Lewis et al., 1996). What social processes might account for these findings? What goes on between children and their siblings or close friends that might foster early understanding of mind and emotion?

Two notable and closely related examples stand out in our longitudinal studies. The first involves children's experiences of shared pretend play, in which roles are taken on, and a story line jointly planned, negotiated, and developed by children playing together. An important predictor of success on the mind-reading and emotion-understanding tasks in our Pennsylvanian study was children's previous experience of cooperative play with older siblings (Dunn et al., 1991); in this, their experience of role enactment in joint pretend play was of special significance (Youngblade and Dunn, 1995). Clearly, the ability to take into account another child's thoughts and intentions greatly facilitates this play, and in turn, efforts to collaborate in sharing and shaping an imaginative world of pretend identities fosters this ability. Other studies confirm that individual differences in children's experiences of sharing and negotiating a pretend world with another are associated with their success on assessments of mind reading or understanding emotion (Astington and Jenkins, 1995).

The second revealing feature of children's interaction with their friends and siblings is their explicit use of mental state terms. Our analyses of children's conversations with their mothers, siblings and friends produced a surprising finding: children talked about mental processes very much more frequently with their friends and siblings than they did with their mothers (Brown, Donelan-McCall and Dunn, 1996). Furthermore, in conversation with their mothers their references to mental states were chiefly to their own thoughts or beliefs, while with siblings and friends they were more likely to talk about shared thoughts and ideas. Pretend play was the interactional context in which beliefs and suppositions were particularly relevant to the children. Importantly, their references to such mental states were correlated with their own performance on mind-reading tasks. When we considered how children employ reference to mental states in their conversations – the pragmatic function – an intriguing role for the 'conversational uses' of mental state terms emerged.

Children (and adults) frequently use phrases such as 'you know' or 'guess what' to gain another's attention or to introduce new topics or actions, and 'I mean' to clarify a statement. Similarly, they may say 'I think' to express uncertainty and 'I know' with the authority of fact. These 'conversational' uses of mental state terms have been excluded from evidence of metacognitive understanding among two-year-olds, the youngest users of these terms (Shatz, Wellman and Silber, 1983; Bloom, Rispoli, Gartner and Hafitz, 1989). The case for discounting statements such as 'I don't know' as not significant is much less convincing, however, among four-year-olds and adults who are credited with a mentalistic understanding of behaviour (Moore, Pure and Furrow, 1990). It has been convincingly argued by Moore and his colleagues that the use of 'know' to strengthen, and 'think' to qualify, an assertion does depend on knowledge that mental states reflect propositional attitudes, and should be regarded as indicating 'true' mental state understanding. They cite evidence from experimental tasks that shows that children whose reasoning included 'think' and 'know' as modifiers of assertions also succeeded on tests of mind reading. We found, too, that such 'conversational' use of mental state terms was correlated with performance on mind-reading tasks (Brown et al., 1996). Furthermore, among the children aged four years and older in our studies these mental terms served important pragmatic functions, facilitating collaboration by resolving differences of perspective, clarifying the other's intentions and sustaining the joint narrative. This is illustrated by the following example in which the two friends are pretending that they are pirates:

F: All the silver things hafta go in here, and then you can use the swords when
     they find the gold.
C: You mean it's gonna be under the bed like that?
F: No, it's gonna be on top of the bed so that we can find it.
C: But we'll still know where it is.
F: I know, that's okay. That's okay, 'cause we're gonna walk from that way.

The references to mental states in the context of pretend play highlight the significance of shared pretend play for children's growing social understanding. They show us that children begin to entertain multiple hypothetical realities (Perner, 1991) and 'decouple' reality from fantasy (Leslie, 1987) not as solitary cognitive enterprises, but through negotiating the social interactions in which these cognitive states are shared. This illustrates how there are multiple and distinct social processes linked to the development of social understanding during the third and fourth years.

For example, role play involves the explicit putting of oneself into someone else's shoes, while the negotiation necessary to joint pretend play – such as resolving a conflict – touches the child's self-interest closely at the same time that she is confronted with another's conflicting interests. Indeed, pretend play between preschool friends is fraught with the negotiation of conflicting perspectives and desires – from divergent plot lines, to the characteristics of fantasy characters, to the sharing of coveted toys. It has been claimed, since Piaget (1932), that children's experience of engaging in arguments where they face the differing views and feelings of another is important to the development of an appreciation of others' thoughts and perspective (Stein and Miller, 1993). In our Pennsylvanian study, children who had taken account of their opponents' views when in dispute with them performed better on later assessments of social understanding than children who had simply reiterated their own demands or views (Slomkowski and Dunn, 1992), as did those children whose mothers and siblings paid attention to others' viewpoints in situations of conflict.

The importance of framing these cognitive developments within the children's social worlds is further highlighted by a second feature of child–child talk about mental states. Individual differences in children's discussion of mental states were linked to the quality of the relationship between the two children. The child–friend pairs who discussed mental states most often in their interactions were those who observers characterized as most cooperative in their play, and the length of their friendship and the frequency of their interaction were positively related to their explicit references to mental processes. Thus, it would appear that the ability to ascribe mental states in order to clarify their thinking or to refine a joint pretend scenario served these friends as a means to the successful resolution of disputes and helped sustain their enjoyment of each other in play.

A further key point concerning these social processes comes to light when we contrast the same children within different relationships. Observations of the same child interacting with his or her mother, sibling and close friend shows us that the child may show strikingly different powers of understanding within these different close relationships, depending on the emotional context of the relationship and the pragmatics of the particular interaction. In the Pennsylvanian study, individual differences in children's engagement in role play, their management of conflict, and their discourse about mental states were not correlated across their interactions with mother, sibling and friend. Some children engaged in elaborate role play with a friend, but not with their sibling or mother; others did so with sibling, but not friend, and so on. Some children when in dispute with their mothers reasoned in a way that took account of her point of view, and rarely did so in disputes with their friends or siblings. And there were no significant correlations across these relationships in the frequency with which children engaged in discourse about mental states. Each of these indices of understanding-in-action nevertheless correlated with false-belief test performance.

These results give us two important kinds of information. First, in measuring children's ability to role play, and to discuss mental states, we are tapping aspects of social understanding at an age well before the children can succeed on formal assessments of the understanding of other minds.

Second, the lack of correlation across their various relationships shows us how children use their social understanding differently in their various real-life relationships. It reminds us, again, that the emotional context of a particular interaction or relationship affects children's ability to marshal their cognitive capacities, and may well influence what is learned from the experience. Children's understanding of their partner's inner states, or at least their use of such understanding, is centrally related to the emotional and motivational colour of the interaction.

Conclusion

This chapter has focused on links between children's discovery of the mind and their social experiences, in particular the pragmatics and emotional quality of those experiences. The relevance of Bruner's vision in *Child's Talk* and *Acts of Meaning* concerning pragmatics and the 'contexts of practice' to the development of mind reading is clear. We can also point to other domains of development where those lessons are equally relevant. A final example, close to the heart of Bruner's arguments, concerns the cultural messages reaching young children through their daily family interactions. In the framework of our studies in England and in the USA, we asked a series of notoriously intractable questions concerning children as cultural selves: In what sense is a preschool child growing up in the USA today an *American* child? How are English preschool children different from their American peers? How do the implicit and explicit prescriptive and moral messages directed to these young children differ in the different cultural worlds of Cambridge, England and Central Pennsylvania?

We learned that already at three years, distinctive cultural messages shape children's lives and their talk. Their fantasies, their narratives and especially the social rules that pattern their lives are not just those of their families, but those of the wider world beyond (Dunn and Brown, 1991). The particulars of the differences are intriguing, and it is tempting to link them with national stereotypes. In the American families, we saw stronger emphases on individual rights, on prescriptions in terms of individual action; in the English, emphasis was on politeness and appropriate behaviour, on avoiding harm to others, on general normative prescriptions.

From a small-scale study of this sort, the particular differences found can only be treated as pilot results; but the general lesson is clear, and reminds us of the centrality of Bruner's emphasis on the constituting role of culture. Questions about cultural selves, about the relation of emotion to cognition in development, about children's conception of the mind are among the most difficult but central issues for developmental psychologists. And the full significance of Bruner's ideas is only now beginning to be fully appreciated. A close look at the daily dramas of children's lives – the epiphanies of the ordinary to which Bruner drew our attention – brings home to us both the early sophistication of children's understanding of others and the significance of the emotional quality of those daily interactions. Bruner began a revolution in *Child's Talk* with his focus on pragmatics and the connections between children's social and intellectual lives. If we are to make progress in understanding children's discovery of the mind we urgently need to heed his message.

Notes

The research in Pennsylvania and London described here was supported by a grant from NICHD (HD 23158).

1 The study was a longitudinal study of 50 second-born children, their families and friends, in central Pennsylvania (Dunn et al., 1991). The families were recruited from sequential birth announcements, were predominantly Caucasian, and included a wide range of socioeconomic backgrounds (the standard deviation and range of fathers' occupational status showed the range and variance was similar to that of nationally representative samples).

   Unstructured naturalistic observations of the children at home with their families were conducted at 33, 40, 47 and 69 months, and the children were also studied playing alone in a room at home with a close friend at 47 and 69 months (Brown et al., 1996). Audiotape recordings of the conversations of the children with their families and friends were made during the observations, transcribed by the observers, and coded for a variety of aspects of interaction, and for reference to inner states. Narrative notes recorded by the observers during the observations (documenting pretend play, conflict incidents, expression of emotion, and a variety of non-verbal behaviours) were incorporated into the transcripts. The observations were targeted on second-born children, and other family members came and went in the course of the observations. Our interest was in observing the children's usual family interactions, capturing what typically happened in the home, rather than imposing a standardized pattern across families. The expression of affect was coded for each speaker turn.

   Assessments of the children's mind-reading abilities (Bartsch and Wellman, 1989) and understanding of emotions (Denham, 1986) were conducted at the 40 and 47 months visits. For further details of the study, and the follow up of the children to the end of their second year at school see Dunn (1995), Brown and Dunn (1996) and Dunn et al. (1996).

References

Astington, J.W. (1994) *The Child's Discovery of the Mind*. London: Fontana.

Astington, J.W. and Jenkins, J. (1995) 'Theory of mind development and social understanding', *Cognition and Emotion*, 9: 151–66.

Bartsch, K. and Wellman, H.M. (1989) 'Young children's attribution of action to beliefs and desires', *Child Development*, 60: 946–64.

Bloom, L., Rispoli, M., Gartner, B. and Hafitz, J. (1989) 'Acquisition of complementation', *Journal of Child Language*, 16: 101–20.

Brown, J.R. (1993) 'Telling "What happened?" A study of children's early conversations about the past'. PhD, Pennsylvania State University.

Brown, J.R. and Dunn, J. (1996) 'Continuities in emotion understanding from three to six years', *Child Development*, 67: 789–802.

Brown, J.R., Donelan-McCall, N. and Dunn, J. (1996) 'Why talk about mental states? The significance of children's conversations with friends, siblings and mothers', *Child Development*, 67: 836–49.

Bruner, J.S. (1983) *Child's Talk: Learning to Use Language*. Oxford: Oxford University Press.

Bruner, J.S. (1990) *Acts of Meaning*. Cambridge, MA: Harvard University Press.

Denham, S.A. (1986) 'Social cognition, prosocial behavior, and emotion in preschoolers: contextual validation', *Child Development*, 57: 194–201.

Dunn, J. (1988) *The Beginnings of Social Understanding*. Cambridge, MA: Harvard University Press.

Dunn, J. (1995) 'Children as psychologists: the later correlates of individual differences in understanding of emotions and other minds', *Cognition and Emotion*, 9: 187–201.

Dunn, J. and Brown, J. (1991) 'Becoming American or English? Talking about the social world in England and the US', in M. Bornstein (ed.), *Cross-Cultural Approaches to Parenting*. Hillsdale, NJ: Erlbaum.

Dunn, J. and Brown, J.R. (1993) 'Early conversations about causality: content, pragmatics, and developmental change', *British Journal of Developmental Psychology*, 11: 107–23.

Dunn, J. and Brown, J.R. (1994) 'Affect expression in the family, children's understanding of emotions, and their interactions with others', *Merrill-Palmer Quarterly*, 40: 120–37.

Dunn, J., Brown, J. and Beardsall, L. (1989) 'Family talk about feeling states and children's later understanding of others' emotions', *Developmental Psychology*, 27: 448–55.

Dunn, J., Brown, J., Slomkowski, C., Tesla, C. and Youngblade, L. (1991) 'Young children's understanding of other people's feelings and beliefs: individual differences and their antecedents', *Child Development*, 62: 1352–66.

Dunn, J., Creps, C. and Brown, J. (1996) 'Children's family relationships between two and five: developmental changes and individual differences', *Social Development*, 5: 230–50.

Feldman, C.F. (1992) 'The new theory of mind', *Human Development*, 35: 107–17.

Goodenough, F.L. (1931) *Anger in Young Children*. Minneapolis: University of Minnesota Press.

Grice, H.P. (1957) 'Meaning', *Philosophical Review*, 66: 377–88.

Hoffman, M.L. (1986) 'Affect, cognition, and motivation', in R.M. Sorrentino and E.T. Higgins (eds), *Handbook of Motivation and Cognition*. New York: Guilford.

Hughes, C. and Dunn, J. (1998) 'Understanding mind and emotion: longitudinal associations with mental state talk among friends', *Developmental Psychology*, 34 (5): 1026–37.

Leslie, A. (1987) 'Pretense and representation: the origins of "theory of mind"', *Psychological Review*, 94: 412–26.

Lewis, C., Freeman, N.H., Kyriakidou, C., Maridaki-Kossotaki, K. and Berridge, D.M. (1996) 'Social influences on false belief access: specific sibling influences or general apprenticeship?', *Child Development*, 67: 2930–47.

Moore, C., Pure, K. and Furrow, D. (1990) 'Children's understanding of the modal expression of speaker certainty and uncertainty and its relation to the development of a representational theory of mind', *Child Development*, 61: 722–30.

Newton, P.E. (1994) 'Preschool prevarication: An investigation of the cognitive prerequisites for deception'. PhD, University of Portsmouth.

Newton, P.E. and Reddy, V. (1996) 'Pseudo-constructs in developmental theorising: the case of pseudo-deception'. Submitted.

Perner, J. (1991) *Understanding the Representational Mind*. Cambridge, MA: MIT Press.

Perner, J., Ruffman, T. and Leekham, S.R. (1994) 'Theory of mind is contagious: you catch it from your sibs', *Child Development*, 65: 1228–38.

Piaget, J. (1932/1965) *The Moral Judgement of the Child*. New York: Academic Press.

Roberts, W. and Strayer, J. (1987) 'Parents' response to the emotional distress of their children: relations with children's competence', *Developmental Psychology*, 23: 415–22.

Rogoff, B. (1990) *Apprenticeship in Thinking*. Oxford: Oxford University Press.

Shatz, M., Wellman, H.M. and Silber, S. (1983) 'The acquisition of mental verbs: a systematic investigation of first references to mental state', *Cognition*, 14: 301–21.

Slomkowski, C. and Dunn, J. (1992) 'Arguments and relationships within the family: differences in children's disputes with mother and sibling', *Developmental Psychology*, 28: 919–24.

Sodian, B. (1991) 'The development of deception in children', *British Journal of Developmental Psychology*, 9: 173–88.

Stein, N. and Miller, C. (1993) 'The development of memory and reasoning skill in argumentative contexts: evaluating, explaining, and generating evidence', in R. Glaser (ed.), *Advances in Instructional Psychology*, Vol. 4. Hillsdale, NJ: Lawrence Erlbaum.

Strichartz, A.F. and Burton, R.V. (1990) 'Lies and the truth: a study of the development of the concept', *Child Development*, 61: 211–20.

Wellman, H.M. (1990) *The Child's Theory of Mind*. Cambridge, MA: MIT Press.

Youngblade, L.M. and Dunn, J. (1995) 'Individual differences in young children's pretend play with mother and sibling: links to relationships and understanding of other people's feelings and beliefs', *Child Development*, 66: 1472–92.

6

EDUCATION: THE BRIDGE FROM CULTURE TO MIND

David R. Olson

Bruner is fond of quoting William Blake's poem, 'With happiness stretch'd across the hills', with its dismissive view of science:

> Now I a fourfold vision see,
> And a fourfold vision is given to me;
> 'Tis fourfold in my supreme delight
> And threefold in soft Beulah's night
> And twofold always. May God us keep
> From single vision & Newton's sleep. (Blake, 1989)

We learn something about Bruner by examining his fascination with Blake's rejection of Newton. Newton represents the discoverer, the great finder of the facts, the truths of nature. Blake, on the other hand, represents the Romantic poet, one who creates new worlds to inhabit. The finder, the prototype for all those who enquire into the natural sciences, is contrasted with the artist, the maker, the prototype for what Harold Bloom has called the 'strong poet' (Bloom, 1973).

Bruner is not so much given to celebrating the well-worn contrast between scientist and poet as to examining their indissoluble relation. Along with such philosophical writers as Goodman, Gombrich and Rorty, Bruner has explored the view that the cognitions of scientist and poet are, at base, not as different as they might seem. Even for scientists, reality does not offer itself up as knowledge. In all cases, as he says, 'knowledge is made not found' (Bruner, 1996: 119).

The idea that knowledge is made not found is at the core of what we may loosely call 'constructivism'. Constructivism is the view that knowledge and truth are products of human enquiry and invention rather than given directly by scripture or nature. Its sources can be seen everywhere. I have already mentioned the Romantic poets. Rorty (1989) locates it in the spirit of the French Revolution when the whole social order, previously taken to be an expression of a fixed divine order, was overturned essentially overnight. Other influential writers who can be seen as sympathetic to the constructivist view are not hard to find. Those nominated by Rorty include Nietzsche, Heidegger, Derrida, James, Dewey, Goodman, Sellars, Putnam, Davidson and Wittgenstein. All reject the view that knowledge is the 'mirror of nature' (Rorty, 1979: 163). Knowledge is the production of statements that may be taken as true and therefore as about reality.[1]

Although Bruner acknowledges his debt to Nelson Goodman (1976) and Ernst Gombrich (1960) (and they their debt to him), Bruner's constructivism in cognitive psychology links most directly to the writings of Piaget and, in the form of social constructivism, to Vygotsky. This involves an important shift in the constructivist agenda, for while the philosophers mentioned above are concerned with the growth of knowledge in a culture – that is, with the production of original knowledge – Bruner's focus is on the growth of knowledge in children. Here the growth of knowledge is new only to the learner not to the culture or the discipline. In spite of this important difference, Bruner assumes that the two processes are similar. Further, Bruner is concerned with the growth of knowledge in children under the impact of systematic education. His theories, like Dewey's and Vygotsky's before him, are basically educational and only by implication general theories of mind. And, again like them, Bruner's emphasis is on how the child constructs knowledge rather than merely assimilates or internalizes it from the environment or culture. Yet, as I mentioned, the child's task is importantly different from that of the scientist: for the child there is an accepted solution towards which his or her constructions must approximate; for the scientist, in contrast, no such accepted solution is available. The assumption underlying constructivist views of learning is that knowledge cannot be simply communicated but must be re-constructed by every learner. One concern of this chapter is to spell out just how this is possible.

In *The Process of Education* (1960) Bruner devoted a chapter to learning by discovery, to the idea that knowledge, if it is to be truly possessed by a learner, cannot simply be learned but must, in some sense, be discovered. Discovery assures understanding, where mere learning may be verbal, superficial, non-transferable, and soon forgotten. Discovery, on the other hand, is possible only by constructing understandings on the basis of extensions, elaborations or reformulations of current or preceding under-standings. Indeed, 'discovery learning' has become something of an official pedagogy in the past three decades.

Both these constructivist assumptions – that scientific knowledge is the product of 'making' and that children's learning is similarly a matter of making and invention – are elaborated in *The Culture of Education*, where Bruner writes:

> science is not something that exists out there in nature, but ... a tool in the mind of the knower ... and you don't really ever get there unless you do it, as a learner, on your own terms. All one can do for a learner en route to her forming a view of her own is to aid and abet her on her own voyage. (1996: 115)

The importance of this 'aiding and abetting' is not only central to Bruner's recent work; it is also what divides a Piaget from a Vygotsky. Although Bruner's emphasis on education leads him to side with Vygotsky, he is swift to acknowledge his debt to both these giants (1997). The second purpose of this paper is to examine more closely how a constructivist orientation can help us address the issues of learning and development and in so doing contribute to a more general understanding of mind and culture.

Internalism and externalism

First, I want to express some reservations about the idea that Vygotsky's cultural theory can be used to fill in a void in Piaget's developmental theory.

It is easy to see that Piaget and Vygotsky provide the foundations for the cognitive developmental theory on which Bruner builds his account of the role of education in human development. All three share three fundamental assumptions: that cognition is best thought of as genetic or developmental, that the mind is constructed by the activities of the subject, and that the structures so constructed are manifest in consciousness. Of these assumptions, constructivism has had the greatest appeal to the current generation of researchers. It is now widely held that knowledge is human-made, that knowledge is not simply the true but the believed, and that theories are at best models of things not the things themselves. And, as a corollary, learning – that is, children's acquisition of knowledge – is constructed through the reorganization of the child's own representational structures.

But the idea that knowledge is made not found leaves psychological theory with the serious problem of just how knowledge could be made. That is, if knowledge is not simply derived from the external world – a position we may call 'externalism' – where does it come from? How is knowledge created? What are the internalist's options?

Internalist views incline towards the innate and genetic. Fodor (1975) provided a detailed argument claiming that neither Piaget nor Vygotsky had an adequate theory of how knowledge was constructed. Fodor distinguished what he called, after Peirce (1955), 'fixation of belief' (acquiring the detailed knowledge of the world through experience) from 'concept formation' (the formation of the basic inventory of concepts in terms of which beliefs can be formulated and expressed). Beliefs, he argued, are acquired through hypothesis testing. Once the requisite stock of concepts is available, they can be used to form hypotheses about the way the world is, and by testing those hypotheses, one can construct appropriate beliefs. The problem, Fodor pointed out, was the absence of any detailed theory of how the concepts needed to formulate hypotheses were formed in the first place. Hence, Fodor was driven to his well-known and extreme nativism regarding basic concepts. How to account for the acquisition of the basic stock of concepts remains a critical problem for constructivists whether Vygotskians, Piagetians or Brunerians. If learning is by means of hypothesis testing, where do the concepts required for the formulation of hypotheses come from? If learning is not by hypothesis testing, how does it occur?

Piaget and Vygotsky tackled this problem quite differently. Piaget remained an internalist, appealing to biological metaphors of assimilation and accommodation as causal mechanisms that reform schemata in such a way that they establish an equilibrium with the external world. Symbolic representations, which are required for hypothesis testing, are constructed once appropriate sensory-motor schema and processing resources are available, roughly in the second year of life. He thus attempted to avoid Fodor's criticism by denying that learning in infancy is by hypothesis testing. Piaget failed, unfortunately, to make clear just how schema elaborate and differentiate if not by hypothesis testing.

Vygotsky's alternative is equally well known but no less problematic. Vygotsky advanced a strict distinction between two levels of mental function. The lower level he characterized as natural, biological, causal and shared with nonhuman animals. The higher mental processes he portrayed as representational, sociohistorical, linguistic, voluntary, conscious and distinctively human. Bruner (1960) extended this argument, suggesting that the development of the elementary functions is Darwinian in kind, whereas the development of the higher is Lamarckian. The former develop through natural selection, while in the development of the latter we see the inheritance of acquired characteristics, making possible the growth of culture and its transmission.

This view is, however, problematic. For the explanation of the growth of culture and the acquisition of culture by children becomes externalist. The new concepts that allow the distinctive properties of human thought are inherited from the culture, first as interpersonal, later as intrapersonal functions (Wertsch, 1993). Admittedly, Vygotsky claims that the concepts are not simply taken up by individuals 'ready-made' from the culture (1986: 146), but undergo development before reaching maturity, and he advanced the notion of a 'zone' that constitutes the intersubjective ground for cognitive growth. And Bruner (1983) proposed the notion of 'scaffolding' and a 'language acquisition support system' by means of which the mature assist the young in their intellectual development. Yet in both cases, the growth of mind is a function of taking over concepts already articulated in the culture as instruments of one's own mind. Because Bruner and Vygotsky both hold that language and other cultural products are first in the culture and then become constituents of children's minds, they both may be charged with what I have called externalism. One is tempted to label Vygotsky a 'naive realist in regard to culture' in that the child is said to 'internalize' or 'appropriate' the cultural environment. This implies a form of cultural determinism seriously at odds with both Piagetian constructivism and with Western notions of privacy and individualism. Indeed, Zinchenko has argued that 'it was the internalization principles that served in Soviet ideological practice as a basis for the system for imprinting communist ideology into people's heads' (1996: 321, n. 1).

That is, although Vygotsky would be among the first to deny that the child 'appropriates' the physical environment – he acknowledges that the child constructs his or her knowledge of the natural environment (exactly how, as we have seen, is not completely clear) – he is willing to say that the child 'appropriates' the cultural environment. Bruner (1996) is more guarded. Although he is an avowed constructivist, who holds firm to the central significance of teaching to intellectual growth, he does claim that teachers, as instruments of culture, are restricted to 'aiding and abetting' intellectual growth.

But if we grant the constructivist assumptions that knowledge is made not found, and that this is true both for cultural knowledge in general, and for the child's acquisition of knowledge in particular, how exactly should we acknowledge the inescapable significance to cognitive growth of culture in general and teaching in particular? Piagetians remain uncompromising in their internalist stance that cognition is the product of the learner's conceptual constructions; teaching provides a complex social environment in which such constructions take place (the child as the solitary scientist in his laboratory, to use a metaphor of Bruner's). Vygotskians, to the extent that they appeal to 'internalization', 'participation' and 'zones' for teaching in an effort to reduce the distance between what the culture offers and what the child constructs, suffer from the externalist perspective – what is 'out there in the culture' comes to be 'in here in the mind.' Some Vygotskians such as Lave and Wenger (1991), Wertsch (1993) and Cole (1996: 104) attempt to shrink the distance between the private and internal, on the one hand, and the social and external, on the other, by appeal to what they describe as 'the mastery or co-construction of mediational means'. But without a theory of construction, co-construction remains utterly mysterious.

Other Vygotskians have moved in a more Piagetian direction. Lawrence and Valsiner, for example, have argued that internalization can misleadingly be interpreted as direct transmission. As Zinchenko points out, 'When one ascribes the driving or originating functions of development to culture, ideal form, or environment, one leaves thereby unclear the role that subjects themselves play in their development' (1996: 314). Lawrence and Valsiner note that, for Vygotsky, internalization is primarily a matter of going from the child's public to private speech and only secondarily as a matter of moving from the external culture to the individual mind. They propose that internalization be replaced by the notion of transformation, allowing the individual mind to be seen as 'the initiating agent of constructive and reconstructive change' (Lawrence and Valsiner, 1993: 165). But what, precisely, is it that subjects themselves do in constructing a representation? Only persons have thoughts. Societies do not have minds nor do they change their minds. Only persons have minds to change even if those changes do occur largely in a social context. Yet a way must be found to acknowledge the fact that what the learner is constructing is, in some sense, the very structures of knowledge that make up a culture.

The problem breaks into two parts, the first concerning the acquisition of the beliefs that the culture as a whole shares. Hypothesis testing, as a form of abduction – or as Bruner prefers, the narrativization of experience – offers what promises to be an adequate theory of belief fixation. Equipped with such powers, the child is in a position to explore not only which beliefs and stories he or she holds true but also which are held by others, both living and long dead. These systems of beliefs, whether organized in terms of theories of biology, mechanics, psychology or history, with appropriate causal explanatory principles, make up the most important legacies of a culture that children can explore by hypothesis formation and evaluation using the symbolic resources of language and notational systems of the culture. The structure and acquisition of these conceptual systems is one of the more promising areas of research in developmental and educational theory (Hirschfeld and Gelman, 1994; Olson and Torrance, 1996).

The second, and much more difficult, problem is how children acquire the concepts out of which the hypothesized beliefs and narratives are to be constructed. Piaget saw these concepts as deriving from the sensory-motor activities of comparing, ordering and the like, these sensory-motor structures giving rise to concepts via the somewhat obscure process of reflective abstraction. Vygotsky saw these concepts as emerging out of involvement in the adult culture, including the language habits of the child's community. Yet just how they do so once we abandon the idea that they can be simply 'internalized' from the culture, remains unclear. Finally, hypothesis testing seems to be ruled out for, as mentioned above, hypothesis testing and narrative formation are applicable only to the formation of beliefs and not to the formation of basic concepts.

Constructing concepts

We are not without options. Old-fashioned learning theory distinguished trial-and-error with reinforcement from hypothesis testing with verification/falsification, and held that only the latter required representation (but see Brewer, 1976; Mandler, 1993). Piaget (1976) exploited this distinction by contrasting the hypothetical thinking of older children, the development of which was made possible by the availability of representations, with the simpler exploration involved in 'making interesting things happen'. That is, he distinguished exploration from hypothesis testing. When a 1-year-old repeatedly drops an object off a ledge he or she is not testing the hypothesis: 'If I drop this it will fall. True or False?' She is simply making interesting things happen. Expectancies, I suggest, are not the same thing as beliefs. Beliefs are couched in the public language of the culture, which, once formed, can engender the much more complex expectancies we think of as hypotheses.

Expectancies, then, are causal states of organisms that may be fulfilled or unfulfilled, whereas beliefs are representational states that are either true or false and can be entertained and revised. Beliefs, unlike expectancies, may be restricted to the conscious processes of symbol-using humans (Carruthers, 1996).

A constructivist orientation should alert us to the possibility that the transition from sensory-motor schemata to language is not a simple matter of explication but a genuine reorganization of experience into culturally acceptable categories. Let me illustrate this reorganization by considering children's acquisition of a meta-representational system: notation systems for representing language and number. That will lead us back to our main concern, the problem of how teaching helps children to make rather than find knowledge.

Bruner, in this a follower of Vygotsky, pointed out that mind is in some sense a cultural artefact and the properties of mind are by-products of the mastery of historically evolved cultural forms. To illustrate, the concept of zero has a distinctive history traceable to Hindu mathematicians living in the second century BC (Danzig, 1954), yet these days every schoolchild by the age of 6 or 7 can represent an empty set by means of a zero. How are we to explain that? As mentioned, Vygotsky handled this by distinguishing lower from higher mental functions and claiming, following Durkheim (see Kozulin in Vygotsky, 1986: 264, n. 15), that the higher functions are 'nothing but social'. Though what this means is not at all clear, the idea is that concepts such as the number zero are historical artefacts, which, once invented, easily find their way into the psychological functions of children. But how to account for these facts? Reflective abstraction of sensory-motor schemata, the Piagetian view, externalization of innate structures, the Fodorian view, seem just as plausible as internalization of external structures, the Vygotskian view. In none of these cases do we have an explicit account of the relation between mind and culture.

Again, we are not without options. Speaking very generally we could say that humans are equipped with biological predispositions for perceiving and acting in the world, and culture is designed so that it can, so to speak, slip through the biological cracks (Gelman and Greeno, 1989; Sperber, 1994; Cole, 1996). Culture, unlike nature, is invented to be learnable, to map onto existing evolutionarily specified categories and relations. In fact in an early paper Vygotsky said precisely this: 'Culture does not produce anything apart from that which is given by nature. But it transforms nature to suit the ends of man' (Vygotsky, 1929: 418; cited in Bruner, 1997).

Consider language learning. Language learning is not merely learning public symbols for previously established sensory-motor knowledge but rather involves a reorganization of that knowledge. One of Vygotsky's most important contributions was his insistence that learning a language, or any other cultural symbolic system, does not merely allow one to 'express' or 'communicate' thoughts that have already been formulated. Rather, in some as yet undisclosed way, language reorganizes those thoughts. As Vygotsky put it: 'Thought does not express itself in words, but rather *realizes* itself in them' (1986: 251; emphasis added). And again:

'Thought is not merely expressed in words; it comes into existence through them' (1986: 219). Words and other symbols provide the categories in terms of which the world is represented in thought. How?

It is widely held that an important reorganization of cognition occurs when children learn a natural language. In learning a language children gain access to a symbolic system that allows for reference, truth, falsity and negation; cognition, it may be argued, becomes logical. But my concern here is more with the cognitive implications of learning representations, for representations such as notations for words, letters and numbers are historical achievements and are widely recognized as the responsibility of the school. What happens when children learn to use notations such as the letters of the alphabet or the numeral zero? Consider first the alphabet. The *abc*s are obviously a purely cultural product. I have discussed their original invention elsewhere (Olson, 1994). What is involved in their re-invention by children? Here is one plausible story. Children first learn letters as mere pattern, discriminated and named but without representational significance. But once acquired these letter names provide an inventory of sounds, a model, in terms of which the constituents of everyday oral speech may be analysed: knowing the sound /b/ associated with the letter name 'b' children may hear the /b/ sound as a constituent of /bat/ which is shared with the word /boy/ and /baby/. The process is neither one of internalizing a concept nor of expressing the already known by means of a public symbol. Rather, it is a matter of representing one set of structures, the sound patterns of speech, in terms of the categories available in some other structure, the alphabet. As they are learning to read they are, at the same time, learning to think, that is, to formulate hypotheses and beliefs, about some of the properties of speech. Before they learn the alphabet, they know that /b/ distinguishes /bat/ from /hat/; what they appear not to know is that there is a property of /bat/ held in common with /boy/ and /baby/, that common property being represented by the letter *b* (Olson, 1996). Vygotsky anticipated this conclusion, arguing that writing makes children conscious of language but he left unanswered the question as to how that could come about (1986: 184). The distinctive process, I suggest, is that of model or metaphor, of seeing one thing in terms of another, and that relation specifies a new concept.

A similar case can be made for children's learning to represent nothing with a something, a zero. In our laboratory, we have observed that when pre-reading children are asked to represent 'No cats' either by writing on a paper or by signalling with their fingers, they are greatly puzzled. Older children, familiar with writing, will attempt to write, print or scribble marks for the expression 'No cats'. Further, they will often signal the number with their thumb against the forefinger forming an *o*, that is, a zero. Younger children offer very different responses, such as saying 'There are no cats so I didn't write anything' or doing nothing (Olson and Homer, 1996; Olson, 1997). A more ingenious response occurs when these children use one finger for 'One cat', two fingers for 'Two cats' and a closed fist for 'No cats'. These performances indicate that many pre-literate children tend to take written signs as corresponding to things, rather than to statements or words or symbols about those things or events. Consequently, no thing is represented by no mark.

How are we to relate such findings to the child's construction of knowledge? On the one hand, children have not yet acquired the cultural convention of using a something, a mark, to represent a nothing, no cats. On the other hand, the children clearly understand the absence of cats. Will reflective abstraction, the Piagetian alternative, give us the cultural product for representing nothing, the zero for example? Not if we are to believe the historical claim that the concept of zero was invented only once, by Hindus in the second century BC, and then widely adopted and widely taught to others. But neither is the concept innate, awaiting triggering conditions to bring it into consciousness, as Fodor would have it, because, were that true, the concept would not have a specific cultural history. The Vygotskian claim that, once invented, the concepts are first cultural forms and only subsequently part of the child's knowledge seems plausible. But the theory lacks an account of how the concept is invented in the first place and, as we have seen, advances an inadequate theory of learning as 'internalization'. How, then, do concepts arise? And how does a concept become part of the child's knowledge?

Concepts, I have urged, cannot pass smoothly from culture to mind. Cultural forms are external to the mind and they have to be connected with something internal, a concept or thought. Consequently, it is not possible for the child to compare two things, one which is in his consciousness, no cats, and the other which is in the culture, the zero. Rather both have to be available in the consciousness of the child. What seems to be required is that the child has two entities available, the knowledge of absence, mentioned above, and the knowledge of a sequence of numerals, perhaps learned, like the alphabet, by rote. The availability to consciousness of these two entities permits the formulation of a hypothesis linking them. Learning, then, consists of applying the memorized sequence of the numerals to the prior knowledge of absence. In so doing the child is not merely making explicit the known but forming a concept applicable to all sorts of nothings.

This proposal is an attempt to fill a gap in all constructivist theories, Bruner's and Vygotsky's in particular, which claim both that knowledge is made rather than found and that development is, in some descriptive sense, the internalization of culture. The child, we wish to say, is the maker of his or her own knowledge even if that knowledge is already a widely shared possession of a culture. The claim that the child has to make his or her own knowledge can thus be reconciled with the idea that the child must be taught if he or she is to be in a position to make that knowledge. To say that the child has to be 'prepared', while true, is unhelpful. To say that the knowledge has to be in a format appropriate for the child's assimilation is to beg the question for we have, hopefully, agreed that knowledge has to be made not found. The solution is not to make it easier to find! How do we, as Bruner says 'aid and abet'?

Knowledge is constructed, I have suggested, when the learner can take one set of concepts and use them as a model for thinking about some other set of events. My example was seeing speech in terms of writing or seeing nothing in terms of a numeral. The basic mode is metaphor, abduction, narrative construal, inference to the best explanation; seeing one thing in terms of another, working with representations rather than things. These representations, accumulated archivally in maps, charts, books and computer programs provide many of these most important models (Olson, 1994; ch. 10).

To see the relevance of this to teaching we must begin by dissolving the distinction between discovery and teaching, terms that apply to forms of pedagogy rather than to processes of cognition. From the point of view of cognition, all knowledge is made not found, hence, the history of equivocation about the possibility of teaching. From the point of view of pedagogy, however, forms of teaching vary only in directness. Teaching, in a sense, defines the problem space in terms of which children construct their knowledge. Discovery provides a large problem space; expository teaching a more delimited one. Each has its risks. Too large a problem space and a child may never hit on a solution; define it too narrowly and a student may simply memorize a solution. Effective pedagogy is a matter of balancing the constraints. But in neither case is knowledge simply transmitted. Successful attempts at direct transmission of knowledge are never simply that. They are cases in which the child was already in a position to construct an interpretation that advanced his or her own knowledge. The successful construction is the result of, so to speak, pouring old wine into new wineskins, of seeing something previously known in one sense in the categories of a new system, and thereby producing new knowledge.

So, constructivism reigns. Children, like adults, make what they find. The emphasis is not just on the children's activity and their engagement but rather on the elaboration and revision of their ideas, beliefs, models and representations generally. But far from minimizing the role of the teacher and teaching, constructivism makes competent teaching even more significant. For it is a much more difficult task to determine that what the children have made is productive and satisfying than to settle for what used to be called 'coverage'. Bruner's insistence on the learner's role in the construction of knowledge is an important step in the development of that revised pedagogy.

Note

1   I do not wish to identify myself with those postmodernists who not only insist that we make knowledge but that we make reality as well. I insist on a sharp distinction between representations (which we do make) and the reals (many of which were there long before we came on to the scene).

References

Blake, W. (1989) *Blake. The Complete Poems*, 2nd edn, ed. W.H. Stevenson. London: Longman.

Bloom, H. (1973) *The Anxiety of Influence*. Oxford: Oxford University Press.

Brewer, W. (1976) 'There is no convincing evidence for operant or classical conditioning in adult humans', in W.B. Weiner and D. Palermo (eds), *Cognition and Symbolic Processes*. Hillsdale, NJ: Erlbaum.

Bruner, J.S. (1960) *The Process of Education*. Cambridge, MA: Harvard University Press.

Bruner, J.S. (1983) *Child's Talk: Learning to Use Language*. Oxford: Oxford University Press.

Bruner, J.S. (1996) *The Culture of Education*. Cambridge MA: Harvard University Press.

Bruner, J.S. (1996b) 'Celebrating divergence: Piaget and Vygotsky', *Human Development*, 40: 63–73.

Carruthers, P. (1997) *Language, Thought and Consciousness: An Essay in Philosophical Psychology*. Cambridge: Cambridge University Press.

Cole, M. (1996) *Cultural Psychology: A Once and Future Discipline*. Cambridge, MA: Harvard University Press.

Danzig, T. (1954) *Number: The Language of Science*. Garden City, NJ: Penguin.

Fodor, J.A. (1975) *The Language of Thought*. New York: Thomas Y. Crowell.

Gelman, R. and Greeno, J.G. (1989) 'On the nature of competence: principles for understanding in a domain', in L.B. Resnick (ed.), *Knowing and Learning: Essays in Honor of Robert Glaser*. Hillsdale, NJ: Erlbaum.

Gombrich, E.H. (1960) *Art and Illusion: A Study in the Psychology of Pictorial Representation*. New York: Bolligen/Pantheon Books.

Goodman, N. (1976) *Ways of Worldmaking*. Indianapolis, IN: Hackett Publishing Company.

Hirschfeld, L.A. and Gelman, S. (eds) (1994) *Mapping the Mind: Domain Specificity in Cognition and Culture*. New York: Cambridge University Press.

Lave, J. and Wenger, E. (1991) *Situated Learning*. Cambridge: Cambridge University Press.

Lawrence, J.A. and Valsiner, J. (1993) 'Conceptual roots of internalization: from transmissions to transformation', *Human Development*, 36: 150–67.

Mandler, J. (1993) 'Representation', in P. Mussen (ed.), *Handbook of Child Psychology*, Vol. 3. New York: Wiley.

Olson, D.R. (1994) *The World on Paper: The Conceptual and Cognitive Implications of Writing and Reading*. Cambridge: Cambridge University Press.

Olson, D.R. (1996) 'Towards a psychology of literacy: on the relations between speech and writing', *Cognition*, 60: 83–104.

Olson, D.R. (1997) 'The written representation of negation', *Pragmatics & Cognition*, 5 (2): 239–56.

Olson, D.R. and Homer, B. (1996) 'Children's concept of "word"'. Paper presented at the XXVI International Congress of Psychology, Montreal, 16–21 August.

Olson, D.R. and Torrance, N.G. (1996) *Handbook of Education and Human Development*. Cambridge, MA: Blackwell.

Peirce, C.S. (1955) *The Philosophical Writings of Peirce*, ed. J. Buchler. New York: Dover.

Piaget, J. (1976) *The Child's Conception of the World*. Totowa, NJ: Littlefield, Adams & Co.

Rorty, R. (1979) *Philosophy and the Mirror of Nature*. Princeton: Princeton University Press.

Rorty, R. (1989) *Contingency, Irony and Solidarity*. New York: Cambridge University Press.

Sperber, D. (1994) 'The modularity of thought and the epidemiology of representations', in L.A. Hirschfeld and S. Gelman (eds), *Mapping the Mind: Domain Specificity in Cognition and Culture*. New York: Cambridge University Press.

Vygotsky, L.S. (1929) 'The problem of the cultural development of the child', *Journal of Genetic Psychology*, 36: 415–32.

Vygotsky, L.S. (1986) *Thought and Language*. A. Kozulin (trans. and ed.). Cambridge, MA: MIT Press.

Wertsch, J.V. (1993) 'Commentary on J.A. Lawrence and J. Valsiner, "Conceptual roots of internalization: from transmissions to transformation"', *Human Development*, 36: 168–71.

Zinchenko, V.P. (1996) 'Developing activity theory: the zone of proximal development and beyond', in B.A. Nardi (ed.), *Context and Consciousness: Activity Theory and Human–Computer Interaction*. Cambridge, MA: MIT Press.

7

TOWARDS A CULTURAL ECOLOGY OF INSTRUCTION

Edward S. Reed

Editors' note: In January 1997, when work on this volume was just beginning, Ed Reed sent us a sketch of the chapter he was writing. He died suddenly later that year. What follows is Reed's draft, to which only a few minor editorial changes have been made, together with commentaries by Howard Gardner and David Bakhurst.

Twentieth-century psychologists have most often described education in terms of supposedly universal aptitudes and capacities on the part of teachers and learners. For example, the spread of public education over the past century paralleled a rise in the transmission theory of culture, the idea that cultures perpetuate themselves by transmitting ideas to children, often through special instructional institutions. Hence, until very recently, most theorists of education have treated culture as if it were a set of ideas – a body of knowledge – to be transmitted from teacher to student, with success to be measured in terms of the student's internalization of that knowledge.

Although couched in the language of universals, these conceptions of education are in fact intimately tied up with specific cultural practices. The transmission theory of education is a parochial view that has seemed universal to many within our culture simply because it is our modern, Western view. It is only in the past decade or two that serious alternatives have been offered. The work of cultural psychologists, especially Jean Lave (1990) and Barbara Rogoff (1990), has shown that transmission is only one aspect of the process of education, and a limited one at that. It is to Jerome Bruner's lasting credit that he immediately appreciated the significance of this work in cultural psychology, and has proved more than willing to modify many of his own ideas about education to take these new insights into account.

Bruner's studies of education thus represent the best in mid-twentieth-century views of education-as-transmission and, in his most recent work, the thoughtful beginnings of a turning away from the transmission view of both education and culture. In this chapter, I try to recast the most useful of Bruner's early ideas about teaching, curriculum and learning by abandoning the transmission concept. In his recent *The Culture of Education* (1996), Bruner has himself begun to rework his earlier views in light of his own variety of cultural psychology, but I argue here that an even more radical – indeed, an explicitly *ecological* – concept of culture is needed to revitalize Bruner's earlier insights.

Bruner's triad

The core insight running throughout Bruner's work on education is what I call 'Bruner's triad': the theory that there are three fundamentally distinct forms of human learning – enactive, iconic, and symbolic. In his earlier writings, Bruner described the triad as three different kinds of 'cognitive process' (1960, 1966, 1971), but in *The Culture of Education*, he hedges, saying that there are 'three ways in which humans represent the world or, better, three ways of capturing those invariances in experience and action that we call "reality"' (1996: 155). The later (vaguer) definition is the better, especially if the goal is to develop a theory of the education process that eschews the transmission metaphor. Educators should be focused on strengthening students' active experiencing of the world, not their representations of it, which are so often little more than by-products of active experience.

Enactive learning concerns the developmental organization of action. This involves the development of increasing skill and flexibility in organizing means–end relations, or what the great Russian physiologist Nicholas Bernstein (1996/1950) called 'dexterity' in its most general sense. Hence, the hallmark of enactive learning is the ability to be flexible in the face of an ever-changing environment, to be able to deploy any one of a number of means to achieve a desired end. It is a fact of fundamental importance for human psychology.

Bruner's adherence to traditional (transmission!) theories of perception led him to treat *iconic learning* in terms of the use of images to guide our developing understanding or action. But, as Bruner himself notes in *The Culture of Education*, this definition is too limited (1996: 156). We perceive the world not as a set of pictures or images, but as a place of possibilities for knowing, doing and interacting with others. Some of these possibilities, because of their ecological importance and frequency, function as criteria for guiding our thoughts, acts and relationships. I suggest we replace Bruner's iconic mode of learning with Eleanor Gibson's concept of active perceptual learning (Gibson, 1969, 1988, 1991, 1994). Perception can and does provide us with information that is sufficiently rich to help us learn about our world. But perceiving is never static; it is always a hunting for more information. The fact that the perceptual process in adults, as well as children, seems to be capable of self-organizing improvement in most situations is another fundamental fact of human psychology.

Bruner's third mode of learning, *symbolic learning*, involves the use of symbols to reorganize previously acquired skills and information. For instance, the acquisition of symbols involved in counting makes possible the development and reorganization of any number of skills, from measuring to playing music, from time telling to skipping rope. The acquisition of that amazing symbolic invention, the alphabet, provides us with an unlimited generative capacity for arranging and rearranging knowledge (Olson, 1994). Symbolic learning is intimately tied to the generativity of human language, another fundamental fact of human psychology.

The Culture of Education betrays Bruner's recent tendency to over-emphasize this last mode of learning. At the outset of the book he more or less subsumes the entire triad under the concept of 'meaning making', which he treats as inherently symbolic, perhaps even hermeneutic (cf. Charles Taylor, 1989). Yet, if meaning making so conceived is the basis of all learning, then there is certainly no such thing as enactive learning, and perhaps no such thing as perceptual learning either.

Worse still, Bruner tends to rest all meaning making on culturally regulated activities and interaction. This is an increasingly common trope in cultural psychology, but one which I believe should be resisted. Bruner himself appears to agree with my concerns when he says that 'if psychology is to get ahead in understanding human nature and the human condition, it must learn to understand the subtle interplay of biology and culture' (1996: 184). But his preoccupation with meaning making conceived as a cultural phenomenon tends to undermine this good intention. In my view, we need to find room for meaning making within individual experience as well as in culturally regulated interactions. To do this, I assert, we must begin with an ecological account of perceiving and acting. Let me explain why.

The ecology of learning

According to the kind of ecological psychology I have been developing, perception is a motivated activity of individuals using resources in their environment. Perception is active, not passive; it is an effortful search for meanings and values (Reed, 1996a). The biological basis of these meanings and values is not our central nervous system, nor yet our genes, but the structured information available in the energy fields of the environment that specify particular affordances to the exploring observer. Ecological information provides a basic biological constraint on meaning making, and the resources for behaviour that I call 'affordances' (following, of course, James Gibson, e.g., 1979) provide a basic biological constraint on meaning and value (Reed, 1991). Observers do not *make* meanings when perceiving their world, they *detect* meanings that emerge from their encounters with the world and with others. Agents do not on their own make the values they strive for and defend, but, like meanings, values are found and used as we encounter our surroundings (Bond, 1983). Neither the detection of information, nor the use of affordances, is biologically fixed. The developmental changes characteristic of enactive and perceptual learning are, as I have stressed, fundamental psychological processes.

To say that meanings and values are biologically – ecologically! – constrained is not to detract from the role played by learning and culture in human experience; on the contrary, it is this grounding in ecological reality that makes symbolic culture possible. Without perceptual or enactive learning, no individuals would live to enjoy the generative symbolic meanings and values of a culture. Perceptual learning is the foundation of both enactive and symbolic learning. However, it is, at least in its pure case, individualistic and without guidance from symbolic knowledge. Exploratory activities that improve an observer's access to the meanings around her are often discovered on an individual basis. And it is frequently the discovery of new meanings that leads the way for later enactive learning (Reed, 1984, 1995).

Of course, human beings' 'effort after meaning' is often a collective process. For example, by 12 months, most infants engage in so-called 'social referencing', where they look to the face of their caregiver for information concerning the meaning of novel events (Fogel, 1993). Caregivers actively guide the exploratory activity of infants and children, organizing their attention by means of gesture, word and action (Zukow-Goldring and Ferko, 1994). But the most important point about our human cooperative (and sometimes competitive) efforts after value and meaning is that, where one person facilitates another's learning, this is not properly character-ized as the transmission of ideas. When I call our attention to an event that you might otherwise miss, I help to educate your perception not by trans-mitting information to you, but by helping you to get the information for yourself. When I point something out to you, or when I say 'look at that', I am not literally *making* you aware of something, but helping you to use your already functioning powers of attention and discrimination to become aware of something. It is a fundamental fact of human psychol-ogy that each of us must individually pick up the information that we use to perceive our world. Others may help us to educate our powers of atten-tion, but the perceptual process is a personal skill. Both what we perceive and how we organize our acts of attention are socialized, to be sure. But, ultimately, each individual is responsible for the information he or she picks up, or fails to pick up.

Ecological psychology thus sees the process of enculturation not as a transmission of ideas or symbols, nor as an inculcation of specific ways of making meanings. Instead, enculturation is the bringing of a person (infant or stranger) into a shared environment, encouraging her to join in the collective efforts after value and meaning of a particular group. Once she begins to enter into this shared environment and collective endeavour, it is possible for her to acquire facility with the symbolic tools of the culture. Such symbolic learning is necessary because it is typically through these symbols that the dimensions of propriety and taboo are specified in human cultures. Through enactive and perceptual learning children acquire abilities to do things, and also to inhibit their doings; but it is only through symbolic learning that children can acquire an understanding of when and where it is *proper* to act, and what acts are *forbidden*.

It is important to note that, from this ecological perspective, the process of meaning acquisition may be inherently *personal*, but it is not inherently *private*. All appreciation of meaning ultimately rests on the individual's ability to use ecological information – that is, information that is available to anyone, if they are willing to learn how to detect and use it. Even the symbols of a culture are embodied in ecological information: language itself must be spoken or signed; all linguistic communication ultimately rests on extremely precise and intricate perceptual discriminations.

It is possible – and often desirable – to conceal one's thoughts, to engage in private cogitation. But the fact is that one has to learn to do this, and that most children cannot hide their cognitive processes from others until at least the age of 3. (I interpret the 'cognitive shift' between 3 and 4 years of age to be largely due to the discovery of privacy, but that is another story (Reed, 1996a: 157).) If the appreciation of meaning is not aboriginally private, then the entire theory of socialization as internalization is misguided. As Vygotsky (1986/1934) perceived, speech is not the 'externalizing' of internalized thoughts, but the coming into existence of a special mode of thinking, one that is inherently socialized. To learn to speak is not to have internalized a grammar, either through an innate language acquisition device or through some form of learning. Rather, learning to speak is learning how to enter the linguistic community within which one is developing. It is only *after* the beginnings of generative language are acquired that children prove capable of internalizing (making private) their thoughts (Reed, 1995).

The self in its environment

The ecological approach taken here suggests that Bruner's concept of 'self' needs radical revision. Like countless philosophers and psychologists since Descartes, Bruner states, 'We know "self" from our own inner experience' (1996: 35). But do we know this? That we have a stream of consciousness is readily verified, but do we 'know our experience'? Is this even a meaningful question, or simply a distorted version of the question of what we have learned via experience? The idea that there exists a stream of consciousness radically separate from our stream of activity was exploded in 1904 by William James's essay 'Does "consciousness" exist?' (James, 1976/1912: 3–19), but it is a tenacious idea.

It is hard to believe, however, that Bruner really intends to revert to this Cartesian conception. For example, he emphasizes that one widespread goal of education is *self-reliance* (1996: 21). Surely he does not mean reliance within our internal self, which we supposedly know through inner experience; instead he must mean something like the ability of individual persons to act competently and resiliently in a variety of settings. Children who work self-reliantly in school do not have stronger Cartesian egos than others – or so I would claim – but they do know better how to fit their actions into their local habitats and social networks. Or consider Bruner's two key properties of self: agency and evaluation. How could these be meaningful and remain solely a function of inner experience? Agency is precisely the guidance of action by external, often shared, meanings and values. Evaluation is, at least as Bruner uses the word, largely an assessment of how well one's agency meshes with others' actions, both in terms of pure utility, and in terms of culturally determined proprieties.

I do not want to deny the existence of a private self – aspects of our experience that we learn to withhold from most or all of those with whom we interact. But this private self is highly derivative, not psychologically primary. Understanding the private self is important for social psychology, and especially important for the psychology of adolescence, because it appears to be during adolescence that most individuals strive to create a characteristic equilibrium between public and private aspects of their activity and experience. A proper understanding of the private self in this sense of the term will not be forthcoming from the kind of simple-minded Cartesianism increasingly common among psychologists and cognitive scientists who now claim to be studying 'consciousness'.

Bruner's later suggestion that a sense of self is more or less equal to the individual's 'conception of his own powers' fits much better with the present perspective (1996: 39). To know one's self is to appreciate one's capacities in different circumstances – to evaluate one's stream of thought and action as they fit into surrounding realities. These personal powers include an ability – or lack of it – to maintain a private sphere despite the various importunities of the social environment.

Education is thus not a change within a private self, but an adaptation of the self within and to a variety of contexts – what Bruner has happily called 'the growth of the self'. Following Bruner (1983) and Fogel (1993) I have argued that this growth occurs within *interaction frames* that are uniquely human in general, and organized in specific ways by different cultures (Reed, 1996a: ch. 9). The fundamental educational interaction frame is triadic: two observers share an object or event in their environment. Although infants as young as 6 months can enter and exit such triadic frames, they contain the seeds of all later forms of learning.

As infants develop they acquire the ability to *indicate topics* for sharing, and to respond appropriately to their caregiver's indications of topics. Much early language and cognitive development emerges within this kind of triadic interaction. It is especially important to note that a child who can reliably comprehend an indication of a topic can engage in shared efforts after both meaning (information) and value (affordances) and thereby begin to join the cultural world around them. Our human ability to share meanings and values thus does not rest on symbolic learning – or at least not on the kind of generative language skills associated with symbolic learning – because children go through a significant phase in which they are capable of dealing with indications but not capable of coping with generative language (Reed, 1996a: 161–4). In fact, I have speculated that generativity emerges from limitations in indicative learning: from a lack of ability to understand complex predications, or to follow the subtle variations of speech acts, and the resultant lack of facility at negotiating conflicts of intention.

Using this interactive and ecological conception of the developing self we can renovate Bruner's earlier and important concept of the *spiral curriculum*. This is a curriculum that spirals through all subjects from the earliest grades on upward, deepening and broadening as students are exposed a second and a third time to each topic. Each topic is shared between teacher and student at a given level of development and interest. As the child develops, increasingly sophisticated forms of working with the topic become possible. Children (and adults!) who are properly exposed to new material come to understand that it is rich in meanings and possibilities even if they cannot yet grasp all the meanings. Pre-readers, for example, display a considerable knowledge of the properties of printed text, even prior to full mastery of the alphabet (Pick, Unze, Brownell, Drozdal and Hopmann, 1978). This is what I call *unfilled meanings*, and they are of great importance in education. A properly organized spiral curriculum is full of unfilled meanings made enticing by sympathetic teachers.

The core idea here is that even the youngest children should be exposed to a broad and ambitious curriculum in the hopes of identifying one or more areas at which each child excels or is motivated to learn. On subsequent exposures to this area, the educator's goals should be to increase the student's 'conception of his own powers' with regard to every subject, but especially to build up identification with those subjects that define the particular student's interests. On this view, built on Bruner's older ideas updated within a cultural ecological framework, the spiral curriculum is seen as a way of developing persons, and helping each individual to a better conception of their selves.

Towards enabling cultures

The best way to move through this spiral growth is by the creation of a community that facilitates the growth of the self, in contrast to an institution that transmits education. Education is here viewed as enlarging, differentiating and enriching shared themes of work and study. This can only be achieved when there is a community-wide agreement over (most of) the themes and commitment to intense teacher–student interaction, which requires dedication, perseverance and other important social resources.

Practice appears to have run ahead of theory in this regard. As Bruner notes, the work of Ann Brown in Oakland and Deborah Meier in Manhattan has shown that even modern urban schools can become communities that foster the growth of selves (though we might note that much of this work is foreshadowed in John Dewey's astonishingly prescient *Democracy and Education* (1916)). We want children's power and mastery to increase in scope and depth, but not at the expense of their ability to cooperate and share ideas and work. In a school setting that is small enough to permit face-to-face interaction and the free exchange of concerns, the paths of self-growth of most of the children can be observed by individual instructors (not just monitored by test instruments). In line with this, Bruner describes his goal as to create:

> school cultures that operate as mutual communities of learners, involved jointly in solving problems with all contributing to the process of educating one another. Such groups provide not only a focus for instruction, but a focus for individual and mutual work. (1996: 81–2)

This is a noble goal, but it is consistent only with an ecological concept of the selves involved, not with the idea that communities are groupings of Cartesian egos.

Bruner's work on education began at the height of the Cold War, at a time when public education in the USA was viewed as a cross between Levittown and the Goddard Space Center. There was little concern for the nature of the children's experience, children's selves, and the differences among children. There was high concern – veritable angst – to fill as many young people as full of as much knowledge as quickly as possible. We in the USA are still paying dearly for the mistakes made over the past three or four decades. Bruner, along with nearly everyone else, made his share of mistakes. Douglas Noble in his important book, *The Classroom Arsenal* (1991), has sketched the history of this Cold War transformation of the institution we call school. Noble shows how bureaucratic constraints and initiatives have greatly influenced educational institutions and ideals at every level in the USA. These trends continue, with the increasing emphasis on corporate involvement and technological restructuring of schools, both of which have proved to undermine the kind of nonbureaucratic, face-to-face environment so important for real education. I believe that we can counter these problematic trends by emphasizing the ecological and cultural understanding of education.

Even when he was writing about education for the RAND Corporation and the Air Force, Bruner's was a voice of caution and concern (e.g., Bruner, 1960). His current preoccupation, and one we would do well to heed, is how to inculcate 'enabling cultures' in our schools and communities. (The community at large cannot be completely separated from concerns of public schooling, especially if we adopt a cultural-ecological point of view.) Here, I believe, Bruner should distance himself from the monolithic view of culture and self characteristic of recent cultural psychology (e.g., Shweder, 1991). American culture is nothing if not heterogeneous and, I would contend, its heterogeneity is not constituted by a myriad of monolithic ethnic subcultures. There is an astonishing interpenetration among Americans, especially among young people (Reed, 1996b). This is all the more remarkable when one considers it in light of the data showing widespread segregation of ethnic groups and especially the hyper-segregation of Afro-Americans from all other subcultures (Massey, 1993).

This multi-valent social world, full of interweaving practices, yet fraught with concepts of appropriate and inappropriate social behaviour, leads to a kind of divided self. To take just one example, but surely the most important one in the USA, that prescient student of William James, W.E.B. DuBois long ago noted that African-American selves were necessarily *double* (DuBois, 1986/1903). The pride and assurance that comes with self-growth and power has always been dangerous for Afro-Americans in a way undreamt of by their White counterparts. Conversely, the success of Afro-Americans within a world that is perceived as 'White' by the Afro-American community can never be enjoyed as success unalloyed, there always being a suggestion of unseemly complicity in it (Gaines and Reed, 1994, 1995).

In the modern world, with people and cultures uprooted and in promiscuous contact, there cannot be one mode of 'enabling culture', nor can there be a single mode of 'self-growth'. The problem for educators is to fashion a set of yardsticks that can measure real growth in a variety of ways. I believe such tools can be constructed only by using something like an ecological version of Bruner's triad, and not Bruner's concept of 'meaning making', which is inherently a culturally loaded notion. Educators need to learn to track the individual learner's abilities in all three areas – enactive, perceptual and symbolic learning. We also need to track the growth of self, conceived, as it is here, as the growth of the ability to learn and perform in many different contexts. Although learning may ultimately be individual, the person who is incapable of entering into the various shared environments of school and community should not be counted as a successful learner.

Bruner's legacy

Bruner's legacy to students of the education process is a rich and varied one. Even where I have criticized him, I have often done so by using ideas taken from Bruner himself. He has taught us that education involves the growth of the self, and that this growth can only occur within a culture as well as within an environment. He has also taught us that this growth is multiform, involving (at least) enactive, perceptual and symbolic modes of learning. Finally, he has taught us that our growth through education is always a spiral, involving a deepening and revising of old themes, as Bruner's own so fruitful career beautifully illustrates.

References

Bernstein, N. (1996 [1950]) *On Dexterity*, ed. M. Latash and M. Turvey. Russian text. Mahwah, NJ: Erlbaum.

Bond, E.J. (1983) *Reason and Value*. Cambridge: Cambridge University Press.

Bruner, J. (1960) *The Process of Education*. Cambridge, MA: Harvard University Press.

Bruner, J. (1966) *Toward a Theory of Instruction*. Cambridge, MA: Harvard University Press.

Bruner, J. (1971) *The Relevance of Education*. New York: Norton.

Bruner, J. (1983) *Child's Talk: Learning to Use Language*. Oxford: Oxford University Press.

Bruner, J. (1996) *The Culture of Education*. Cambridge, MA: Harvard University Press.

Dewey, J. (1916) *Democracy and Education*. New York: Macmillan.

DuBois, W.E.B. (1986 [1903]) *The Souls of Black Folk*. New York: Library of America.

Fogel, A. (1993) *Developing Through Relationships*. Chicago, IL: University of Chicago Press.

Gaines, S.O. and Reed, E.S. (1994) 'Two social psychologies of prejudice: Gordon W. Allport, W.E.B. DuBois, and the legacy of Booker T. Washington', *Journal of Black Psychology*, 20: 8–28.

Gaines, S.O. and Reed, E.S. (1995) 'Prejudice: from Allport to DuBois', *American Psychologist*, 50: 96–103.

Gibson, E.J. (1969) *Principles of Perceptual Learning and Development*. New York: Appleton-Century-Crofts.

Gibson, E.J. (1988) 'Exploratory behavior in the development of perceiving, acting, and the acquiring of knowledge', *Annual Review of Psychology*, 39: 1–41.

Gibson, E.J. (1991) *An Odyssey in Learning and Perception*. Cambridge, MA: MIT Press.

Gibson, E.J. (1994) 'Has psychology a future?', *Psychological Science*, 5: 69–74.

Gibson, J. (1979) *The Ecological Approach to Visual Perception*. Boston: Houghton Mifflin.

James, W. (1976/1912) *Essays in Radical Empiricism*. Cambridge, MA: Harvard University Press.

Lave, J. (1990) 'The culture of acquisition and the practice of understanding', in J.W. Stigler, R. Shweder and G. Herdt (eds), *Cultural Psychology: Essays on Comparative Human Development*. New York: Cambridge University Press.

Massey, D. (1993) *American Apartheid: Segregation and the Making of an Underclass*. Cambridge, MA: Harvard University Press.

Noble, D. (1991) *The Classroom Arsenal: Military Research, Information Technology, and Public Education*. New York: Falmer.

Olson, D. (1994) *The World on Paper*. Cambridge: Cambridge University Press.

Pick, A., Unze, M., Brownell, C., Drozdal, J. and Hopmann, M. (1978) 'Young children's knowledge of word structure', *Child Development*, 49: 669–80.

Reed, E.S. (1984) 'What develops when action develops?' Symposium on Motor Learning. American Association for the Advancement of Science, New York, April.

Reed, E.S. (1991) 'Cognition as the cooperative appropriation of affordances', *Ecological Psychology*, 3: 135–58.

Reed, E.S. (1995) 'The ecological approach to language development: a radical solution to Chomsky's and Quine's problems', *Language and Communication*, 15: 1–29.

Reed, E.S. (1996a) *Encountering the World: Toward an Ecological Psychology*. New York: Oxford University Press.

Reed, E.S. (1996b) 'Cultures, values, selves', in E. Reed, E. Turiel and T. Brown (eds), *Knowledge and Values: Their Development and Interrelation*. Hillsdale, NJ: Erlbaum.

Rogoff, B. (1990) *Apprenticeship in Thinking*. New York: Oxford University Press.

Shweder, R.A. (1991) *Thinking Through Cultures*. Cambridge, MA: Harvard University Press.

Taylor, C. (1989) *Sources of the Self*. Cambridge, MA: Harvard University Press.

Vygotsky, L.S. (1986 [1934]) *Thought and Language*. A. Kozulin (trans. rev. and ed.) Cambridge, MA: MIT Press.

Zukow-Goldring, P. and Ferko, K. (1994) 'An ecological approach to the emergence of the lexicon: socializing attention', in V. John-Steiner, C. Panofsky and L. Smith (eds), *Socio-cultural Approaches to Language and Literacy*. New York: Cambridge University Press.

COMMENTARIES

JEROME BRUNER AS EDUCATOR: PERSONAL REFLECTIONS

Howard Gardner

Recently, as part of a written survey, I was posed a number of questions about my educational philosophy. Included among the items were 'important educational experiences', 'publications that influenced my thinking about education', and 'individuals who influenced my thinking about education'. In filling out such forms, one strives for variety. I was, however, caught in a dilemma. Only if I were to dissemble could I provide a suitably variegated set of responses. Were I to be truthful, I would be forced to submit a response sheet that invoked, over and over again, the name of Jerome Bruner.

For scholars and practitioners who became interested in the improvement of precollegiate education in the 1960s, Jerome Bruner is the central figure. In my case, Bruner looms so large that he dwarfs everyone else. I first heard about Bruner when, as an undergraduate at Harvard College, I read about the illustrious professor in an article in a national magazine. Immediately after my graduation from college, I had the good fortune to work with him on the memorable social studies curriculum, 'Man: A Course of Study'. Joining his team of educational reformers, then enrolling as a student in his graduate courses, and then serving as a 'fellow traveller' in the fabled Center for Cognitive Studies, I received extensive exposure to Bruner's educational ideas and was subject as well to his powerful influence as teacher, mentor, Director of the Center and public figure. Happily, these influences have continued to this day.

I have a confession to make. Bruner had such a powerful effect on my 'formation' as a psychologist and educator that, for years, I did not recognize his influence. Perhaps I could not afford to. Only as I passed into middle age, and acquired a measure of distance on my own development and persona, was I able to recognize Bruner's enormous impact on my activities and my educational philosophy.

In light of my close professional and personal relationship to Bruner, I find it an odd experience to read Edward Reed's essay. While Reed clearly respects Bruner and has learned from him, nowhere in his text can the living, breathing Bruner be found. For him, Bruner is a set of published texts, and a clutch of positions, to be critiqued and opposed to Reed's ecological perspective. My brief remarks here have a different purpose: to record some impressions of Jerome Bruner as an educator and to consider his own educational contributions in that light.

Few scholars of our time have so exemplified the permanent student and perennial teacher. For over 60 years, Bruner has pursued the study of psychology in its multitudinous facets. Invading one area of psychology (and neighbouring disciplines) after another, and shaping more than a few, he has mastered the relevant bodies of knowledge even as he has asked questions that have captured wide attention and advanced a spectrum of disciplines. Because Bruner is always reflecting on what he is doing, and sharing his reflections with others, the line between student and teacher seems arbitrary, indeed wrongheaded. Bruner is the teacher that he is because he is the student that he is; as he learns he teaches not just himself but others, and one of the most important lessons that he teaches is how to ask questions and how to arrive at productive answers. As he notes in *The Culture of Education*, 'Not knowing is what makes you into a true teacher' (Bruner, 1996: 115).

Bruner's approach to teaching is vivid and unforgettable. His infectious curiosity provides the entry point, affecting all those who are not completely jaded. In his own words, 'Intellectual activity is anywhere the same, whether at the frontier of knowledge or in a third-grade classroom' (Bruner, 1960: 14). Accordingly, individuals of every age are invited, sometimes even seduced, to join in the enquiries. Logical analysis, technical distinctions, rich and wide knowledge of subject matter, asides to an even wider orbit of information, intuitive leaps, pregnant enigmas pour forth. Bruner asked ten-year-olds in Newton, Massachusetts, and in many other cities and countries as well, the questions he was asking in his own research: What is human about human beings? How did they get that way? How can they be made more so? And, in the manner of an inspired teacher, he listened carefully to the words of the youngsters and learned from them.

Broadly speaking, Bruner is situated in the tradition of great American pragmatists and progressive thinkers: William James, Charles Sanders Peirce, James Mark Baldwin, and above all, John Dewey. His sentiments are Deweyian at a fundamental level; the curricula he helped to create, and the classes that he taught and inspired, fit comfortably under the rubric of progressive education – America's gift to the wider educational world. For Bruner, knowing is never inert; it emerges from genuine concerns about the world, and it feeds back to that world, enriching it in the process.

But Bruner approaches education neither as an armchair philosopher, nor as a perennial inhabitant of the classroom. He has been an active psychological researcher as well as a reflective social scientist and humanist, and the fruits of his own never-ending research and learning have continued to inform his educational philosophy. Perhaps Bruner began his work in education as a Deweyian and a Piagetian. But he became involved in new lines of study – investigating the varying modes of representation to which Reed refers, the evolution of tool use in primates, the role of schooling in the formation of cognition, the impact of diverse media, technology and symbol systems, the nature of social supports, the power of dialogue and narrative, the formative role of culture – each of these in turn found its way into an ever-evolving educational philosophy.

What is striking to me, as someone who has known Bruner for over 30 years, is that in many ways his educational practices foreshadowed his theoretical notions. One might say that, in his bones, Bruner appreciated Vygotskian support systems, the humanistic narrative mode, and the Geertzian stress on the making of meaning before these concepts made their appearance in his formal writings on education. I consider this a merit. Those educational ideas that have been forged in the smithy of experience have generally proved more robust than those that are merely derived from theoretical debates or, worse, from the jargon-laden pages of educational publications.

For those of us who have had the privilege of knowing Jerry Bruner well, and of counting him as a friend, he has been and remains a role model of the Compleat Educator in the flesh: in his own words 'communicator, model, and identification figure' (Bruner, 1960: 91). As he plunges forward in his ninth decade, one month in the classrooms of New York University Law School, the next in the preschools of Reggio Emilia, he remains the most eager student in the class.

References

Bruner, J.S. (1960) *The Process of Education*. Cambridge, MA: Harvard University Press.
Bruner, J.S. (1996) *The Culture of Education*. Cambridge, MA: Harvard University Press.

REED ON BRUNER ON EDUCATION

David Bakhurst

Edward Reed's principal target in this paper is what he calls 'the transmission theory of culture'. This view, he claims, dominated our conceptions of education until very recently. It portrays culture primarily as a set of ideas, or a body of knowledge, to be conveyed by teachers and 'internalized' by learners. Reed objects to this model on the grounds that transmission is only one of many aspects of learning. In addition, he argues that the model encourages us to see learning as a matter of the acquisition of representations, rather than the cultivation of modes of experience or action, and thus places undue emphasis on symbolic forms of learning. Finally, it is prone to adopt an excessively monolithic view of culture.

Reed maintains that Bruner's influential early thinking about education was cast in terms of the transmission model, which was lent a peculiar plausibility by the circumstances of the Cold War. After the Russian successes in space in the late 1950s and early 1960s, many Americans felt that an effective education system was vital if their country was to keep pace with its adversary. As Bruner put it, American concerns about education were 'accentuated by what is almost certain to be a long-range crisis in national security, a crisis whose resolution will depend upon a well-educated citizenry' (1960: 1). Since scientific expertise was deemed of paramount importance to America's future, education was naturally seen as a matter of transplanting the maximum amount of knowledge into children's heads as efficiently as possible. Reed suggests that, though Bruner has recently tried to distance himself from the transmission model, he still remains enamoured of many of its elements. Bruner's notion of meaning making, for example, while it helps portray children as participants in the educational process, perpetuates the preoccupation with the representational and the symbolic. Bruner's many valuable insights on education, Reed argues, must be disentangled from the transmission theory and placed in a more satisfying theoretical framework.

The framework Reed recommends is the form of ecological psychology he expounds in *Encountering the World*, the first book of the trilogy he published shortly before his death (Reed, 1996a, 1996b, 1997). Ecological psychology, as Reed understands it, rejects the mechanistic explanatory principles so commonly deployed in psychology and cognitive science, putting in their stead the 'organic metaphor of regulation'. Its central focus is the organism's activity in its environment and, specifically, how that activity is regulated. Following Eleanor and James Gibson, Reed treats the environment, not as a kind of neutral setting for action, but as a context laden with objective value and significance. Any creature's environment is structured by affordances, resources the environment offers creatures of that kind, and by ecological information about those affordances. Awareness and behaviour are understood as a creature's ability to pick up such information and to change its relation to its surroundings in light of its awareness of affordances. Ecological psychology naturally incorporates an evolutionary perspective: affordances are treated as constituents of a species' fundamental niche and the foci of selection pressures.

Reed holds that this approach can nicely encompass human psychology, so long as we appreciate how the human environment is shaped by culture and language, and how human efforts after value and meaning are so often collective. This at least sounds like a position congenial to a cultural psychologist. But Reed distances himself from the constructivism he detects in Bruner's view. The human environment is not something we simply find, but neither is it something we make. Rather, it is 'selected and transformed' (1996a: 125). It is also misleading to speak of 'meaning making'. Meaning is not made, but detected. And although the search for meaning is often collaborative, its detection is always individual. I can draw something to your attention but I cannot make you attend: I cannot, as it were, give you its significance. Learning is thus not best seen as the transmission of ideas, nor as inculcation into patterns of meaning making, but as inauguration into a shared environment. In this, Reed sees the development of the child's capacity for primary experience – for first-hand engagement with the world – as the crucial educational aim, rather than the acquisition of representational systems, which so often embody second-hand forms of knowledge constructed to pass in lieu of direct experience (this is an important theme in Reed, 1996b). Since the development of the capacity for primary experience is central to personal growth, Reed urges that we replace the transmission metaphor with another – one that is also found in Bruner's work – the idea of the growth of the self (e.g., Bruner 1966: 1). It is growth, Reed argues, and not the conveying of bodies of knowledge, which is education's true end.

I must confess that I find Reed's ecological approach hard to assess. His writings abound with challenging insights and stimulating conjectures, but his project is so ambitious in scope and radical in perspective that, as Reed would have admitted, what he gives us is the shape of a position rather than a finished theory. It is to be hoped that others will continue the work Reed started. It is possible, however, to evaluate his critique of Bruner. In his commentary, Howard Gardner reacts to Reed's critique with disbelief, arguing that Reed fails to see the significance of Bruner's contribution to our understanding of education. Bruner's contribution lies, not so much in what Bruner has written about education, important though that may be, but in the way the whole of Bruner's legacy expresses his voracious appetite for learning and his infectious enthusiasm for teaching. Bruner teaches us about education by example, and we would do better to appreciate Bruner's genius as an educator than to set out his written views and subject them to academic criticism.

Gardner writes as a longstanding friend and colleague of Bruner. But one doesn't need to have known Bruner personally to appreciate his point. There is much in Bruner's works to support Gardner's reaction, both in the manner of Bruner's writing – his qualities as an educator come across in the way he addresses his audience – and in the letter of the text. Consider, for example, the following passage from *Toward a Theory of Instruction*:

> A body of knowledge, enshrined in a university faculty and embodied in a series of authoritative volumes, is the result of much prior intellectual activity. To instruct someone in these disciplines is not a matter of getting him to commit results to mind. Rather, it is to teach him to participate in the process that makes possible the establishment of knowledge. We teach a subject not to produce little living libraries on that subject, but rather to get a student to think mathematically for himself, to consider matters as an historian does, to take part in the process of knowledge-getting. Knowing is a process, not a product. (Bruner, 1966: 72)

There is not much here to suggest an undue preoccupation with learning as transmission. On the contrary, we are treated to Bruner's familiar enthusiasm for empowering students to think autonomously within a living tradition of enquiry.

Yet it would be a mistake, I think, to dismiss Reed's criticisms out of hand, for they contain something deep. For instance, I believe Reed is right to hint that Bruner's point of departure has a fundamentally Cartesian aspect. For Bruner is certainly inclined to portray the relation of self and reality as one between two worlds: the 'inner' world of the subject and the 'external' world beyond the mind that the subject strives to represent. Of course, Bruner has always been concerned with the degree to which the self is active in the construction of its world (in this he is more Kantian than Cartesian) and he has increasingly stressed the vital mediating role of culture in the relation of the two 'worlds'. For all that, however, much of Bruner's writing preserves a rather traditional picture of the self, organizing its private experiences in its own 'inner world'. This is evident, for example, when he writes that: 'The heart of the educational process consists of providing aids and dialogues for translating experience into more powerful systems of notation and ordering' (1966: 21). Reed is also right in thinking that Bruner's view of culture's contribution contains a profound emphasis on the symbolic and the representational (an emphasis with its origins, of course, in the early days of the cognitive revolution). For culture is portrayed not just as a 'tool kit' of resources that facilitate the way we structure our experiences into a representation of reality but as a repository of shared meanings, collectively created and sustained.

In fact, Bruner's recent treatments of meaning making tend to undermine his dualistic point of departure, for they show an increasing emphasis on the idea that the 'external world' is itself a cultural construction.[1] The effect of such an emphasis on Bruner's view of learning, however, is that we find ourselves arguing that what inauguration into culture gives the child access to is culture itself. By embracing a kind of social phenomenalism, we lose a sense of the appropriation of culture as empowering the child to engage with a reality that is something over and above our collective conceptions. Culture is alpha and omega. Many may find this view appealing, but it stands in dramatic contrast to the realist assumptions of Reed's ecological perspective. Indeed, Reed would no doubt argue (as I do, this volume) that from the infelicitous commitment to a dualism of self and world we are led naturally into constructivism. Reed would have us begin elsewhere, from an ecological vision of embodied organisms in interaction with their environments that eschews the whole Cartesian starting point.

Thus, Reed's critique does raise genuine issues of substance about the nature and plausibility of Bruner's cultural psychology and Reed's own ecological alternative. The conflict between them occurs, however, at the level of high theory; it concerns their respective pictures of the fundamental relation of mind and world. It might therefore seem rather remote from issues of pedagogy. Yet there is a sense in which such theoretical conceptions have a crucial, if often indirect, influence on our ideas of education. First, they help define the metaphors by which we teach, metaphors which shape our views of learning and instruction, and of the ends of education more generally. Second, our culture's prevailing conceptions of mind and world embody concepts of knowledge and objectivity that can profoundly influence what we think we should teach and how it should be taught. The more constructivist dimensions of Bruner's position are unquestionably informed by postmodern ideas that, in turn, raise challenging questions about the nature of history (*Whose* interpretations define the past as we teach it to our children?), about the objectivity of science (Does science have a special authority, or is it just one discourse among others?), and about the coercive elements of any institutional regime for the propagation of knowledge. Such questions are now certainly raised in the most practical of educational contexts, and it is important to be aware of their origins in theory.

One might wonder, indeed, how Bruner's increasing interest in postmodern themes can be reconciled with the kind of single-minded progressivism that informs his earlier writings. In 1966, Bruner wrote that the question of how 'we are to evolve freely as a species by the use of the instrument of education' is one about the optimal design of the education system and that the 'mission' of educational psychology is to address this question and, by so doing, to explore 'the limits of man's perfectibility' (1966: 37–8). Such perfectionism sits ill with the ironic stance of postmodernism, but it still has a presence in Bruner's thinking (though I am sure he is far less sanguine today about psychology's mission). Indeed, such a tension is arguably found not just in Bruner's thought, but in the culture at large, especially in the United States.[2] It is vital to think these issues through, and impossible to do so without appreciating their origins in high theory.

For these reasons, I am inclined to think that there is much to be gained by reflecting on how our theoretical conceptions of the relation of mind and world, abstract and obtuse though they may be, influence our ideas about education. Indeed, I believe it is far more important for philosophers and psychologists to engage in such reflection than to try to secure the application, in real educational contexts, of their pet theories about the mechanics of the learning process. Educational psychology certainly has something to contribute to the vexed issues of curriculum design and the assessment of students' performance, though in these areas it should be only one voice among many. But the fact is that our everyday, entrenched, practical understandings of learning[3] carry greater conviction than any current general theories in developmental and educational psychology. So we are better engaged in educational reforms that pay attention to how teachers, students and their parents conceive their situations in the terms in which they assess them, rather than try to import solutions minted in the academy in the theoretical terms of educational psychology.[4] We already know the most important things we need to do to improve our education systems. We want to create environments that encourage in children a voracious enthusiasm for learning, a love of knowledge, and the willingness to exercise their intelligence creatively and critically. And we want children to develop into responsible and self-confident individuals who respect others and are concerned about others' well being. It is no mystery what such environments are like. Indeed, the obstacles to their creation reside largely in the culture at large. Schools cannot flourish without adequate resources and if their teachers and pupils habitually confront significant social problems in their daily lives.

It is a great merit of Bruner's work that he appreciates this broader context very well. His interest is genuinely in the culture of education in all its dimensions. Thus for all his early talk of the 'mission' of educational psychology, his own writings on education, though they are full of insights to inspire educators, actually recommend little in the way of systematic theory. The politics of education is a far greater presence, for the generous humanism that Bruner's writings communicate so forcefully has a profound moral and political dimension. This is something that must have been congenial to Reed, who sought to set the insights of ecological psychology in political and historical perspective (see Reed 1996b and 1997 respectively) and was very much attuned to the political context of educational practice. Had Reed lived, we could have anticipated a fruitful debate about the respective contributions of ecological and cultural psychology to the high theory of education and to our understanding of its politics. What we have here are merely Reed's first thoughts about his first move in that debate. I hope I have shown that even this contains much to provoke worthwhile reflection on issues of significance and much to make us regret that the debate that might have been now cannot be.

Notes

1   Though, as I argue elsewhere (Bakhurst, 1995, and this volume), Bruner's commitment to radical constructivism is hardly wholehearted: he often retreats to the much weaker view that our *conception* of reality, rather than reality itself, is a cultural construction.

2   It is important to bear in mind that both Bruner and Reed write very much as American scholars. Their conception of the failings of present educational practice (and theory) and their prescriptions for the future are both influenced greatly by American realities and American ideals.

3   I hesitate to say 'folk psychology of education', for the word 'folk' in these contexts ('folk psychology', 'folk physics') rarely strikes the right tone. It either belittles our practices by setting them in invidious contrast to something scientific, and hence superior, or it conveys a romantic idea of a kind of unselfconscious, popular wisdom (almost rustic in association). Obviously, neither image is appropriate to the knowledge teachers and students have about education.

4   Gardner's remarks suggest he would agree.

References

Bakhurst, D. (1995) 'On the social constitution of mind: Bruner, Ilyenkov and the defence of cultural psychology', *Mind, Culture, and Activity*, 2 (3): 158–71.

Bruner, J.S. (1960) *The Process of Education*. Cambridge, MA: Harvard University Press.

Bruner, J.S. (1966) *Toward a Theory of Instruction*. Cambridge, MA: Harvard University Press.

Reed, E.S. (1996a) *Encountering the World: Toward an Ecological Psychology*. New York: Oxford University Press.

Reed, E.S. (1996b) *The Necessity of Experience*. New Haven, CT: Yale University Press.

Reed, E.S. (1997) *From Soul to Mind. The Emergence of Psychology from Erasmus Darwin to William James*. New Haven, CT: Yale University Press.

8

INFANCY AND THE BIRTH OF COMPETENCE: BRUNER AND COMPARATIVE-DEVELOPMENTAL RESEARCH

Duane Rumbaugh, Michael Beran and Christopher Elder

No treatment of Jerome Bruner's wealth of contributions to behavioural science would be complete without considering his exemplary influence upon the creation of a comparative-developmental framework. Humans are primates and, back in 1974, Bruner correctly anticipated that we will better understand ourselves through studies that compare and contrast the patterns of development across the more than 200 species that comprise the Primate order (Bruner, 1974).

In this chapter, we will selectively consider research of the past quarter century that vindicates Bruner's comparative-developmental perspective of the early 1970s. His views have had a major impact, and a salutary one, upon the course of that research. Bruner anticipated that comparative studies of social, cognitive and motor skills during the protracted development of primates, notably the great apes (e.g., the chimpanzee, *Pan*; the gorilla, *Gorilla*; and the orang-utan, *Pongo*), would enhance our understanding of child development. Such studies, he felt, would help us evaluate the interactions of heredity and environment as they are expressed in the acquisition of competence. He further perceived that observational learning, within the societal structures of various primates, becomes increasingly significant to the development of competence during infancy as one moves from the relatively small prosimian primates to monkeys and then to the great apes. Bruner noted that human infants are more socially interactive than any of the great apes to the same degree that the great apes are more socially interactive than monkeys (Bruner, 1983). This is, in his opinion, a function of their unique and prolonged period of dependent immaturity. Human infants are highly attuned to communicative interactions with others and observational learning is very important to their development. This perspective has certainly been vindicated.

In what follows, we first consider various factors in infant development that are illuminated by a comparative perspective. We then focus on the lessons of recent work on language development and tool use by apes. Finally, we discuss the significance of the concept of emergent behaviour, an idea in harmony with Bruner's contribution to the comparative-developmental perspective and, indeed, his psychology as a whole.

Elements of development in comparative perspective

Observational learning

Even Bruner could not anticipate just how much we would learn about the pervasive influence that observational learning has upon the development of nonhuman primates. Following his suggestions, we now search to understand the parameters of observational learning within social contexts to attain a more refined understanding of communication and language, the acquisition of motor skills, and the relationship between brain complexity and methods of rearing. We view this search as necessary to understand the emergence of various specific dimensions of competence. We also look for homologues in brain structure and function between humans and apes as they process the speech that they hear and interpret word-lexigrams that they see. From all this, we are encouraged to define anew our conceptions of learning and reinforcement theory (Rumbaugh, Savage-Rumbaugh and Washburn, 1996).

Learning in animals is no longer viewed as a highly mechanistic process in which responses are conditioned to specific stimuli because of the influence of reinforcers, such as pellets of food. Rather, the size and complexity of primate brains determine the kind of information that primates can garner from interactions with their environments. It is this interaction, in all its complexity, that enables the great apes, and possibly monkeys as well, to behave in ways that suggest that they can become sentient, insightful, creative, symbol-using and, indeed, thinking beings. Accordingly, the great apes provide, as Bruner has suggested throughout the years, a uniquely valuable resource for developmental study.

Play

Bruner has always stressed the significance of play in providing rich occasions for observation and learning. Great ape infants are as dependent on their parents or social groups as are human children. Prolonged dependency provides the opportunity for the myriad lessons afforded by social play to become based on generalized principles and not just on the specifics of a given context. Similarly, in social play the infant can observe its mother interacting with other members of its group. General lessons are derived from this that later prove essential to the individual's survival and reproductive success in novel situations.

Early environment and neural development

Although human brains contain all of the neurons they will ever have at birth, it is their stimulation that determines how those neurons will function and which of them will survive until adulthood (Purves, 1994). At the cellular level, synapses are constantly forming or dying off depending on the amount of electrical or chemical stimulation received during development. Without proper stimulation by target tissues, cell death is increased in a population of cells so that the neuronal number at adulthood is lower than would be expected due to natural cell death (Caldero, Prevette, Mei, Oakley, Li, Milligan, Houenou, Burek and Oppenheim, 1998).

Appropriate and timely stimulation of the brain's neural systems is thus essential to normal development. At the extreme, the development of the ape's visual system is dependent upon the eyes receiving patterned light stimulation from birth. Denied appropriate and timely stimulation, the visual system suffers irreparable damage (Riesen, 1982). Nursery-reared infant chimpanzees deprived of light stimulation from 8 to 24 months of age showed a marked decrease in the number of ganglion cells in the retina. This decrease in cell number resulted in poor form and movement vision. Even with a return to normal levels of light stimulation for a period of four years, there was not a significant improvement in the vision of these chimpanzees. The same holds true for cognitive development. Denied appropriate and timely stimulation by peers and adults for the first two years of life, the ape suffers irreparable deficits in the development of cognition, intelligence, social communication skills, breeding and parenting skills (Menzel, Davenport and Rogers, 1970; Davenport, Rogers and Rumbaugh, 1973).

Early environment and social-cognitive development

It is clear that there are critical periods in primates' cognitive and social development. Harlow and Mears (1979) showed that rhesus monkeys (*Macaca mulatta*) that are socially isolated early in life fail to form proper social relationships as adults; in fact they become fearful of other monkeys. As noted earlier, impoverished rearing induces irrevocable cognitive and social deficiencies in chimpanzees (Davenport et al., 1973). In contrast, rhesus monkeys that were reared in impoverished environments showed only minimal cognitive deficiencies compared with control subjects (Harlow, Harlow, Schlitz and Mohr, 1971). This difference is attributed to the fact that the chimpanzee brain is both larger and more complex than the rhesus monkey's brain and hence more vulnerable to the effects of an impoverished environment.

Observation and social interaction also influence the infant primate's ability to respond to and to produce calls that announce the appearance of various kinds of predators (Seyfarth and Cheney, 1986; Cheney and Seyfarth, 1990). Whereas adult vervet monkeys (*Cercopithecus aethiops*) are able to distinguish between different predator species within more general predator classes, infants distinguish only between general predator classes. Seyfarth, Cheney and Marler (1980) reported that infants gave leopard alarm calls rather indiscriminately to terrestrial mammals, eagle alarms to birds, and snake alarms to long thin objects on the ground (as well as to snakes). Adults were much more discerning in producing alarm calls. Thus, an infant's experience with these calls, as well as possible observational learning from adults, leads it to become more discriminating in making appropriate predator calls as it grows older.

Within the order Primates, there is an increasing premium on the length of time that infants remain dependent on their mothers and engage in social play and observation of other group members. In the prosimians and monkeys, relatively rapid rates of growth and development serve to limit play, both in time and variety, when compared to the play behaviour of the great apes. As Bruner notes (1974), it may be that the prosimians and monkeys spend so much time watching or avoiding confrontations with dominant group members that there is little attentional capacity left for other kinds of learning. And their relatively small and primitive brains probably constrain learning to the most basic forms of stimulus–response associations, through processes of conditioning. By contrast, the great apes' more flexible social structures provide for a wider variety of learning opportunities. There is more play, adults participate more often in play behaviour – both with infants and with other adults – and there is generally less use of force as a means of social control. There is also a greater emphasis on experimentation with novel items and with new ways of interacting with old items. Bruner is right that, where opportunities are enhanced for infants and juveniles to learn through the observation of adults, there is an increased potential for new learning capacities to emerge: ones that facilitate flexible behaviour in the apes.

The evolution of primate body and brain for size

Primates have evolved larger bodies and, with them, increasingly large and complex brains. With the enlargement of the primate brain, the potential for extraordinary competence in complex learning is systematically increased (Rumbaugh, Savage-Rumbaugh and Washburn, 1996). The primate brain is noted both for its high weight relative to the body and for the complexity of the cortex and other structures (Deacon, 1997). Along with this increase in brain size and complexity come qualitative changes in the way that primate species use differing amounts of learning during training phases to improve their performance on test phases when reward values of discriminative cues are switched (i.e., positive becomes negative and vice versa). As the primate brain gets larger and more complex – as one progresses from the prosimians and monkeys to the great apes – there is a change in the effect that additional learning has on performance when the cue valences are altered for tests of transfer of learning. The larger-brained monkeys (e.g., macaques) and the great apes can use even small amounts of additional learning to their leveraged (i.e., more than expected) advantage in transfer tests when the reward values of discriminative cues are reversed and they must alter their choices if a reward is to be obtained. By contrast, the smaller primates, with their relatively smaller brains, are profoundly handicapped and do worse in transfer tests as prior learning is increased (Rumbaugh, 1997). In this regard, only big brains pay big dividends. At the same time, however, the larger the brain, the more its normative development is dependent upon rearing in an ecologically appropriate and orderly environment.

The emergence of competence

Disorderly stimulation enhances the development of the human infant's brain no more than it does for the ape's. Indeed, we see that reliable, interesting, relevant and predictable environmental contexts serve to enhance the orderly development of both the human infant's and the ape's brain in ways that Bruner could not have anticipated 25 years ago. As will be discussed later, given rearing in a logical and language-structured environment, the infant ape even has the potential for understanding novel sentences of spoken English! In sum, prolonged periods of immaturity lead to new behaviours and cognitive competence. If these newly formed behaviours are adaptive, the neurobiological bases both for those behaviours, and the immaturity which facilitated them, may be selected for genetically.

Studies in recent years have provided many examples of how competencies previously thought unique to humans can develop in apes if an environment can be created appropriate to the sustained and orderly development of the ape's complex brain. Strong empirical evidence supports the development of language (Savage-Rumbaugh, 1986; Savage-Rumbaugh, Sevcik, Brakke, Rumbaugh and Greenfield, 1990; Brakke and Savage-Rumbaugh, 1996), numerical competence (Rumbaugh, Hopkins, Washburn and Savage-Rumbaugh, 1989; Boysen and Capaldi, 1993; Beran, Rumbaugh and Savage-Rumbaugh, 1998), culture (McGrew, 1992), hunting (Boesch and Boesch, 1989), politics (de Waal, 1992), tool use (McGrew, 1993), mirror self-recognition (Povinelli, Rulf, Landau and Bierschwale, 1993), and theory of mind (Premack and Woodruff, 1978).

Language acquisition and tool use in apes

Language acquisition

Initial enquiries into ape language used either signs (Gardner and Gardner, 1969; Patterson, 1978; Miles, 1983) or artificial symbols (Premack, 1971; Rumbaugh, 1977). Such attempts focused on the strict training of each symbol or sign as words for various referents. These efforts met with limited success in getting apes to produce various symbols and provoked great controversy (Terrace, Pettito, Sanders and Bever, 1979). The emphasis of this work was on the production of symbols; little attention was paid to the 'passive' comprehension of symbol use. Later, serendipitous events at the Language Research Center at Georgia State University established that language comprehension could emerge without explicit training of symbol meaning (Savage-Rumbaugh et al., 1990).

The prime example is the case of the male bonobo (*Pan paniscus*), Kanzi (Savage-Rumbaugh, McDonald, Sevcik, Hopkins and Rubert, 1986; Savage-Rumbaugh et al., 1990). Savage-Rumbaugh and her associates (Savage-Rumbaugh, Murphy, Sevcik, Brakke, Williams and Rumbaugh, 1993) reported attempts to train Matata, a female bonobo of about 14 years of age, to use lexical symbols to represent items in a manner similar to that used previously with the common chimpanzees Sherman and Austin (Savage-Rumbaugh, 1986; Savage-Rumbaugh and Lewin, 1994). Whereas Sherman and Austin came to learn many of these lexigrams and to use them in a referential manner, Matata did not. Her failure is likely a consequence of the fact that she spent the first six years of her life in the forest, where the 'lessons of life' are quite foreign to those of laboratory tests and procedures. By contrast, her adoptive son, Kanzi, learned what she did not. His competence was discovered when his adoptive mother was separated from him so that she might be bred. At the time he was about two years old. Even though no direct attempts had been made to teach Kanzi how to use the symbols, or their meanings, he was always present to observe his mother's training. Thus, Kanzi acquired his knowledge of word-lexigrams not by formal training, but spontaneously, through the complexities of observational learning. By the age of seven years, Kanzi could comprehend novel sentences of request that were spoken to him in controlled tests (Savage-Rumbaugh et al., 1993).

Bruner (1974) states that incorporating what one observes into one's own behavioural repertoire in a way that is intelligent, rather than mere mimicry, depends on matching the effects of behaviour, not just its specifics, to that of the model. Quite probably Kanzi did precisely this as he learned by observation how to select and use individual lexigrams in ways that were in principle similar to the ways in which others used them. By so doing, he would have learned from the behaviour of others the importance and meaning of each lexigram.

Deacon (1997) has suggested that a crucial factor in Kanzi's learning language is that he was so immature at the time: a view with which we concur. Deacon argues that the existence of a critical period for language learning is the expression of the advantageous limitations of an immature nervous system for the kind of learning problems that language poses. Language capitalizes upon the fertile ground provided by immaturity. If early exposure to language is critical to the emergence of language in apes, then this explanation for Kanzi's language acquisition must be attributable to something about infancy in general, regardless of language. Immaturity itself is the key to Kanzi's advantage.

Deacon proceeds to argue that, paradoxically, the inability to remember the details of specific word associations, slowness in mapping words to objects that occur in the same context, and difficulties in holding more than a few words of an utterance in short-term memory, may all be *advantages* for learning language. These constraints might serve to enhance the remembering of only the most global structure–function relationships of utterances, permitting language to 'pop out' of the background of details too variable for young children (and apes) to follow. Rumbaugh, Savage-Rumbaugh and Washburn (1996) would agree, stating that Kanzi's extensive opportunities to observe the reliable, predictable, meaningful, consistent and communicative patterns of language afforded his spontaneous acquisition. Despite everything else occurring around him,

> it was through Kanzi's reliable access to the patterned experiences afforded by the *logical structure* of his environment (e.g., the speech of the experimenters and their use of word-lexigrams on a keyboard that structured his mother's instructional sessions) that he perceptually *discerned* and *learned* the relationships between symbols and events that provided for him the basic processes and competencies with language. (Rumbaugh, Savage-Rumbaugh and Washburn, 1996: 119, italics in original)

Savage-Rumbaugh (1991) states that daily routines are important to the emergence of language in bonobos. As the routines become familiar to the bonobo, so the underlying vocal, gestural and lexical markers come to signal various parts of the routine. Through this interaction of the routines and the markers referring to them, the referents of the symbolic markers are clarified. When comprehension of these markers later becomes fully separated from the routine (and the ape can then deal with the details of specific word associations, remember the most global structure–function relationships of utterances, and hold more than a few words of an utterance in short-term memory), the ape can pass formal tests of word recognition and match spoken words to their lexical and visual equivalents – and without specific training!

As we noted above, Bruner stresses how play behaviour in human cultures makes a distinctive contribution to human immaturity. Games provide opportunities for children to engage in systematic use of language with adults, and they demonstrate how to get things done with words. Games and play behaviours also provide an opportunity for distributing attention over an ordered sequence of events: a valuable process in learning the rules of language (Bruner, 1983). Although it is true that no other species plays the number and variety of games that human infants engage in, the great apes are known for their playfulness. The apes at the Language Research Center have been raised in an environment in which play and specific games (such as hide-and-seek, chasing, keep-away, and peek-a-boo) make up a significant part of an infant's day.

Deacon argues that learning even a simple symbol system requires the learner to postpone commitment to the most obvious and immediate associations until various less obvious distributed relationships are acquired. When the learner's attention is shifted from the details of word–object relationships to patterns of combinatorial relationships between symbols, there is likely to be a shift from an indexical strategy to a symbolic one.

The initial stages of this shift are almost certainly more counter-intuitive for a quick learner, who learns details easily, than for an impaired learner who grasps the big picture but has trouble with detail. This initial move to reliance on symbolic relationships is most likely to succeed if it occurs at a relatively young age. Again, Deacon suggests that immaturity itself provides the answer to the time-limited advantage for language learning that is evident in Kanzi's case. Kanzi's immaturity made it easier to shift from indexical to symbolic reference and to learn the logic behind the surface structure of spoken English (through focusing on routines that are predictable and the markers that accompany those routines). If this is true for Kanzi, then it may follow that the appeal to a critical period is not in itself a valid explanation for language acquisition in human children. Rather, the critical period itself follows from the advantageous limitations of an immature nervous system for the kind of learning that language involves.

Brakke and Savage-Rumbaugh (1995, 1996) provide further evidence that early rearing influences the development of language use in apes. By raising Panzee, a female chimpanzee, and Panbanisha, a female bonobo, in a language-structured environment similar to that in which Kanzi was raised, they demonstrated that exposure to language in structured, daily routines is sufficient to increase both the comprehension of spoken English and production of lexical phrases. As an example of these routines, Panzee and Panbanisha were included daily in the 'evening' routines in which the lab began to quieten down and caregivers prepared the evening meal, made milk for the apes, cleaned blankets for their night nests, and groomed the apes. Each of these routines was made up of smaller sub-routines, such as retrieving the milk from the refrigerator, pouring it into bowls, heating it in the microwave, and giving it to the apes. Throughout all these routines, caregivers and apes communicated through the use of the lexigram keyboard, and caregivers communicated verbally to the apes. As the routines became familiar, so Panzee and Panbanisha began to initiate them more and more.

Panzee and Panbanisha came to take a greater role in many such routine activities and to communicate frequently about them. Again, these apes were exposed to language very early in life, and they remained in that type of environment throughout their lengthy immature period. As they matured, the components of the routines were behaviourally and linguistically encoded by the apes (Brakke and Savage-Rumbaugh, 1995). During a three-year period in which utterances were recorded for Panzee and Panbanisha (when they were both between 1.5 and 4.0 years of age), the bonobo Panbanisha responded correctly to 92 per cent of the utterances directed to her, while the chimpanzee, Panzee, responded correctly to 81 per cent. Their accuracy rates remained consistent over this time period, and they were able to respond equally well to utterances consisting only of spoken English as well as utterances containing spoken English and lexigrams (Brakke and Savage-Rumbaugh, 1995). These results indicate that chimpanzees and bonobos learn by participating in routines with lexical markers used by adults (in this case, caregivers) and, as they mature, achieve decontextualization of symbol comprehension (Brakke and Savage-Rumbaugh, 1995).

Tool use

Apes also demonstrate a capacity for tool use both in the wild and in the laboratory. Bruner has suggested that the emergence of tool use requires a long period of opportunity for combinatorial activity. An increased period of immaturity allows the infant more time to experiment and play with objects in novel ways and circumstances, play that involves combinations of behaviours that would never be performed under functional pressures (Bruner, 1974).

Important in this process is experimentation with learned skills in new contexts. This may involve a loss of interest in the goal itself and a greater preoccupation with the means. Kanzi proved capable of making stone tools when given the opportunity to observe an experienced flint knapper (Toth, Schick, Savage-Rumbaugh, Sevcik and Rumbaugh, 1993), and his tools were appropriate in sharpness and size to the object to be cut – which could be anything from thick rope to thin lengths of string or leather. Kanzi was not taught a series of actions to produce a flake. Rather, the researchers' strategy was to motivate Kanzi to want to produce a flake in order to obtain a reward by cutting a piece of rope and opening a box. The researchers simply demonstrated some basic flint knapping principles and left him to work out his own method of tool production so as to attain the reward. Kanzi immediately learned the utility of a flake, and he was highly motivated by the general testing situation. When he discovered that a tool site had been baited with food rewards, he became very interested in the task. His initial tool manufacture and use was based on observational learning, but he then began to experiment with methods to produce a flake that were entirely his own and the outcome of trial-and-error learning.

Kanzi eventually developed his own preferred method of producing a flake: he would throw one rock against a hard floor or (if the floor was covered with a rug or he was outdoors) against another rock. He had previously shown little interest in throwing objects, but he came to learn the utility of such an action to produce a flake and attain the food reward. This behaviour seemingly emerged from nowhere, yet was context appropriate. Such 'emergent behaviour' is evident not only in Kanzi's knowledge that throwing is an effective means to produce a needed tool but also in his understanding that the tool itself is the important outcome, not the manner through which the tool is attained. Kanzi was never taught to throw one rock at the floor or another rock. He was only shown how to make a tool in the traditional hard-hammer, free-hand percussion method. But throwing worked for him, and, for a time, became his preferred method (Toth et al., 1993).

Immaturity and emergent behaviour

Bruner's interest in the emergence of new processes and abilities has stimulated the definition of a new category of behaviour: emergents. Recently, Rumbaugh, Washburn and Hillix (1996) have proposed that emergents should be seen as a third class of behaviour in addition to the operant and respondent behaviours defined by Skinner (1938). This third category is deemed necessary to explain forms of behaviour that do not neatly fall into the respondent–operant dichotomy of the behaviourist tradition and cannot be explained in terms of the conditioning of specific responses. The introduction of the concept reflects the new focus on the complex processes and determinants of behaviour that lead to the development of new patterns of interacting with the environment.

Emergent behaviours have several distinctive attributes that set them apart from respondents and operants. Emergents are *new competencies* and *new modes of responding* that were never intentionally reinforced/ trained/conditioned via prior regimens. Emergents frequently come as a surprise to the observer. Rather than being specific responses prompted by conditioning procedures, emergents represent new patterns of behaviours. They are based on the syntheses of diverse experience, knowledge and principles, and require operations more complex than those of basic stimulus–response association. Emergents develop frequently as a consequence of interactions between organismic and treatment variables during early rearing. The more complex the brain of the species, the more probable, it seems, that emergent capacities will appear; and their attributes appear as logical extensions of the logic-structure inherent in the rearing environment.

Selected examples of emergents (including some discussed above) are: language acquisition, stimulus-equivalence (Sidman, 1994), relative numerousness judgements, counting, transfer of learning to a leveraged advantage, shifts in learning processes as a consequence of extended systematic training, and invention of new modes of solving problems. Rumbaugh, Washburn, and Hillix (1996) state that these emergents have four attributes:

1 Emergents are forms of silent learning: the learning or acquisition of new response patterns can progress with no obvious manifestation until several months or even years later. Emergents are acquired by a passive subject through observation.
2 Emergent behaviours are not, and cannot be, specifically reinforced via training regimens that condition specific responses to specific stimuli.
3 Emergent behaviours are established through induction by the organism.
4 Emergent behaviours are noted for their appropriateness to novel situations. They generalize between contexts, not on the basis of the specific stimulus dimension (as in stimulus generalization) but rather, on the basis of relationships between stimuli and/or rules.

Emergents are further illustrated by the development of numeric competence, which can include both judgements of relative numerousness and counting. Washburn and Rumbaugh (1991) report that rhesus macaques can correctly choose the larger of two numerals in a novel pair as a consequence of learning the ordinal values of those numbers through their pairings with other numerals from 0 to 9. Thus, though never intentionally trained to do so, the rhesus learned the ordinal values of all nine numerals and could then choose the larger of any two presented, based on the matrix of relationships between all the numerals. They could do this even if the two being presented had never been paired on previous trials. In other tests, these monkeys successfully and spontaneously selected numerals sequentially, from arrays of five at a time, in a manner that reflected their comprehension of the numerals' rank-ordered values (e.g., $9 > 8 > 7 > 6 \ldots$).

Beran, Rumbaugh and Savage-Rumbaugh (1998) report counting in a chimpanzee, Austin. Through the use of a computer program, Austin was trained to select the Arabic numerals in the correct order to reach a target number. In later sessions, Austin had to select dots in place of the Arabic numerals. The dots were placed linearly around the bottom edge of the computer monitor and Austin simply had to select dots to a certain location for each target number. However, when the dots were randomly arranged on the computer screen in the final test sessions, Austin was still able to select the correct number of dots to match the target numbers 1 to 4, even though the linear pattern arrangement of the dots was no longer available. Although never specifically taught to ignore the pattern and look for the quantity, Austin none the less learned that quantity was the variable of interest rather than the pattern by which the dots were displayed on his monitor.

Conclusion

Prolonged periods of immaturity, Bruner has emphasized, are crucial to the formation of emergent behaviours. Emergent capacities, abilities and behavioural patterns are seen most readily in the larger-brained primates as a reflection of the logic-structure of the rearing environment. It is suggested that relatively large-brained primates have a great deal of neural plasticity which can serve to organize and interrelate broad arrays of learning and experiences. An extended period for development provides time in which to observe, to experiment and to interact with the environment so as to afford a primate the opportunity to make associations, not just among individual items within the environment, but also between the rules of the environment and how they interact. It is knowledge of these rules that later manifests itself in new behaviours – new modes of solving problems that are appropriate, adaptive and creative – without having ever been tested before in the environment. A prolonged period of immaturity, quite simply, provides the time for an animal to 'learn how to learn'.

Bruner was quite correct to postulate the importance of prolonged periods of immaturity in the development of the rich behavioural repertoires seen in the primates, and in the great apes in particular. Rumbaugh, Hopkins, Washburn and Savage-Rumbaugh (1991) propose that developmental structures for cognition in apes are plastic and reflect in substantial measure the essence of the early environment. Cognitive development reflects patterns that are in accord with complex, structured aspects of the environment in which development takes place. Rumbaugh and colleagues (1991) state that competence for language, numbers and other cognitive domains are reflections of genetically possible modes of development in interaction with complex environments and are limited only by the 'object lessons' encountered by the organism across the days and years of its maturation to adulthood. This view would most certainly be welcomed by Bruner who championed it both in principle, and in many specific dimensions, more than 25 years ago.

Bruner's early formulation of this dynamic view of primates has given strong impetus to comparative-development studies that have produced new methods of enquiry, new findings and new theories of emergent behaviours. These studies help us understand the parameters of the early environment that serves to provide the requisite foundation for what we cherish in our children: social and cognitive competence. For that and his illustrious career, we are thankful.

Note

Preparation of this chapter and much of the work summarized in it were funded by a grant from the National Institute of Child Health and Human Development (HD-06016) and other support from the College of Arts and Sciences, Georgia State University.

References

Beran, M.J., Rumbaugh, D.M. and Savage-Rumbaugh, E.S. (1998) 'Chimpanzee (*Pan troglodytes*) counting in a computerized testing paradigm', *Psychological Record*, 48: 3–19.

Boesch, C. and Boesch, H. (1989) 'Hunting behavior of wild chimpanzees in the Tai National Park', *American Journal of Physical Anthropology*, 78: 547–73.

Boysen, S.T. and Capaldi, E.J. (eds) (1993) *The Development of Numerical Competence: Animal and Human Models*. Hillsdale, NJ: Erlbaum.

Brakke, K.E. and Savage-Rumbaugh, E.S. (1995) 'The development of language skills in bonobo and chimpanzee – I. Comprehension', *Language and Communication*, 15: 121–48.

Brakke, K.E. and Savage-Rumbaugh, E.S. (1996) The development of language skills in Pan – II. Production', *Language and Communication*, 16: 361–80.

Bruner, J.S. (1974) 'Nature and uses of immaturity', in K. Connolly and J. Bruner (eds), *The Growth of Competence*. London: Academic Press.

Bruner, J.S. (1983) *Child's Talk: Learning to Use Language*. Oxford: Oxford University Press.

Caldero, J., Prevette, D., Mei, X., Oakley, R., Li, L., Milligan, C., Houenou, L., Burek, M. and Oppenheim, R. (1998) 'Peripheral target regulation of the development and survival of spinal sensory and motorneurons in the chick embryo', *Journal of Neuroscience*, 18: 356–70.

Cheney, D.L. and Seyfarth, R.M. (1990) *How Monkeys See the World*. Chicago, IL: University of Chicago Press.

Davenport, R.K., Rogers, C.W. and Rumbaugh, D.M. (1973) 'Long-term cognitive deficits in chimpanzees associated with early impoverished rearing', *Developmental Psychology*, 9: 343–7.

Deacon, T.W. (1997) *The Symbolic Species: The Co-evolution of Language and the Brain*. New York: W.W. Norton.

de Waal, F.B.M. (1992) *Chimpanzee Politics*. London: Jonathan Cape.

Gardner, R.A. and Gardner, B.T. (1969) 'Teaching sign language to a chimpanzee', *Science*, 165: 664–72.

Harlow, H.F. and Mears, C. (1979) *The Human Model: Primate Perspectives*. Washington: Winston & Sons.

Harlow, H.F., Harlow, M.K., Schlitz, K.A. and Mohr, D.J. (1971) 'The effects of early adverse and enriched environments on the learning ability of rhesus monkeys', in L.E. Jarrard (ed.), *Cognitive Processes of Nonhuman Primates*. New York: Academic Press.

McGrew, W.C. (1992) *Chimpanzee Material Culture*. Cambridge: Cambridge University Press.

McGrew, W.C. (1993) 'The intelligent use of tools: twenty propositions', in K.R. Gibson and T. Ingold (eds), *Tools, Language and Cognition in Human Evolution*. Cambridge: Cambridge University Press.

Menzel, E.W. Jr., Davenport, R.K. and Rogers, C.M. (1970) 'The development of tool using in wild born and restriction reared chimpanzees', *Folia Primatologica*, 12: 273–83.

Miles, H.L. (1983) 'Apes and language: the search for communicative competence', in J. de Luce and H.T. Wilder (eds), *Language in Primates: Perspectives and Implications*. New York: Springer.

Patterson, F.G. (1978) 'The gestures of a gorilla: language acquisition in another pongid', *Brain and Language*, 5: 72–97.

Povinelli, D.J., Rulf, A.B., Landau, K. and Bierschwale, D. (1993) 'Self-recognition in chimpanzees (*Pan troglodytes*): distribution, ontogeny, and patterns of emergence', *Journal of Comparative Psychology*, 107: 347–72.

Premack, D. (1971) 'Language in a chimpanzee?', *Science*, 172: 808–22.

Premack, D. and Woodruff, G. (1978) 'Does the chimpanzee have a theory of mind?', *Behavioral and Brain Sciences*, 5: 515–26.

Purves, D. (1994) *Neural Activity and the Growth of the Brain*. Cambridge: Cambridge University Press.

Riesen, A.H. (1982) 'Effects of environments on development in sensory systems', in W.D. Neff (ed.), *Contributions to Sensory Physiology*. New York: Academic Press.

Rumbaugh, D.M. (ed.) (1977) *Language Learning by a Chimpanzee*. New York: Academic Press.

Rumbaugh, D.M. (1997) 'Competence, cortex, and primate models: a comparative primate perspective', in N.A. Krasnegor, G.R. Lyon and P.S. Goldman-Rakic (eds), *Development of the Prefrontal Cortex: Evolution, Neurobiology, and Behavior*. Baltimore, MD: Brookes Publishing.

Rumbaugh, D.M., Hopkins, W.D., Washburn, D.A. and Savage-Rumbaugh, E.S. (1989) 'Lana chimpanzee learns to count by "NUMATH": a summary of a video-taped experimental report', *Psychological Record*, 39: 459–70.

Rumbaugh, D.M., Hopkins, W.D., Washburn, D.A. and Savage-Rumbaugh, E.S. (1991) 'Comparative perspectives of brain, cognition, and language', in N.A. Krasnegor, D.M. Rumbaugh, R.L. Schiefelbusch and M. Studdert-Kennedy (eds), *Biological and Behavioral Determinants of Language Development*. Hillsdale, NJ: Erlbaum.

Rumbaugh, D.M., Savage-Rumbaugh, E.S. and Washburn, D.A. (1996) 'Toward a new outlook on primate learning and behavior: complex learning and emergent processes in comparative perspective', *Japanese Psychological Research*, 38: 113–25.

Rumbaugh, D.M., Washburn, D.A. and Hillix, W.A. (1996) 'Respondents, operants, and emergents: toward an integrated perspective on behavior', in K. Pribram and J. King (eds), *Learning as a Self-organizing Process*. Hillsdale, NJ: Erlbaum.

Savage-Rumbaugh, E.S. (1986) *Ape Language: From Conditioned Responses to Symbols*. New York: Columbia University Press.

Savage-Rumbaugh, E.S. (1991) 'Language learning in the bonobo: how and why they learn', in N.A. Krasnegor, D.M. Rumbaugh, R.L. Schiefelbusch and M. Studdert-Kennedy (eds), *Biological and Behavioral Determinants of Language Development*. Hillsdale, NJ: Erlbaum.

Savage-Rumbaugh, E.S. and Lewin, R. (1994) *Kanzi: The Ape at the Brink of the Human Mind*. New York: John Wiley & Sons.

Savage-Rumbaugh, E.S., McDonald, K., Sevcik, R.A., Hopkins, W.D. and Rubert, E. (1986) 'Spontaneous symbol acquisition and communicative use by pygmy chimpanzees (*Pan paniscus*)', *Journal of Experimental Psychology*, 115: 211–35.

Savage-Rumbaugh, E.S., Sevcik, R.A., Brakke, K.E., Rumbaugh, D.M. and Greenfield, P.M. (1990) 'Symbols: their communicative use, combination, and comprehension by bonobos (*Pan paniscus*)', in C. Rovee-Collier and L.P. Lipsitt (eds), *Advances in Infancy Research*, Vol. 6. Norwood, NJ: Ablex.

Savage-Rumbaugh, E.S., Murphy, J., Sevcik, R.A., Brakke, K.E., Williams, S. and Rumbaugh, D.M. (1993) *Language comprehension in ape and child*, Monographs of the Society for Research in Child Development, 58 (3–4, serial no. 233).

Seyfarth, R.M. and Cheney, D.L. (1986) 'Vocal development in Vervet monkeys', *Animal Behavior*, 34: 1640–58.

Seyfarth, R.M., Cheney, D.L. and Marler, P. (1980) 'Monkey responses to three different alarm calls: evidence of predator classification and semantic communication', *Science*, 210: 801–3.

Sidman, M. (1994) *Equivalence Relations and Behavior: A Research Story*. Boston: Authors Cooperative.

Skinner, B.F. (1938) *The Behavior of Organisms: An Experimental Analysis*. New York: Appleton-Century-Crofts.

Terrace, H.S., Pettito, L.A., Sanders, R.J. and Bever, T.G. (1979) 'Can an ape create a sentence?', *Science*, 206: 891–900.

Toth, N., Schick, K.D., Savage-Rumbaugh, E.S., Sevcik, R.A. and Rumbaugh, D.M. (1993) 'Pan the tool-maker: investigations into the stone tool-making and tool-using capabilities of a bonobo (*Pan paniscus*)', *Journal of Archaeological Science*, 20: 81–91.

Washburn, D.A. and Rumbaugh, D.M. (1991) 'Ordinal judgments of numerical symbols by macaques (*Macaca mulatta*)', *Psychological Science*, 2: 190–3.

9

NORMS IN LIFE: PROBLEMS IN THE REPRESENTATION OF RULES

Rom Harré

Why are there still unsettled philosophical problems about the understanding of human behaviour? Why have so many who have reflected on how to make human behaviour the topic of systematic study become wary of using the methods of physics and chemistry to achieve this end? The importance of Jerome Bruner's many contributions to the understanding of human life lies, at least in part, in the answers they have prompted to these big questions.[1]

The natural sciences have alternated between two main ways of conceiving of enquiry into nature – positivism and realism. Positivism treats only observable phenomena as real and reduces the role of theory to a logical auxiliary of prediction. Causality is a mere regularity of patterns of observable events. Realism accords theory not only a logical role; theory can also describe unobservable processes that underlie observed regularities. Causality involves the powers of potent entities. The respective attitude of these traditions to the entities and processes postulated by theory is thus quite different. Positivists deny theoreticians the right to make existence claims for the 'hidden' entities that they postulate. Realists, however, insist that there is a well-founded distinction between, on the one hand, hypothetical entities that are merely psychological aids to thought and, on the other, things that really exist.

Behaviourism, and its descendant, American experimental empiricism, were textbook examples of positivism in application to human behaviour. In contrast, the first cognitive revolution, and its contemporary offspring 'cognitive science', was realist in spirit. According to behaviourism, mental states, even if they exist, are irrelevant to a science of behaviour. According to cognitive science, mental states do exist, and do so unobserved, like the quarks and intermediate vector bosons of physics. Hence behaviourism and cognitive science exemplify different interpretations of natural science. Whether philosophy of science directly influenced the architects of these two approaches I cannot say. But the parallels do suggest an interesting problem for historians of ideas.

Bruner was one of the instigators of the first cognitive revolution. His studies of word recognition, succinctly recalled in his autobiography (Bruner, 1983), demonstrated that stimuli were never adequate to the experience they supposedly occasion. A store of knowledge was clearly implicated in a wide variety of psychological processes (Bruner, 1979). Bruner was able to show that what we perceive involves not only the optical stimulus, but also our beliefs about the nature of the object perceived. Thus a circular coin seen at an angle is perceived as a broader ellipse than its geometrical projection on the retina (Bruner, 1974). Among other examples, Bruner noticed that word recognition involves knowledge of matters other than the auditory or graphical representation of the word. Yet just how the knowledge in question is stored and implemented remained a puzzle. The first cognitive revolution suggested that it is stored and implemented in the way that computers store and implement information.

Bruner has recently been very critical of this supposed 'solution' (Bruner, 1990: ch. 1) and his criticisms have played an important role in stimulating a *second* cognitive revolution, one which involves a radical departure from natural-scientific models and turns to other explanatory paradigms and modes of enquiry (Bruner, 1990, 1992). In this chapter, I develop an argument designed to expose the shortcomings of all computer models of the mind, an argument with which, I hope, Bruner should be sympathetic. If the argument is correct, the legitimacy of the second cognitive revolution is established.

The first cognitive revolution: theories, models and type-hierarchies

To see the full force of the second cognitive revolution it is helpful to look closely at the structure of contemporary continuations of the first.

In cognitive science, the key metaphysical notion is that of a 'mental state' and the key hypothesis is that there are both conscious and unconscious mental states. Hypotheses about unconscious mental states are invoked to account for mental activities, both private and public, of isolated human beings (see Shannon (1991) for an insightful analysis). This pattern of reasoning has a familiar ring. It is exactly what we encounter in the natural sciences. Unobserved states, of the same kind as those that can be observed, are invoked to account for observed states and processes.

Theory construction in physics and chemistry exploits two distinct facets of our cognitive powers. A theory exemplifies one of the common formats of deductive logic. The hypotheses are among the premises and the phenomena that we try to explain figure in the conclusions of deductive inferences from those premises. It has long been realized that this format cannot account for the rationality of natural science, since deductions of the same phenomena can be derived from indefinitely many logically equipollent theories. This point was first noticed by the renaissance astronomer Christopher Clavius (1602) and has been often revived in recent years as the 'underdetermination of theory by data'.

Choice among logically adequate options is achieved in practice by controlling the ontological content of theories. This involves a second facet of our cognitive powers – our capacity to construct models and employ metaphors. A model is a set of objects and relations that allows the austere logical structure of a theoretical discourse to be interpreted as an 'as if' reality. A model is both an interpretation of a theory and a model of the reality that the theory purports to describe. But how are these 'as ifs' constrained? In principle there could be a second sort of 'underdetermination', since there exists the possibility of an indefinite proliferation of models. In real science, a restriction on the scope of possible models is provided by an ontology of unobserved entities, states and processes. This catalogue of possible existents derives from an ontological type-hierarchy that expresses the most general beliefs we have about the nature of the material world. For example, if 'Newtonian entity' is the defining supertype of a working type-hierarchy, then among its subtypes are planets, cannon balls and gas molecules. The former two are observables, the latter an unobservable, since actual gas molecules are imperceptible. We can use the type-hierarchy to fix the properties of the unobservable molecules, since, as a subtype of this hierarchy they must inherit the properties encapsulated in the supertype, such as position, motion and mass.

Ontological type-hierarchies are supported by the empirical evidence for instances of many of their subtypes, and by their long-run success in underwriting fruitful models of unobserved generative processes. It is on the basis of their observable properties that planets and cannon balls are located where they are under the Newtonian supertype. It is the ubiquity of instantiations of subtypes of that type-hierarchy that supports its use in constructing the concept 'gas molecule' – the unobserved constituent of observed samples of gases.

If we take into account both our logical and our model-building skills, then there is no threat of local underdetermination. The illusion that there is comes from taking too narrow a view of our cognitive capacities. Of course, ontological type-hierarchies have changed, but like the stony part of Wittgenstein's river bed, they change not often and do so slowly.

The key point is that advanced science is possible because we can test our working type-hierarchies. It is because we can observe the behaviour of cannon balls and planets that we can assign a sharply defined set of properties to the supertype, 'Newtonian entity', and thus constrain the many subtypes of this ontology. The final step in building a theory is to show that an instance of the subtype that our model exemplifies is a possible existent in the material environment to which our theory assigns it. Our model, tightly restricted by its location in the relevant type-hierarchy, and taken as a representation of what is responsible for the phenomena we observe, leaves us with only one theory. We thus avoid underdetermination by the confluence of logical coherence of the theoretical discourse and ontological plausibility of the best model. When the ontological constraints are weak, as in the case of sixteenth-century cosmology, then we do indeed have real cases of underdetermination, as recorded by Clavius and other astronomers of the period.

Cognitive science invokes its own double-branched ontological type-hierarchy, the respective supertypes of which are 'mental state' and 'mental process'. We know what attributes to assign to the supertype 'mental state' because we are aware of some of our own. The key attribute is *intentionality*: an intentional state is one that is experienced as directed to something other than itself. Since all the subtypes in the type-hierarchy must inherit all the attributes of its supertype, cognitive science is committed to the existence of unconscious intentional states. We also know what attributes to assign to the supertype 'mental process' because we are familiar with them. The key attribute is *normativity*: a state or process is normative if it is routinely subject to the possibility of assessment according to standards of correctness. Since all subtypes must inherit the properties of the supertype, unconscious mental processes must be normatively structured.

The idea is to create models for our explanatory theories of cognition (for example word recognition and remembering) by subsuming the concepts we need to invoke under one or other branch of the general type-hierarchy for cognitive science. But to do this we must subject ourselves to its discipline: any phenomenon we invoke, which is to be understood as a possible existent and not just as a heuristic device, must be a possible existent of which we could be unaware.

In the physical sciences tectonic plates, gas molecules, viruses, dark matter and so on are existentially certified by virtue of their places in type-hierarchies that are well grounded in observation. The viability of cognitive science rests on whether we can invoke unobserved mental phenomena to play an analogous explanatory role. The parallel strictly requires states unobservable only to the psychologist as scientist. But from its beginning, mental states and processes of which the subject herself is unaware played a key part in the ontology of cognitive psychology. For example, 'implicit memory' was introduced as the set of memories that were unavailable consciously to the person making use of them. But can there be 'unobserved mental states', of which he or she who 'has' them is unaware? And can there be 'unobserved mental processes' going on when someone remembers something? The whole of cognitive science rests on affirmative answers to these questions. But mental states are intentional states: the type-hierarchy admits and orders states according to whether they are intentional, that is, whether they have meaning for the person who 'has' them. But how can such states be unobserved by their 'owners'? How can there be an emotion of which the person who has it is unaware, when emotions are feelings expressing judgements and are directed towards some intentional object? We may be wrong about the interpretation of our feelings, but we can hardly be said to have feelings of which we are not aware. How could one have a memory of which one was not conscious? To remember something is to bring it to awareness. Unobserved mental states cannot find a place in the ontological type-hierarchy of mental states in the way that gas molecules can find a place in the ontological type-hierarchy of material entities. 'Unconscious mental state' is an ill-formed concept.

This is the style of argument developed by Searle (1983) against the pretensions of cognitive science to be a plausible psychology. If Searle is right then one branch of the type-hierarchy on which cognitive science rests fails to generate acceptable models. I want to turn now to an examination of the other branch of cognitive science's type-hierarchy, which concerns mental processes. Taking the notion of a *rule* as central to the explication of the normative constraints on cognition, I shall argue that computer models of the mind cannot capture the normativity of mental processes. Normativity cannot be modelled as processes in machines, and hence, if the brain is a computational device, it cannot be modelled in brains.

Towards the second cognitive revolution: preliminary considerations

The duality of rules

In his recent writings – those that have helped inaugurate the second cognitive revolution – Bruner portrays cognition as a discursive process conforming, context by context, to many different standards of correctness and propriety (Bruner, 1986, 1990). Logic, in the formal sense, is only one among many 'grammars' that we use to give order to discourses. In his studies of narrative conventions (Bruner, 1991), Bruner has emphasized the role of story telling in shaping people's actions and attitudes. One concept which is implicit in these writings, but which is crucial, is the concept of a rule. Narrative conventions can be expressed as rules, as can our standards of correctness and propriety.

There is a duality in the notion of rule that needs to be made explicit. We must distinguish cases of *rule-following*, where the rule is explicitly formulated and used in the management of action, from cases of *acting in accordance with a rule*, where people behave in an orderly way simply because they have acquired a habit of so acting. In the latter case, the behaviour can be represented (by a psychologist, perhaps) as conforming to rules. It is important, however, not to conflate acting in accordance with some rule with unconscious rule-following.

We can say that a rule is *immanent* in a practice if the normative character of what is being done comes from simply learning the practice, but a rule could be formulated to express the normative character of the practice. In contrast, a rule is *transcendent* to a practice if the rule exists in the same symbolic realm as the practice, such as when an actor attends to a rule and uses it as an instruction for performing certain actions, or a teacher deploys a rule to guide the actions of a pupil. A rule may be transcendent to the practice for the trainer but immanent for the learner, if the latter is not taught the practice by being given the rule as an instruction.

The determinacy of cognitive processes

In order for a phenomenon to be a proper topic for scientific investigation it must be sufficiently determinate to be provisionally assigned to a category in a working type-hierarchy (of course, a new but provisional category might be needed to accommodate it). According to an implicit principle of the second cognitive revolution, when it comes to psychological states and processes, determinateness for purposes of scientific investigation coincides with determinateness for the actor whose psychological functioning is being studied. A process or state is 'determinate' if it has a sufficiently definite meaning for the actors in a certain situation to accomplish joint actions successfully. For people to bring off a social act, their actions must have the same meaning, *ceteris paribus*, for everyone in that cultural matrix who is a participant in the act or a spectator. The intended outcome should also be sufficiently well specified for questions of its correctness or appropriateness in the relevant circumstances to be settled, at least in principle. If we cannot make out what someone meant by their actions, the issue of their correctness, as the performance of the contextually required act, cannot arise. This is a general constraint on the intentionality and normativity of human actions. Social life is full of devices for ensuring this requirement, even so drastic as the ordering of a retrial by an appellate court. In real life, however, it is rare that issues of determinateness of actions or acts are pushed to extremes. But at whatever degree of determinateness an act-creating sequence of actions is left unchallenged there is an intimate relationship between context and meaning.

The requirement that cognition be relevantly determinate, within the paradigm defining the first cognitive revolution, raises the well-known 'frame problem'. A cognitive process is determinate only relative to a set of framing assumptions, which reduce the ambiguity and spread of the possible meanings of a cognitive act. The determinateness of every cognitive act presumes certain background assumptions not specified in the description of the cognitive act itself. This is the distinction Wittgenstein drew between frame and picture, or in another well-known image, between grammatical and descriptive propositions. Since there are indefinitely many such background framing conditions, some selection from among them must be implicit in any cognitive process, in order for the two requirements of intentionality and normativity to be met in a determinate way. The selected assumptions constitute the 'frame' or grammar within which the cognitive process is intentionally and normatively determinate, relative to the task in hand.

In real human cognition, such as remembering or problem-solving, these abstractions from the indefinitely complex background are ad hoc and only locally valid. It is only in *this* place and at *this* time that *this* selection from among the conditions is relevant to a locally valid pattern of cognitive acts. Rules for the admissibility of evidence, as administered by a particular judge in a particular trial, are a case in point. Each trial is managed by a unique 'frame'. In the absence of such abstractions, the background is both huge and indeterminate; each assumption within it dependent for its meaning upon other as yet unspecified assumptions. Cognition is possible only if the proliferation of conditions is constrained, either deliberately, as in the trial of 'O.J.', or implicitly, as in everyday encounters. We can never tell, however, whether unacknowledged assumptions are at work, which will surface only when some novel decision or inference is made in the light of a particular frame constraint, or some well-established discursive convention is overthrown.

Performances and their enabling conditions
Without racquets, balls, a court, an agreed set of rules, and so on, it would not be possible to play tennis. Yet the playing of tennis cannot be reduced to a function of these. Tennis is a performance, an activity that is done by people, insofar as they have the necessary skills to take part. The actions of tennis players have meaning and are judged for correctness by reference to a socially maintained system of customs and rules. To play tennis people use an array of tools. Should we include their bodies and brains among them? Racquets behave according to the laws of physics and brains according to the laws of biochemistry and neurophysiology. The tools enable the playing of tennis. But the rules of tennis are not some conjunction of laws of physics and neurology.

The distinction between the enabling conditions for an activity and the activity as performed is frequently overlooked in psychology, particularly by those who see scientific psychology as involving reduction to the physiological or material aspects of human performances. Physics enables tennis but the rules of tennis are not laws of physics. Likewise, while remembering is something people do – a symbolic/discursive performance – it has neurophysiological enabling conditions. One uses a structure in one's brain to recollect a past event in which one had a role. People need molecular-based long- and short-term 'memory' stores to achieve this, and if these fail they resort to such things as written records, videotapes from security cameras, old photographs, and so on. From a psychological point of view the role of the molecular basis of memory and the diary are not so dissimilar. My diary is part of a prosthetic memory and if I have mislaid my diary I must use my brain-based memory instead. Remembering is an intentional and normative activity. Molecular goings on in brains or other computing machines cannot be intentional, if Searle is right.

But may we not represent the social and normative component of remembering in a set of rules that could be input as a program into the machine, or learned as unthinking habits by a person, becoming in that respect machine-like? Let us focus on the crucial concept of a 'skill'. Here the distinction between enabling conditions and performance must be very sharply drawn. A skill, say the ability to play a musical instrument, is individuated and characterized by reference to intentions and norms that exist in the practices of a community, 'outside' the agent. The exercise of the skill, however, is enabled by the existence of a certain brain structure brought into being by the training necessary to acquire the skill. The skill 'exists', we might say, when not being exercised, in that relatively permanently existing bodily state.

It should be obvious that skills cannot be reduced to their enabling conditions. Yet it is surprising how frequently the contrary assumption is made. Francis Crick, for example, claims that consciousness just is a condition of the brain. But this conflates a skill with its enabling conditions. The criteria of identity that pick out the neurophysiological states that ground a skill are quite different from those that pick out the skill they enable. The former involve patches of dendrites, areas of the brain and so on, none of which is relevant to identifying the particular skill. We can tell whether someone can ride a bicycle, or is conscious, knowing nothing about the actual states of the brain and nervous system of the rider. Are they unobserved mental states and processes invisible not only to a psychologist but also to the actor him or herself?

The founding insights of discursive psychology

If we adopt the principle that psychological phenomena are characterized by intentionality and normativity, we have thereby pre-selected the type of model that will be most enlightening in the analysis of human behaviour. The most obvious (though not the only) model that a discursive psychologist might take for a public, collective cognitive process would be conversation, as Bruner and others have suggested. A conversation is an exchange, in which the performances of each participant are meaningful, and assessable as appropriate or correct, relative to the conventions of the particular discursive context. A great deal of cognition (though not all) is literally conversation. And it is a central insight of discursive psychology that we can usefully use conversation as a model for studying complex forms of social interaction. For example, the growth and confirmation of a friendship, or a game of tennis, are not conversations, but can be illuminated by being considered as conversation-like. In the terms of philosophy of science, conversations can serve as a super-type for creating an ontological type-hierarchy for a great variety of activities, with respect to their intentional and normative character. The generalization of this model to all cognitive activities, both private and individual and public and collective, founded upon the developmental psychology of Vygotsky (1962) and that independently developed by Bruner, marks the most ambitious reach of the second cognitive revolution.

The use of the term 'discursive' for a psychology grounded in intentionality and normativity highlights the dominant role of the idea of conversation in the explanation of human behaviour.

Types of action

As a first approximation, we can now classify patterns of human action and interaction into three major categories:

1 *Causal:* A fixed action pattern, say smiling, as a neuromuscular spasm, in response to someone else's smile, as stimulus, can be exhaustively described in physiological terms. The stimulus triggers an inherited, genetically sustained, neurological mechanism that produces the effect. Such a causal process is experienced by the person in whose body it occurs (if it is attended to at all) as if he or she were a spectator.
2 *Habitual:* Once fully trained, a person's habits, such as depressing a certain pattern of keys on a clarinet to produce Middle C, are similar to causal patterns. In some of the early presentations of the discursive point of view, these were called 'enigmatic', since it would not be clear from a mere description of the phenomenon whether it was causal or habitual, inborn or ingrained. Habits are cases of 'acting according to rule', rather than 'rule-following'. There are rules in the background of habits, since habits are acquired by training. But once trained, habitual behaviour is like causal behaviour. Indeed, in training we are building micromechanisms in the brain and nervous system. The experienced player feels her fingers move towards a new key pattern almost like a spectator.
3 *Monitored:* Some patterns of action, such as performances in job interviews, and especially in the course of acquiring or improving a skill, are self-consciously managed by the actor or actors, by reference to a meta-conversation in which meanings and rules are considered 'on line'. Here we have a paradigm of rule-following.

I believe that the whole of psychology, as a discipline, hinges on whether we should assimilate habits to causes or to monitored actions. Nothing but confusion can arise from extending the notion of cause to cover every regular temporal pattern of antecedent and consequent without further qualification. If it is so extended then we are forced to distinguish different versions of causality. In (1) above we must invoke nonconscious mechanisms, eschew the concept of choice, and expect to find some form of determinism. We might call this 'mechanistic causation'. In (3) we need to invoke a complex hierarchy of choices, including one's adherence to rules as the appropriate guides to action, and we must eschew determinism, since the possibility remains of misapplying the rules in question.

Monitored actions absolutely require the concepts of 'meaning' and 'rule' as explanatory devices, but what of the habitual? Should we use the latter concepts to understand habitual actions or assimilate the habitual fully to the causal? One of the reasons that psychology has proved difficult to found on an agreed ontology and methodology is, I believe, that there is no simple answer to this question. Habits partake of the causal and they partake of the monitored, in different circumstances in different ways. In the origins in some individual's life they are tied closely to rules, while in their immediate activation their basis in the brain and central nervous system may be very like the instigation of an inherited fixed action pattern, a paradigm of caused behaviour.

Wittgenstein's observations on psychology (1953, 1980) may seem to push us towards the assimilation of the habitual to the monitored, and so to the adoption of 'rule' as the most powerful and basic analytical and explanatory concept. But this would be a superficial interpretation. To see how this concept can play a role in both habitual and monitored patterns of action we must return to the distinction between (1) following a rule, where the rule is explicit and the action managed by a meta-conversation, be it private or public, in which the rule is attended to as such, and (2) acting in accordance with a rule, where the rule is implicit and the action is habitual.

One way in which discursive psychology differs from 'mainstream' is that the latter has been built up on a largely unexamined assumption that habits should be assimilated to the domain of mechanistic causes. This has tended to obscure the cultural relativity of habits, leading to unjustified claims for the existence of universal psychological laws on the basis of locally observed regularities in patterns of human thought and action. There has been some movement away from an exclusively mechanistic causal interpretation in mainstream psychology. For example, in a recent presentation, Berkowitz (1996) described the effect of watching violence on television as playing a part 'in patterns of thought related by meanings'. The distinction between mechanistic cause/effect patterns and sequences of thoughts and feelings ordered semantically is clear enough to suggest that the task of a scientific psychology is to make explicit the implicit rules of human action, and the structures of meaning that they sustain and that sustain them.

Let us now turn to computer models of the mind.

The problem with GOFAI

Rules and machines

Much the most successful branch of AI, as a branch of knowledge engineering, has been its application in the creation of 'expert systems'. There now exist programs that can control machines that can paint cars, diagnose diseases, and perform a host of other tasks that once were the preserve of well-trained and talented human beings. The issue here is what GOFAI (Good Old-Fashioned Artificial Intelligence) can teach us about human cognition.[2] Crucial here is the role of rules in causal, habitual and monitored patterns of behaviour. In my view, they have no role in the first, a complex and obscure role in the second and an unproblematic role in the third. Whatever happens in a machine (or in a brain for that matter) is causal.

Much that happens 'in' a person is intentional and normative, calling for the use of a different explanatory paradigm.

In response to the question of how intentionality and normativity can be represented in a machine simulation, we should answer boldly that they cannot be represented at all. And this is not a factual observation, but the result of a conceptual analysis of the relation between rules and causes, as the sources of order or pattern in human action. I shall show that, when it is claimed that a rule is represented in a computer, via an instruction in a program, what is represented is not in fact a rule at all, since what corresponds to it is not normative, but causal in the mechanistic sense.

If these arguments are persuasive, then the Turing Test cannot be invoked to link AI (a branch of engineering working on artificial tools for cognitive tasks) and cognitive psychology (a branch of the human sciences working on how human beings perform cognitive tasks, using both natural and artificial tools). Discussion of the working of a material process in a machine cannot involve normative questions of correctness, whereas discussions of human thought and action in cognitive psychology must involve such questions. 'He is using a saw but is he using it correctly?' is the sort of question that could not be answered by any description of motor mechanisms, whether genetic in origin or ingrained by training. Similarly 'She is counting sheep but is she getting the right total?' takes us out of her brain and into the culture at large. It is said that Australian aboriginals used a numbering system that lumped together all aggregates above five as 'many'. An aboriginal stockman and a grazier on an Australian sheep station each counts sheep by the use of some ingrained neural mechanism, but their results, though each uses his brain correctly according to the standards of his culture, are different.

The significance of Wittgenstein's distinction

Let us reflect again on Wittgenstein's dichotomous conception of 'rule'. As we have seen, he distinguishes 'following a rule' from 'acting in accord' with one. The former is a deliberate action, much like obeying an order. A rule, in this sense, is overt and explicit. It specifies the kind of thing that would satisfy it, and in that respect it is very like many ways of anticipating the future in thought. In giving an order in a restaurant, for instance, we are specifying the type of dish we want, not its unique particularity. To determine what to do, a person consults or recites or otherwise attends to the rule, treating it as one might treat a command. In contrast, actions 'in accordance with rules' are patterns of human action that are neither cases of rule-following nor cases of automatic, genetically programmed responses to stimuli. To act in accordance with a rule is to engage in a trained procedure subject to normative constraints. It makes sense to say that a certain person has got some habitual procedure wrong. And this of course implies that they might have got it right. The dichotomy 'right/ wrong' applies to performances of this type. But contrast those behaviours that are brought about by the automatic workings of a neural mechanism, for example a spasmodic cough. 'Right' and 'wrong' have no application to them. There are complexities here, since we human beings impose certain standards on the way our bodies work, summed up in the concept of 'health'. Though a blink is just the outcome of a certain mechanism, we might judge the blink reflex defective relative to our conception of how the system should work. It might be normatively construed within a cultural matrix of 'appropriate bodily appearance' as a tic.

It is a mistake to think that habitual action in accord with some rule is brought about by an unobservable version of conscious rule-following. This was Wittgenstein's great insight. His anti-mentalism is easily misunderstood. Some thought that he denied the existence of subjective experience altogether, particularly those who had not read his 'private language argument' carefully (Wittgenstein, 1953: §§243–315). The mentalism he denied was that pilloried by Ryle (1947). It was the idea that there is a shadow mental world behind the world of experience and action. Acting in accordance with a rule is not made possible by unconscious rule following. It is a quite different way of acting from following a rule, but related to it. Those who act in accordance with rules have usually at some time followed those rules (though not always). Habits involve rules, in both their training and in later criticism of habitual performances, but they do not involve rules in their moment-by-moment implementation. In training people we create in them artificial neural mechanisms. In this way habits partake of the causal. But in that their origin is cultural and their assessment overt, they partake of the monitored. It is in this double-sidedness that there lies the greatest danger of misinterpreting AI and of slipping into a form of cognitive science modelled too closely on the invocations of unobserved processes (e.g., Fodor, 1975).

When we say that someone is acting in accordance with a rule, the appeal to rules serves to remind us of the way that his or her habit was acquired. It also opens the way for a suitable means for representing, in psychological discourse, what it is that someone acting habitually and competently must know so to act.

Programming expert systems

To express an expert's skill we might write down a set of rules with the conditions under which they should be applied. These rules would express 'norms of correctness'. The very notions of 'skill' and 'expert' are normative notions. But, and here we approach the nub of our analysis, experts can make mistakes, even though they are well acquainted with the rules and are masters of the techniques of the trade. Some wine tasters, for example, are better than others. Such distinctions make sense only if there can be a gap between actual performance and the acknowledged norms. Thus to write down rules that express expertise is not to conduct an inductive survey of how people do things, but to abstract the norms for the procedure in question. This fits nicely with the Wittgensteinian distinction drawn above. An implicit rule is not a cause of an action, but a norm for actions of that type. 'Acting in accordance with a rule' partakes of causation; however, it is not the rule that causes the action, but the material enabling conditions for the habit, the artificial mechanisms built into the body by training.

Representing the norms of the skill as 'rules' (as conditionals like 'If such and such occurs, do so and so'), enables an AI expert to write a program which, when run on a computer, simulates the performance of the expert, say in wine tasting. But in programming the machine the 'rule' becomes a causal mechanism, and as such is no longer a rule (Harré, 1996).

A machine simulation for wine tasting (or for assembling a car) is two steps away from the normativity of the psychology of persons. The first step is to express the skill as a set of explicit rules. The second step is to program the machine, at which moment the rules are replaced by artificial causal mechanisms.

More about habits

We identified above three categories of behaviour evident in human affairs – the causal, the habitual and the monitored – and we raised the question of whether habitual or trained behaviour should be assimilated to causes or to norms. It became clear, however, that we should resist this dichotomous question. We must now examine this insight in more detail.

First, habits or trained performances partake of causality because the training brings into being neural mechanisms that a person can use without consciously monitoring his or her performance. A top class tennis player just plays the backhand passing shot that has the right direction and the right amount of topspin, 'without thought'. But her very next serve is planned, calculated and monitored in execution. So the distinction between habitual and monitored performances does not coincide with the distinction between skilled and novice stages of competence. Second, habits partake of the normative or monitored because the performance is subject to standards of correctness that are, in general, exterior to the trained performer. These norms are embodied in the judgements of teachers, trainers, critics, or exist in the community at large. Although a player may not at that moment be monitoring the performance, someone else may be. In the wine tasting competition there are judges. And in the matter of remembering – that is, recollecting the past correctly – there are others who may have documentary, forensic, or other evidence, and who can criticize our efforts at remembering.

Of course, the assessments of teachers and judges may themselves be habitual. They too have been trained. The question of whether they are good teachers or competent judges can arise and direct our attention to matters exterior to the teacher or judge. The judges may themselves be judged.

Better or worse explanatory discourses

The more extreme advocates of a postmodern interpretation of science have claimed that every psychology represents just one story amongst a slew of others, all of which have claims to our attention. That is, in a sense, true, as I have been arguing for decades. Conforming to the discursive conventions of 'science' may not be the best strategy for certain purposes. If you want to know the subtleties of misery and joy you would be better to read Tolstoy. But radical relativism does not follow from the postmodern insight. For relative to the task in hand stories can be ranked according to rational criteria. They are not all of equal value when judged in the light of a specific project. I think we have to see people as engaging in joint tasks and projects, adopting positions in the local moral order, and guided in what they do, publicly or privately, by story lines that are appropriate to the task. The natural sciences are not just one genre of stories among others with respect to the task of comprehending the material world, when what is in question is building bridges, synthesizing useful chemicals and explaining the array of products in an atom-smashing machine. But with respect to the task of finding our place, as human beings, in that world then indeed science is one among other genres and less compelling than some.

There could be a preferred scientific psychology, provided that the honorifics 'scientific' and 'psychology' have some philosophical respectability. Calling questionnaires 'instruments' and the results of answering them 'measures' to which statistical analysis is applied does not make psychology a science. The irony is that studying the answers people give to questions is a possible scientific method, provided that it is seen for what it is, a study of some of the discursive conventions for answering certain kinds of questions. Modelling some of this in a computer offers a method of testing whether we understand the rules for conversing on this particular subject matter in this context. It does not give us access to an abstract model of unobserved cognitive processes (though it might help us find the neurophysiological bases of the relevant skills, that is, the bodily mechanisms a skilled performer uses to accomplish tasks).

The Turing Test reconsidered

The Turing Test for the 'mentality' of a computer can be run as follows: a person, A, interacts sometimes with another person, B, and sometimes with a computer by some communication device. The computer can be said to have a mind if A cannot tell from their responses which is the computer and which is B. A natural extension of this test to assess the adequacy of the machine modelling of a cognitive function would be to see if the outcomes, suitably 'matched', of a person performing a specified cognitive task and a computer running a program to perform the 'same' task (*ceteris paribus*), are comparable. If a computer, programmed on the basis of explicit rules extracted from a study of an expert's performance, passed this extended Turing Test, we could say that it serves as a model for the state of the trained performer, for whom the skill is habitual. The reason is simple. Programming the computer and training the human performer create miniature causal mechanisms, in the first case in the registers of the machine, in the second in the dendritic nets of the person, which are activated in fulfilling the task.

However, striking though this parallel is, running a Turing Test assesses only the degree to which the engineer has managed to capture the implicit rules immanent in the expert's habit. It cannot test whether those rules are correct. This is Wittgenstein's point in the famous example of the pupil who has learned a rule of addition, and then after a certain point applies it differently (Wittgenstein, 1953, 1980). An expert exterior to the machine or the well-trained pupil assesses correctness. The pupil is behaving like a machine. We must make reference to the form of life within which these processes are occurring to find the criteria for assessing their agreement with norms. This may require consultation of a complex network of social institutions to resolve a question of propriety.

The criteria for correctness no doubt could themselves be expressed as a set of explicit rules, which could be re-expressed as a program and programmed into another computer, during which process they would create yet another layer of miniature causal mechanisms. These mechanisms would mimic the performances of trained judges only if their assessments were habitual, trained into them. Only then would the judges embody miniature causal mechanisms of the appropriate type. If they had not been so habituated they would be followers of rules, not actors behaving in accordance with rules. The psychology of the former, as I have argued, requires the invocation of different ontological type-hierarchies.

At each level of these assessment-hierarchies the basic dichotomy at the heart of this paper reappears. Are the actors following rules or are they acting in accordance with them? Only in the latter case is there a parallel with the computer suitably programmed to do the same job. Those who follow rules know that they are to attend to rules; those that act in accordance with them just possess good habits. I claim that assessment regresses cannot end in cases of 'acting according to a rule' for these cases are indistinguishable from mechanistic causal patterns of behaviour. If this were so, the corresponding performance by a computer would not express the fact that acting in accordance with a rule ensures that what is done is correct.

We can see this more clearly if we consider what it would take to disobey a rule. This can occur only at the level where behaviour can be assessed as following a rule. Otherwise departing from the rule would just be a glitch in the mechanism. A fault in a machine is not the same thing as a fault in a person. When the latter is interpreted as an instance of the former then it escapes censure as improper, immoral or incompetent conduct.

The 'frame problem' revisited

This feature of assessment hierarchies and skilled performances is a special case of the frame problem. To see this, consider the question of whether, in tennis, that way of hitting a ball back and forth across the net is correct. To begin to judge whether a particular way of hitting the ball is correct, the behaviour must be abstracted from a complex and indeterminate background. For example, until recently what a tennis player said when they struck the ball was not part of the game, in that it did not fall under criteria of propriety in tennis. Players' remarks were not occasions for rule-work until Mr John McEnroe's sayings were abstracted from the background of custom and included explicitly in the normative context of the game. The frame problem is just the problem of whether it is possible to frame an activity in such a way that questions about it always have answers which, context by context, settle issues according to local standards. The problem of representing normativity, as it appears in the relationship between the necessities for programming GOFAI machines with the rules of some skilled activity and the background within which that activity is assessable, cannot be solved, save ad hoc and for the moment.

Conclusions

The parallel between a person and surrogate machine is at best partial. This is because something is known by the community of human users that not only is not known by the machines, but could not be known. This epistemological point is the core of this chapter. Machines can mimic people acting in accordance with a rule, acting out of habit, but they cannot mimic people following rules. This is not because it is too hard, but because people use rules for certain jobs, just as they use their arms, racquets, brains and computers for other jobs. In most cases rules are primarily in the possession of the community or institution and only secondarily taken up by individuals. The normative stance to the understanding of human performance is a different 'take' on these activities from studies of the ways the tools people use work in the various tasks of everyday life. According to the proponents of the second cognitive revolution, this is the ontological foundation on which all of psychology must depend.

Bruner's first cognitive revolution invited us to take account of more than any behaviourist possibly could. But the mentalism of his early studies, that spurred the AI engineers to pursue the computational analogy, is set aside in his later narratological writing. To find the narrative conventions at work in a form of life is to make explicit the rules in accordance with which people live. Just how those rules are related to the explicitly formulated rules of conduct of a social group is a question yet to be fully investigated. But we can be sure that when people are busy thinking and acting, the former are not involved in some invisible and shadow version of the latter, but have been replaced by miniature causal mechanisms. When rules are turned into programs and input as bit-strings in registers into silicon machines, or turned into instructions and trained as habits into protoplasmic machines, they cease to have any cognitive standing at all. My brain is no more remembering or deciding or worrying than my racquet is playing tennis or my car steering.

Notes

An earlier version of this paper was given at Aarhus University in August 1996.

1   Bruner has been concerned principally with mistaken conceptions of psychology derived from mythical ideas of the *physical* sciences. The status of biology as a model science is quite another matter; I shall not address the relation of biology and psychology in this chapter.

2   There are of course rivals to GOFAI as computer models of cognition. But I believe that in respect of the issues of intentionality and normativity they are equally flawed. Searle has, for example, upgraded his famous Chinese Room Argument to the Chinese Gym, in which a multiplicity of 'prisoners' perform the coding and decoding tasks of meaningless marks, that was required of the original inhabitant of the Chinese Room. Here the model parodies the architecture of connectionist systems just as effectively as the original thought experiment parodied GOFAI. So for simplicity's sake I focus here on GOFAI, but what I have to say about normativity is equally applicable to connectionist systems.

References

Berkowitz, L. (1996) 'The effects of television on the tendency to aggression'. Paper delivered to the 50th Anniversary Conference of the Korean Psychological Association, Seoul.

Bruner, J.S. (1974) *Beyond the Information Given*. London: Allen & Unwin.

Bruner, J.S. (1979) *On Knowing: Essays for the Left Hand*. Cambridge, MA: Harvard University Press.

Bruner, J.S. (1983) *In Search of Mind: Essays in Autobiography*. New York: Harper & Row.

Bruner, J.S. (1986) *Actual Minds, Possible Worlds*. Cambridge, MA: Harvard University Press.

Bruner, J.S. (1990) *Acts of Meaning*. Cambridge, MA: Harvard University Press.

Bruner, J.S. (1991) 'The narrative construction of reality', *Critical Inquiry*, 18: 1–21.

Bruner, J.S. (1992) 'On searching for Bruner', *Language and Communication*, 12: 75–78.

Clavius, C. (1602) *In sphaeram de Ioannis de Sacro Bosco*. Lyon.

Fodor, J.A. (1975) *The Language of Thought*. New York: Crowell.

Harré, R. (1996) 'AI Rules OK?', *Journal for Empirical and Theoretical Artificial Intelligence*, 8: 109–20.

Ryle, G. (1947) *The Concept of Mind*. London: Hutchinson.

Searle, J. (1983) *Intentionality: An Essay in the Philosophy of Mind*. Cambridge: Cambridge University Press.

Shannon, B. (1991) 'Representations: senses and reasons', *Philosophical Psychology*, 4: 355–74.

Vygotsky, L.S. (1962) *Thought and Language*. Cambridge, MA: MIT Press.

Wittgenstein, L. (1953) *Philosophical Investigations*. Oxford: Blackwell.

Wittgenstein, L. (1980) *Remarks on the Philosophy of Psychology*. 2 Vols. Oxford: Blackwell.

10

TOWARDS A THIRD REVOLUTION IN PSYCHOLOGY: FROM INNER MENTAL REPRESENTATIONS TO DIALOGICALLY-STRUCTURED SOCIAL PRACTICES

John Shotter

It is then that the reader asks that crucial question, 'What's it all about?' But what 'it' is, of course, is not the actual text ... but the text the reader has constructed under its sway. And that is why the actual text needs the subjunctivity that makes it possible for a reader to create a world of his own.

Bruner, *Actual Minds, Possible Worlds*

The present – the concreteness of the present – as a phenomenon to consider, as a *structure*, is for us an unknown planet; so we can neither hold on to it in our memory nor reconstruct it through imagination. We die without knowing what we have lived.

Kundera, *Testaments Betrayed*

Only in the stream of thought and life do words have meaning.

Wittgenstein, *Zettel*

Just as in writing we learn a particular form of letters and then vary it later, so we learn first the stability of things as a norm, which is then subject to alteration.

Wittgenstein, *On Certainty*

One of our tasks in understanding another person is to do justice to the uniqueness of their otherness. But this is not easy, for it is only in the particular, dialogically-structured events that occur between us in fleeting moments, that we can grasp who and what they are. What is involved in making sense of people's behaviour by focusing on its unique and unrepeatable aspects is the central topic of this chapter.

Jerome Bruner refers to the nature of such fleeting moments in his essay, 'Two modes of thought'. There he contrasts the 'paradigmatic mode of thinking', employed in mathematics and logic, with the 'narrative mode of thought', which in its 'imaginative application ... leads to good stories, gripping drama, believable (though not necessarily "true") historical accounts'. Narrative 'strives', he says, 'to put its timeless miracles into the particularities of experience, and to locate the experience in time and place', and he adds that Joyce 'thought of the particularities of the story as epiphanies of the ordinary' (Bruner, 1986: 13). This focus on the innumerable and subtle details in each transitory moment, and on the special nature of the ordinary, will be crucial in what follows.

Milan Kundera, writing on the novel, also emphasizes the significance of the unique and the transitory. He writes:

> It is a *discovery* that might be termed *ontological*: the discovery of the present moment; the discovery of the perpetual coexistence of the banal and the dramatic that underlies our lives.... [I]n a single second, between two lines of dialogue, endless numbers of things occur ... [and] a single second of the present becomes a little infinity. (Kundera, 1993: 131)

In the reality of each present moment, continuously created and re-created as we spontaneously respond to others and otherness around us, is a whole complexly structured set of rich and meaningful relations, a world. The strange and surprisingly comprehensive consequences of these claims will become clear as we proceed. But let me straightaway link them to further aspects of Bruner's recent work to locate him in the current dialogue on the dialogical.

In *Acts of Meaning*, Bruner discusses the problem of how 'cultural psychology', as he calls it, should 'go about posing the problem of the Self'. (1990: 116). He suggests this imposes two related requirements. First, we must focus 'upon the *meanings* in terms of which Self is defined *both* by the individual *and* by the culture in which he or she participates'. But this, he adds, is insufficient. For if we are to grasp how we can each negotiate a 'Self' with those around us, we must also understand the continuously changing 'opportunities for', and 'constraints upon', self-development that we present each other as the living exchanges between us unfold. Thus his second requirement is that we 'attend to the *practices* in which "the meanings of Self" are achieved and put to use', and he adds that a focus on these practices will lead us to a view of the self 'distributed in action, in projects, in practice' (1990: 116–17).

Also relevant here is Bruner's emphasis on what he calls the 'subjunctivizing' strategies (talk of possibility) so often used in literary texts (Bruner, 1986: 26). These strategies are also of great importance in our practices of Self. For, in rendering what we say 'indeterminate', the use of such strategies allows (as Bruner points out, quoting Iser, 1978), '"a spectrum of actualizations" ... [so that] literary texts initiate "performances" of meaning rather than actually formulating meanings themselves' (Bruner, 1986: 25). Such indeterminate expressions allow those communicating to render their meanings uniquely determinate between themselves, to make their meanings fit their own particular circumstances. It is in such performances of meaning, in our bodily living-out of our specific reactions and rejoinders to another's expressions of possibility, that we not only create unique meanings between us, but also co-author new Selves for ourselves. As George Steiner puts it, 'The "otherness" which enters into us makes us other' (1989: 188). Alone, as isolated individuals, we cannot create any new meanings for our actions; such meanings are made in the living activities between ourselves and others. Only those who are 'other' to us can call out from us responses we could never call from ourselves.

Meaning in motion: boundary crossings

The need for new practices of enquiry

Bruner's approach to our practices of Self draws our attention to important issues in these increasingly multicultural times. Almost all of us are now members of more than one active culture. Thus the experience of having to 'cross' cultural boundaries, to 'shift one's stance', to view one's surroundings, fleeting aspect by fleeting aspect, from more than a single perspective, has become 'normal'. We have now to make sense of our surroundings, while continually being ourselves 'in motion'. But how should academics and intellectuals respond to the dialogical, aspectival circumstances in which we now live in order to heed the 'practices of Self' that Bruner outlines? Can we apply our old and well-tried methods to this new topic? Or must we invent novel methods, different modes of enquiry?

Our current intellectual methods require us to set ourselves apart from those we study and view them as if from afar. We aspire to look upon their activities as already completed achievements, aiming to predict the future by finding regularities in the past. But can we any longer even pretend to do this? Should we not find a more participatory way in which to relate ourselves to the phenomena of our studies, one that allows a better awareness of our own relations to, and involvement in, what we are studying? Must we not recognize the unfinished, incomplete, ongoing nature of all of our engagements?

Bruner and Kundera remind us that our current methods are monological and individualistic, and that we moderns think we are fully ourselves only when set over against our surroundings as solitary thinkers. But they also show that we import mythic abstractions of our own making into our accounts of what happens around us. It is as if we observed some turn-taking game – say tennis – and, failing to realize that the players act in response to each other, tried to explain their activities as if they originated solely from within them as self-contained individuals (Sampson, 1993).

It is the hegemony of this method over us – that of trying to explain the causes of events in terms of our own abstractions from them – that I seek to undo in what follows. Instead of arguing like Rom Harré (this volume) that it is a second, discursive revolution that we now require, I suggest that we abandon these individualistic and monological, theory-driven methods. Only if we institute a third revolution of a dialogical kind, one that suggests wholly new intellectual practices and institutions to us, can we begin to fashion forms of enquiry that will do justice to the uniqueness of the being of others. But first, let me recount some history, for such institutional changes have their own problems, as Bruner's own history illustrates (Bruner, 1983).

The institutional dominance of the paradigmatic

I first met Jerry in 1972 when I was in the Psychology Department in Nottingham, soon after he came to England to the newly established Watts Professorship at Oxford. Our paths had already become intertwined, as I had earlier arranged for my then research student, David Wood, to do postdoctoral work with Jerry in Harvard (they later produced Wood, Bruner and Ross, 1976). Nottingham at that time had a lively child development research unit established by John and Elizabeth Newson (its work is well represented in Newson and Newson, 1975). From 1969, prompted by the feeling that Chomsky's (1957, 1965) brilliant analyses of linguistic structure were somehow beside the point to the real life of language acquisition, we focused on detailed videotape analysis of mother–child interaction, looking at mothers showing their children, of 10 to 20 months, how to put shapes into form boards. This work was pioneered by Susan Treble (later Susan Gregory; see Shotter and Gregory, 1976). Influenced by Vygotsky's (1962) notions of instruction, mediation, and the internalization of the social, and by Merleau-Ponty's (1962) account of intersubjectivity, we discussed the amazing social, joint, relational (or 'distributed' as Bruner (1996: 154) now calls them) phenomena that were created between caregiver and child, for which neither could be seen as individually responsible.

But we were still somewhat at sea, aware that we were not doing experiments or testing hypotheses as such, that we were not able to present measurements or 'objective data'. It was clear that there was something here of great importance not captured in previous, more hard-nosed approaches, but we did not know how publicly to present what we were observing. We badly lacked a leader and protector. Jerry's arrival in England gave us the focus we needed. The Developmental Psychology Section of the British Psychology Society was formed. Nottingham, Cambridge, Edinburgh and Oxford combined to run a kind of travelling workshop/seminar. Suddenly, the field of social-developmental psychology was up and running, and – to those of us within it between 1972 and 1976 – it was the most intellectually exciting arena in the whole of psychology. As Bruner remarks in his autobiography, the workshop/seminar meetings 'shine in memory!' (Bruner, 1983: 166). But something went wrong, and for 20 years the movement lost the shine it is only now beginning to regain. It succumbed to tendencies at work, not just in academic psychology, but also in the institutions of our modernist, Western societies at large: the repression of the dialogical by the monological, the practical by the theoretical, the particular by the universal, and the unique moment by the repeatable.

Acutely aware of the dialogical, the concrete and the particular, and of their tension with the mainstream, Bruner has none the less given expression to them in his writings 'for the left-hand' as he calls them (Bruner, 1962/1979). However, he has never allowed both 'right-' and 'left-handed' sides of his intellectual character to be equally present in his professional thinking at once. Instead of pursuing the conversation with otherness, instead of seeing it as a continual source of new possibilities, he has always switched to seeing it as a 'problem-requiring-a-solution'. In other words, he has always privileged the paradigmatic over the narrative mode of thought, quelling the tendency to disorderly playfulness in favour of order, seeking the mastery of meaning by form, while never fully articulating the consequences of so doing. Thus, although Bruner has continually identified important, new departures for our investigations in academic psychology – new topics to which we have all, sooner or later, come to pay attention – he has also too quickly sought to corral his own unruly, left-handed encounters with the particularities of otherness. He has not dwelt long enough on their strangeness. To use his own words in describing the paradigmatic mode of thought, he has sought 'to transcend the particular by higher and higher reaching for abstraction', to privilege explanation over description (Bruner, 1986: 13). As a result, he has also drawn back from giving us the dialogical, relational psychology I think we need – a psychology in which both left and right hand work in concerted action.

Psychology technicalized and demoralized

We find Bruner's unruly 'left-handed' tendencies at work at the beginning of his 1990 book, *Acts of Meaning*. It opens with strong criticism of 'the cognitive revolution' – the most long-lived and successful of all of psychology's revolutions, which Bruner himself helped engineer (Baars, 1986; Gardner, 1987). He points out that its original impulse was 'to bring "mind" back into the human sciences after a long cold winter of objectivism'. But he proceeds to remark that cognitive psychology 'has now been diverted into issues that are marginal to the impulse that brought it into being' (Bruner, 1990: 1). For, what he, George Miller and others sought to realize in establishing the Harvard Center for Cognitive Studies in 1960, was 'to establish meaning as the central concept of psychology – not stimuli and responses, not overtly observable behavior, not biological drives and their transformation, but meaning' (Bruner, 1990: 2). Thus, in attempting to bring 'mind' back into psychology, Bruner did not just want to add 'a little mentalism' to behaviourism, but something much more profound: to discover and describe 'what meaning-making processes were implicated' in people's encounters with the world, 'to prompt psychology to joining forces with its sister interpretative disciplines in the humanities and the social sciences' (1990: 2). But even in the early stages of the cognitive revolution, he laments, the 'emphasis began shifting from "meaning" to "information", from the *construction* of meaning to the *processing* of information. These are profoundly different matters' (1990: 4). And in *Acts of Meaning*, and also *The Culture of Education* (1996), he begins to outline how he thinks that original impulse can be recaptured and revitalized. For, as he sees it, the revolution in psychology 'has been technicalized in a manner that even undermines that original impulse' (1990: 1).

But how can it be recaptured? Precisely by attending to many points that Bruner himself has made, but without, I suggest, succumbing to his temptation to turn too early to the requirements of our current institutionalized academic practices. In other words, instead of trying to *explain* what makes our performances of meaning possible by theories, we must turn to another approach, one to do with achieving a much more direct form of understanding, the kind of relational understanding in fact at work, spontaneously, in our everyday practices.

The movement of meaning in dialogic encounters

The performance of variational meanings

The kind of understanding at issue can be grasped from a story Bruner relates from Italo Calvino's *Invisible Cities* (1972, quoted in Bruner, 1986: 35–7). Marco Polo tells Kublai Khan of a stone bridge, which he describes stone by stone. Kublai Khan gets impatient and asks what supports the stones? 'The bridge is not supported by one stone or another', Marco answers, 'but by the line of the arch that they form.' 'Why do you speak to me of the stones?', Kublai Khan demands. 'Without stones there is no arch', Polo replies, for the arch is in the *relations* between the stones. As Bruner points out, in her reading of the story, the reader herself: 'goes from stones to arches to the significance of arches to some broader reality – goes back and forth between them in attempting finally to construct a sense of the story, its form, its meaning' (1986: 36). Sometimes in reading stories, we move from their particularities to something more general, to a structure constituted by the relations between them. As Wittgenstein might have said, we grasp something which is 'shown' in the text rather than explicitly 'said'. But, what kind of textual structures invite such a kind of understanding? And how is it achieved?

It is, Bruner claims, texts of a *narrative* kind that allow us to gain a sense of otherness that is strange and novel to us. In reading such texts, we begin to construct a 'virtual text' of our own. It is as if readers

> were embarking on a journey without maps.... [Where] in time, the new journey becomes a thing in itself, however much its initial shape was borrowed from the past. The virtual text becomes a story of its own, its very strangeness only a contrast with the reader's sense of the ordinary.... [This] is why the actual text needs the subjunctivity that makes it possible for a reader to create a world of his [or her] own. (Bruner, 1986: 36–7)

To repeat: It is the way in which such texts 'subjunctivize reality', by 'trafficking in human possibilities rather than settled certainties', that makes possible the co-creation of such virtual worlds by authors and their readers.

Such trafficking in possibilities is occasioned, Bruner suggests, by making use of the conventions, maxims and regularities constitutive of our cultural being, though he certainly does not have in mind the mechanical or repetitive observance of such rules. On the contrary, the existence of conventions and maxims provides 'us with the means of violating them for purposes of *meaning more than we say* or for meaning other than what we say (as in irony, for example) or for meaning less than we say' (Bruner, 1986: 26). The stability of this background, and the possibility of deviation, is emphasized again in *Acts of Meaning*, where Bruner comments on his own efforts to describe a people's 'folk psychology' as follows:

> I wanted to show how human beings, in interacting with one another, form a sense of the canonical and ordinary as a background against which to interpret and give narrative meaning to breaches in and deviations from 'normal' states of the human condition. (Bruner, 1990: 67)

It is the very creation of indeterminacy and uncertainty that makes it possible for people to co-create new and unique meanings as their dialogical activities unfold. 'To mean in this way', suggests Bruner, 'by the use of such intended violations ... is to create "gaps" and to recruit presuppositions to fill them' (1986: 26). Indeed, our unique responses to our own unique circumstances are carried by the subtle variations in how we use these constitutive forms of response as we bodily react to what goes on around us. This is what it is for us to *perform meaning*. Our 'performed meanings' are 'shown' in our ways of 'going on' with others around us in practice.

I shall call such joint, first-time meanings – meanings which are expressive of the 'world' of a unique 'I' – *variational* meanings. For they are only intelligible as variations within the already existing, ongoing, background flow of activity constitutive of our current forms of life. Bakhtin calls such events *'once-occurrent events of Being'* (1993: 2).[1] The very indeterminacy in a narrative text allows 'readers' to render their meanings uniquely determinate themselves, to make their meanings relate to their own particular circumstances.

Bruner's emphasis on the living 'playing out' of understanding is central to Wittgenstein's whole philosophy, and to Bakhtin's (1981) and Voloshinov's (1986) dialogical approach to speech communication (Shotter and Billig, 1998). What I want to pursue further here is the nonreferential, nonrepresentational, nonconceptual, 'moving', 'poetic' nature of these practical forms of meaning and understanding.

In exploring how we perform meaning in practice, in the context of a discussion of 'intention', Wittgenstein suggests that we might feel tempted to say that an intention 'can do what it is supposed to only by containing an extremely faithful picture of what it intends'. He continues, however,

> That that too does not go far enough, because a picture, whatever it may be, can be variously interpreted; hence this picture too in its turn stands isolated. When one has the picture in view by itself it is suddenly dead, and it is as if something had been taken away from it, which had given it life before ... it remains

isolated, it does not point outside itself to a reality beyond. Now one says: 'Of course, it is not the picture itself that intends, but we who use it to intend something'. But if this intending, this meaning, is in turn something that is done with the picture, then I cannot see why it has to involve a human being. The process of digestion can also be studied as a chemical process, independently of whether it takes place in a living being. We want to say 'Meaning is surely essentially a mental process, a process of conscious life, not of dead matter' ... And now it seems to us as if intending could not be any process at all, of any kind whatever. – For what we are dissatisfied with here is the grammar of *process*, not with the specific kind of process. – It could be said: we should call any process 'dead' in this sense. (Wittgenstein, 1981: §236)

And he adds: 'It might almost be said: "Meaning *moves*, whereas a process stands still"' (1981: §237).

Meaning as movement

Wittgenstein sees meaning, not as a cognitive process of statically 'picturing' something, but as part of a dynamic, interactive process in which embodied agents continuously react in a living, practical way to each other and to their circumstances. Thus, even as a person is speaking, the responses of the others around her influence her moment by moment in shaping her unfolding talk. In such circumstances, we inevitably do much more than talk 'about' something; we continuously live out changing 'ways of relating' of our own creation; or as Wittgenstein would say, we create particular 'forms of life'.[2]

Thus, we perform meaning in practice as we tack back and forth between the particular words of a strange, newly encountered, meaning-indeterminate text, and the whole of the ongoing, unsayable, dynamic cultural history in which we all are in different ways immersed. In 'bridging the gaps' with our responsive movements as we read, we creatively 'move' over what Bruner (1986) calls the 'landscapes' of a 'virtual text'. And these 'ways of moving' of our spontaneous creation are what is general in our reading, what we can 'carry over' into other activities. They are ways of 'orchestrating' our ever-changing relations to our past, our future, others around us, our immediate physical surroundings, authorities, our cultural history, our dreams for the future – ways of relating ourselves in these different directions perceptually, cognitively, in action, in memory, and so on (Vygotsky, 1978: 1986). We can 'carry over' into new spheres of activity what we 'carried in' in our initial ways of responding, bodily, to the text.

Such meaning-indeterminate texts, viewed as calling from us new responsive movements rather than as being *about* something in the world, are a special part *of* the world to which we cannot but relate in a living way. So, although such texts may seem to be similar to those purporting to be 'about' something – texts with a representational-referential meaning that 'picture' states of affairs in the world – their meaning does not reside in such picturing. We must relate to them differently. For their meaning is more practical, pre-theoretical, pre-conceptual; they provide us with a style of knowing, rather than with knowledge of something in particular. Such texts are exemplary *for*, not *of*, certain ways of going on. They exemplify new ways of relating to our circumstances; they provide not representations *of* things already in existence, but new poetic images *through* which to make sense of things.

Consider Susan Sontag's remarks on the creative effects of works of art upon us:

> To become involved with a work of art entails, to be sure, the experience of detaching oneself from the world. But the work of art itself is also a vibrant, magical, and exemplary object which returns us to the world in some way more open and enriched.... Raymond Bayer has written: 'What each and every aesthetic object imposes on us, in appropriate rhythms, is a unique and singular formula for the flow of our energy.... Every work of art embodies a principle of proceeding, of stopping, of scanning; an image of energy or relaxation, the imprint of a caressing or destroying hand which is [the artist's] alone'. We can call this the physiognomy of the work, or its rhythm, or, as I would rather do, its style. (1962: 28)

Such a 'moving' form of communication not only makes a unique, previously unwitnessed other or otherness present to us, but enables a new 'way of going on' that only *it* can call from us. But this requires us to encounter its distinct nature in all its complex detail. If we turn too quickly to its *explanation*, we miss what it alone can teach us. And the turn is pointless, for we literally do not yet know *what* we are talking about.

Only if we enter into an extended, unfolding set of living relations with an other (say, another person, or with a picture like Van Gogh's *Sunflowers*, or a text) can we come to a full grasp of what it means to us. And what we sense in such a set of relations, we sense *from inside* those relations. As Wittgenstein puts it, when a picture has meaning for us, it is as if 'we looked at a picture so as to enter into it and the objects in it surrounded us like real ones.... In this way, when we intend, we are surrounded by our intention's pictures, and we are inside them' (1981: §233). Indeed, he says elsewhere:

> It often strikes us as if in grasping meaning the mind made small rudimentary movements, like someone irresolute who does not know which way to go – i.e., it tentatively reviews the field of possible applications. (1981: §33)

In going up to someone to meet them, in writing about an experience, or in intensely studying a work of art there is an oscillating, shifting, fluid inner complexity that until recently psychology has ignored.

Describing (and explaining?) the dialogical – 'the difficulty here is: to stop'

The temptation to explain

Why has psychology ignored the fleeting fullness of the present? Because it is terribly difficult to focus on the details of a practice in the course of doing it. Crucial in our early work in Nottingham was our use of videotape recordings. We watched the same transitory moments over and over again to capture ever more detail, and once we had learned to see such events on videotape, we learned to see them in the everyday world as well. In the same way, ethnomethodology could not have established itself without audiotape recorders. For crucial encounters with each other and our surroundings flit by so quickly and are distributed between us to such an extent that we have no distinct sense of their effect on us or our effect on them. It is thus difficult to focus on the performance of meaning as a social practice, to see the 'events of meaning' as they are. Thus, we assume that there must be something mysterious within them that cannot be observed and we *theorize* about their nature. This is where Wittgenstein's work is so important, for he points to how, in our ordinary social practices, we draw each other's attention to aspects of our own on-going practices. Attending to previously unnoticed aspects of our practices is the major way we elaborate and refine them. Indeed, this is crucial in our learning such practices in the first place. Hence Wittgenstein's admonition 'don't think but look!' when we feel tempted to assume that our practices *must* have a certain character to them (1953: §66).

Although the task of looking for the fleeting, once-occurrent details of our interactions is not easy, it is the crux. For, as Wittgenstein puts it, the problems we face are not empirical problems to be solved by giving *explanations*:

> they are solved, rather, by looking into the workings of our language, and that in such a way as to make us recognize those workings: *in spite of* an urge to misunderstand them. The problems are solved, not by giving new information, but by arranging what we have already known. (1953: §109)

It is not that we seek the *nature* of an object already in existence, but how we ourselves *constitute* our relations to each other and to our surroundings. We want a better understanding of our own forms of life, for so far in our everyday dealings with each other they have passed us by unnoticed. Thus, for Wittgenstein, our task is not to imagine, and then to investigate empirically the 'mechanisms' within us, which we suppose responsible for our communicative abilities. Instead, we must *describe* how in fact we do it in practice, for after all, meaning is a human achievement. Everything of importance in our practices of meaning must always have been in some way available to us. Wittgenstein writes, 'How do sentences do it? Don't you know? For nothing is hidden' (1953: §435).

But, even if 'nothing is hidden', how can we describe our practices if we cannot view them from outside, if we have only our being within them? All we can do is point out further, previously unnoticed characteristics from within. And we can only do it with the indeterminate, 'poetic' forms of talk we ordinarily use in everyday activities. That is, we can do it with a great deal of first-person, once-occurrent, variational, dialogical talk (Shotter, 1996, 1998). Thus, to gain a better grasp of our practices, we must be content with merely pointing to their crucial aspects from within our own ongoing involvement in them. And, though it is extremely difficult to accept this fact, once such pointing out has achieved its practical purpose, there is nothing more that can be said with any clarity or distinctness. Thus, the essential aspects of a practice cannot be explained, but only described – that is, pointed out in the course of our talk about it – for intelligible explanations can be provided only from within the confines of already established forms of life with their associated language-games. Hence Wittgenstein's remark:

> You must bear in mind that the language-game is so to say something unpredictable. I mean; it is not based on grounds. It is not reasonable (or unreasonable). It is there – like our life. (1969: §559)

Once we go beyond the confines of established language-games, we are again in the realm of the indeterminate, where our meanings are ambiguous and can be made determinate only by 'playing them out' within a practice. Our language-games cannot themselves be explained, for they set the terms in which explanation is possible.

Explaining joint action: a 'theory of mind'

I think Bruner finds the temptation to explain hard to resist, for he seems to find the need to be a scientist hard to resist also. Thus, to apply what he says about the paradigmatic or logico-scientific mode of thought to his own tendencies, he ultimately 'seeks to transcend the particular by higher and higher reaching for abstraction, and in the end disclaims in principle any explanatory value at all where the particular is concerned' (Bruner, 1986: 13). We can see this at many points in his work, but nowhere is this tendency more apparent than in his treatment of *joint action* (a topic in which I have a special interest; see Shotter, 1980, 1984, 1993a, 1993b, 1995).

In *Acts of Meaning*, Bruner writes that:

> The division between an 'inner' world of experience and an 'outer' one that is autonomous creates three domains, each of which requires a different form of interpretation.... In the first domain we are in some manner 'responsible' for the course of events; in the third not.
>
> There is a second sphere of events that is problematic, comprising some indeterminate mix of the first and third. (Bruner, 1990: 40–1)

In social theory, we have called the first, the sphere of *action*, to be explained by giving people's *reasons* for their actions, and we have called the third sphere *behaviour*, to be explained by its *causes*. Elsewhere, I have called Bruner's second sphere *joint action*, and related it to Bakhtin's account of dialogically structured activity, claiming that it is a distinct sphere of activity *sui generis* (Shotter, 1984, 1993a, 1993b; see also Bakhtin, 1981). Bruner, however, writes that this second sphere:

> requires a more elaborate form of interpretation in order to allocate proper causal shares to individual agency and to 'nature'. If folk psychology embodies the interpretative principles of the first domain, and folk physics-cum-biology the third, then the second is ordinarily seen to be governed either by some form of magic or, in contemporary Western culture, by the scientism of physicalist psychology or Artificial Intelligence. (Bruner, 1990: 41)

In other words, Bruner not only misses the special dialogically structured nature of the second sphere, but assimilates the unique to the repeatable, the particular to the universal, and the practical to the theoretical.

Rather than treating events within the second realm as unique occurrences – new bodily responses that might originate new language-games within which new Selves might be co-created – Bruner treats them as something to be *explained* by extending our 'folk psychology' into what could be called a 'folk human science' (Bruner, 1990: 67). This involves accepting the everyday mental terms we use to talk of psychological matters in our culture, and seeking to discover empirically how we live out our lives in these terms and how children acquire a knowledge of them. Thus, he views us as structuring our psychological lives in terms of 'beliefs' and 'desires', in the following sense:

> we *believe* that the world is organized in certain ways, that we *want* certain things, that some things *matter* more than others, and so on .... [W]e also believe that people's beliefs and desires become sufficiently coherent and well organized to merit being called 'commitments' or 'ways of life'.... [And] personhood is itself a constituent concept of our folk psychology. (Bruner, 1990: 39)

And to account for how we develop such a 'folk psychology', how we make our 'entry into meaning', Bruner hypothesizes that even very young children to some extent possess a 'theory of mind'. He writes that:

> Nobody doubts that four- or six-year-olds have more mature theories of mind that can encompass what others who are not engaged with them are thinking or desiring. The point, rather, is that even before language takes over as the instrument of interaction one cannot interact *humanly* with others without some protolinguistic 'theory of mind'. (Bruner, 1990: 75)

Bruner is not the only originator of these proposals, as he is the first to admit. Consequently, the fact that they are now at the heart of a major tradition of empirical research in child psychology, cannot be credited wholly to him. Indeed, we can see how the institutional structure of our current academic and intellectual methods and practices 'requires' such notions. Such research is deemed necessary because it is assumed that, as a leading source in the field puts it,

> perceptions, emotions, physiological states, and more – are a part of the web of psychological constructs used [by adults and children] to understand and explain action and mind.... [They] are centrally organized by consideration of the actor's thoughts and desires. These two sorts of generic mental states are, of course, internal and unobservable. But unobservable mental states can often be inferred. (Bartsch and Wellman, 1995: 6)

And it is further taken for granted that adults' everyday talk 'about' mental states, such as beliefs and desires, is unproblematically definitive of their 'commonsense conception of mind' (Bartsch and Wellman, 1995: 5). Given these assumptions, children's everyday talk is inspected for what it reveals about their knowledge of such theoretical states, in themselves and in others. A typical hypothesis under study is the suggestion that 'children go from understanding subjective connections to a later understanding of representational mental states' (Bartsch and Wellman, 1995: 14), as if the 'proper' or 'natural' set of developmental stages was 'already there' awaiting discovery.

Dwelling on joint action instead of trying to explain it

If Wittgenstein is right, this kind of research is utterly misguided. Our beliefs and desires are not, as Bartsch and Wellman claim, 'of course, internal and unobservable', but are in fact *shown* in our acting. And what we 'show' in our actions cannot be explained: it is part of the background that makes explanation possible. We have just not yet taught ourselves to see such fleeting 'showings'. That is perhaps more easily said than done. For, in practice, the temptation to solve the puzzles we face by seeking explanations is not easy to avoid, for we do not recognize the character of the puzzles we face.

Exploring the temptation to invoke hidden mental processes in the explanation of meaning, Wittgenstein remarks:

> the difficulty – I might say – is not that of finding [a] solution but rather that of recognizing as the solution something that looks as if it were only a preliminary to it.... This is connected, I believe, with our wrongly expecting an explanation, whereas the solution of the difficulty is a description, if we give it the right place in our considerations. If we dwell upon it, and do not try to get beyond it. The difficulty here is: to stop. (1981: §314)

Instead of attempting to see behind or beyond events or phenomena, casting them as indicators of something hidden, we must dwell on them, looking ceaselessly over them, responding to them, bodily and dialogically, so that we continuously create within ourselves, not new insights, but new responses and reactions – new language-games, new forms of life, and, as a result, new *movements* of thought. It is in such reactions and their refinements, rather than a protolinguistic theory of mind, that we find the origins and beginnings of children's entry into meaning. As Wittgenstein wrote, 'It is so difficult to find the *beginning*. Or better: it is difficult to begin at the beginning. And not to try to go further back' (1969: §471).

If we express ourselves, not by simply reproducing the 'normal' background activities constitutive of our form of life, but by deviating from them in unique, joint action, our task cannot be to develop 'a more elaborate form of interpretation in order to allocate proper causal shares to individual agency and to "nature"' (Bruner, 1990: 41). Instead, we must simply attend to the detailed character of such beginnings, and not be tempted to explain them in theoretical terms. This is the importance of Wittgenstein's way of talking, the point of his remarks, which aim, he says, to change our *'way of looking at things'* (1953: §144), to give 'prominence to distinctions which our ordinary forms of language easily make us overlook' (1953: §132). He is not concerned 'to hunt out new facts', but 'to *understand* something that is already in plain view. For *this* is what we seem in some sense not to understand' (1953: §89). And, through his 'poetic' remarks, he wants to draw our attention to 'observations which no one has doubted, but which have escaped remark only because they are always before our eyes' (1953: §415).

What Wittgenstein draws to our attention is that, strangely, we can gain the new kind of *practical understanding* required by using many of the self-same methods we use in our everyday lives, such as the methods adults use to 'instruct' children how to be the kind of persons required in our community (Vygotsky, 1978, 1986; Shotter, 1984, 1993a, 1993b). So although his methods are as many and various as those we use in life itself, they do in fact have something in common: they all work in just the same way as our 'directive', 'instructive', 'organizational' and 'educative' forms of talk in everyday life. For example, we 'give commands' ('Do this!', 'Don't do that!'); we 'point things out' to people ('Look at this!'); 'remind' them ('Think what happened last time'); 'change their perspective' ('Look at it like this …'); 'organize' their behaviour ('First, take a right, then …'), and so on. All these *instructive* forms of talk 'move' us to do something we would not otherwise do. In 'gesturing' or 'pointing' towards something, they 'move' us to relate ourselves to our circumstances in new ways, to 'orchestrate' our relations to each other and our surroundings in novel and complex ways. The key feature of these forms of talk – what gives them their life – is their *gestural* function in 'calling out' new, dialogical responses from us, responses of a kind shared by others around us, as we spontaneously 'answer to' events occurring around us. These are the reactions, the new beginnings, from which more complicated 'ways of going on' can be developed.

Conclusions

In social theory, two major spheres of activity have occupied our attention: individual *actions*, and *behaviour*. But now, dialogical phenomena (what Bruner focuses on as narrative), occurring in a sphere between these other two, are coming to constitute a distinct realm of activity requiring its own distinct attention. Such phenomena cannot be accounted for simply as *actions* (for they are not done by individuals and cannot be explained by giving a person's *reasons*), nor can they be treated as 'just happening' *events* (to be explained by discovering their *causes*). As Bruner himself points out, such events occur in a chaotic zone of indeterminacy between the other two spheres, and, as such, occurrences in this sphere do not seem amenable to any clear characterizations at all. Yet, although Bruner is at pains to point out that these joint, first-time, variational activities consist of 'some indeterminate mix of the other two', that is, of actions or happenings, he does not in the end treat them as a distinct realm of events, as an otherness to be endlessly dwelt on if justice is to be done to its uniqueness. In his 'folk human science', he seeks a specific, explanatory account of this in-between realm.

In celebrating Jerome Bruner's distinguished career, I have sought to display what I see as some of the contradictory and irresolvable tendencies in the twists and turns it has taken – twists and turns, I might add, Bruner has made in response to the contradictory tendencies in the institutional practices in academic psychology and the rest of the social sciences. However, one feels the full contradictory nature of these tendencies only if, like Bruner, one lives one's professional psychology in a morally engaged way. Clearly, Bruner does take psychology very seriously, and not just as an academic discipline, but as one of our hopes in passing beyond 'the malaise of futurelessness ... the unspoken despair in which we are now living' (Bruner, 1986: 148–9). Thus on the horizon of his understandings, determining how he positions himself in psychology, is his concern with our human condition. Hence he worries about psychology becoming too technicalized, for it will then make us once again treat the cultural knowledge of ordinary people as:

> *just* a set of self-assuaging illusions, [rather than as] the culture's beliefs and working hypotheses about what makes it possible and fulfilling for people to live together, even with great personal sacrifice. (Bruner, 1990: 32)

This is why he sees the denigration or neglect of our cultural knowledge as disastrous.

In outlining the strangeness of our cultural activities, Bruner draws our attention not only to the realm of first-time, variational events, to our violations of the normal, but also to the fact that such 'violations' only have their significance against the constitutive background of our normative activities. If we lose our grasp on this background, then anything goes! We will not only lack a shared basis on which to judge the adequacy and relevance of people's claims to knowledge, but we will lose the basis on which we can proclaim ourselves as beings worthy of respect and civility. For us to acquire and retain a grasp of its nature, to achieve insight into our practices of Self, is not easy. To repeat: Instead of a theoretical, explanatory account, we need first to come to a practical understanding of the joint, dialogical nature of our lives together. And if we are to do that, if we are to see the ways in which we 'violate' the norms of our everyday institutions, then we must also violate the norms of our professional institutions. And this is what Bruner has done over and over again, while at the same time always wanting to make amends while still, luckily, not quite being able to prevent himself from yet further violations.

Notes

1 Bakhtin writes

> An act of our activity, of our actual experiencing, is like a two-faced Janus. It looks in two opposite directions: it looks at the objective domain of culture and at the never-repeatable uniqueness of actually lived and experienced life. But there is no unitary and unique plane where both faces would mutually determine each other in relation to a single unity. It is the once-occurrent event of Being in the process of actualization that can constitute this unique unity; all that which is theoretical and aesthetic must be determined as a constituent moment in the once-occurrent event of Being. (1993: 2)

2 Intertwined into our forms of life are different 'language-games' (by this famous term Wittgenstein means 'to bring into prominence the fact that the speaking of language is part of an activity, or a form of life' (1953: §23)). The playful, game-like nature of our forms of talk is most apparent when we are learning, or developing, new language-games. At such times, when meanings are vague, gestures and other more bodily forms of expression are particularly important. We cannot but be spontaneously responsive to the bodily activities of those around us, and are thus always in a living relation to our surroundings. Indeed, such relations constitute the source of all our later, more deliberate activities. We can thus agree with Wittgenstein when he says, 'The origin and the primitive form of the language game is a reaction; only from this can more complicated forms develop. Language – I want to say – is a refinement, "in the beginning was the deed"' (1980: 31).

References

Baars, B.J. (1986) *The Cognitive Revolution in Psychology*. New York: Guilford Press.

Bakhtin, M.M. (1981) *The Dialogical Imagination*, ed. M. Holquist, trans. C. Emerson and M. Holquist. Austin, TX: University of Texas Press.

Bakhtin, M.M. (1993) *Toward a Philosophy of the Act*, M. Holquist (ed.), with trans. and notes by Vadim Lianpov. Austin, TX: University of Texas Press.

Bartsch, K. and Wellman, H.W. (1995) *Children Talk about the Mind*. New York: Oxford University Press.

Bruner, J.S. (1962/1979) *On Knowing: Essays for the Left Hand*. Cambridge, MA: Belknap Press.

Bruner, J.S. (1983) *In Search of Mind: Essays in Autobiography*. New York: Harper & Row.

Bruner, J.S. (1986) *Actual Minds, Possible Worlds*. Cambridge, MA: Harvard University Press.

Bruner, J.S. (1990) *Acts of Meaning*. Cambridge, MA: Harvard University Press.

Bruner, J.S. (1996) *The Culture of Education*. Cambridge, MA: Harvard University Press.

Calvino, Italo (1972) *Invisible Cities*, trans. William Weaver. New York: Harcourt, Brace Jovanovich.

Chomsky, N. (1957) *Syntactic Structures*. The Hague: Mouton.

Chomsky, N. (1965) *Aspects of the Theory of Syntax*. Cambridge, MA: MIT Press.

Gardner, H. (1987) *The Mind's New Science: A History of the Cognitive Revolution*. New York: HarperCollins.

Iser, W. (1978) *The Act of Reading*. Baltimore, MD: Johns Hopkins Press.

Kundera, M. (1993) *Testaments Betrayed: An Essay in Nine Parts*. New York: Harper Perennial.

Merleau-Ponty, M. (1962) *Phenomenology of Perception*, trans. C. Smith. London: Routledge & Kegan Paul.

Newson, J. and Newson, E. (1975) 'Intersubjectivity and the transmission of culture', *Bulletin of the British Psychological Society*, 28: 437–46.

Sampson, E.E. (1993) *Celebrating the Other: A Dialogic Account of Human Nature*. Boulder, CO: Westview Press.

Shotter, J. (1980) 'Action, joint action, and intentionality', in M. Brenner (ed.), *The Structure of Action*. Oxford: Blackwell.

Shotter, J. (1984) *Social Accountability and Selfhood*. Oxford: Blackwell.

Shotter, J. (1993a) *Cultural Politics of Everyday Life: Social Constructionism, Rhetoric, and Knowing of the Third Kind*. Milton Keynes: Open University Press.

Shotter, J. (1993b) *Conversational Realities: Constructing Life through Language*. London: Sage.

Shotter, J. (1995) 'In conversation: joint action, shared intentionality, and the ethics of conversation', *Theory and Psychology*, 5: 49–73.

Shotter, J. (1996) 'Living in a Wittgensteinian world: beyond theory to a poetics of practices', *Journal for the Theory of Social Behavior*, 26: 293–311.

Shotter, J. (1998) 'Social construction as social poetics: Oliver Sacks and the case of Dr P.', in B. Bayer and J. Shotter (eds), *Reconstructing the Psychological Subject: Bodies, Practices and Technologies*. London: Sage.

Shotter, J. and Billig, M. (1988) 'A Bakhtinian psychology: from out of the heads of individuals and into the dialogues between them', in M. Mayerfield and M. Gardiner (eds), *Bakhtin and the Human Sciences: No Last Words*. London: Sage.

Shotter, J. and Gregory, S. (1976) 'On first gaining the idea of oneself as a person', in R. Harré (ed.), *Life Sentences*. Chichester: Wiley.

Sontag, S. (1962) *Against Interpretation and Other Essays*. New York, NY: A Delta Book.

Steiner, G. (1989) *Real Presences*. Chicago, IL: University of Chicago Press.

Voloshinov, V.N. (1986) *Marxism and the Philosophy of Language*, trans. L. Matejka and I.R. Titunik. Cambridge, MA: Harvard University Press.

Vygotsky, L.S. (1962) *Thought and Language*, ed. and trans. E. Hanfmann and G. Vakar. Cambridge, MA: MIT Press.

Vygotsky, L.S. (1978) *Mind in Society: The Development of Higher Psychological Processes*, ed. M. Cole, V. John-Steiner, S. Scribner and E. Souberman. Cambridge, MA: Harvard University Press.

Vygotsky, L.S. (1986) *Thought and Language*. A. Kozulin (trans. and ed.). Cambridge, MA: MIT Press.

Wittgenstein, L. (1953) *Philosophical Investigations*. Oxford: Blackwell.

Wittgenstein, L. (1969) *On Certainty*. Oxford: Blackwell.

Wittgenstein, L. (1980) *Culture and Value*, introduction G. von Wright, trans. P. Winch. Oxford: Blackwell.

Wittgenstein, L. (1981) *Zettel*, 2nd edn, ed. G.E.M. Anscombe and G. von Wright. Oxford: Blackwell.

Wood, D., Bruner, J.S. and Ross, G. (1976) 'The role of tutoring in problem solving', *Journal of Child Psychology and Psychiatry*, 17: 89–100.

11

MEMORY, IDENTITY
AND THE FUTURE
OF CULTURAL PSYCHOLOGY

David Bakhurst

I begin with two examples. The first is a case of experiential memory.[1] Whenever I hear the opening of the Beatles' *All my Lovin'* I experience an uncanny sensation of the past. I am transported to my early childhood in the 1960s, when the song was new. Unlike paradigmatic cases of experiential remembering, this memory does not involve determinate imagery or the reliving of specific events. The sensation is a seemingly unmediated presentiment of the past; one so bare that my present self cannot impose itself upon it and domesticate it. I am somehow able to recapture the mood of how things were, to be fleetingly 'back then'. This brings me nostalgic pleasure, tinged with sadness, as one might feel coming across a scrap of handwriting of a long-dead relative.

This case brings out the close relation between memory and identity. Just as the sensation reminds me intimately of who I am, so the example reminds us that our identity depends on an enduring stream of self-conscious experience that rests, in turn, on memory's power to place present experience in a temporal continuum.[2] Our personal histories are histories of lived experience. This fact is central to our understanding of ourselves.

Now an example of collective remembering. Consider the following passage:

> In March 1979 the strangeness began. I called on him one day and was immediately struck that he appeared peaceful, reconciled. His usual state was one of inner turmoil, as if he felt all the sorrows of the world as a sharp pain in his soul. Now suddenly he was lighter. I was even more surprised to find, sitting at his trusty typewriter, his three year old nephew, Van'ka, banging at the keys with all his might. I voiced concern for the machine. He replied, 'Ah, it doesn't matter'.
>
> His melancholy worsened. He began to ignore meetings at the Institute of Philosophy. One day, as I left the Institute, I phoned him. He answered my questions in monosyllables. When I suggested that he get some rest (as if

anyone were forcing him to work) he answered, 'Yes, yes, for good'. And when
I said goodbye, he replied abstractedly, 'Farewell'.

Why farewell? After all, he wasn't going anywhere .... It seems, however, that
he had long known where he was going. He just wasn't clear about the method.
But soon that was decided too. The pathologist examining his body asked
suddenly, 'Did this man know anatomy?' (Mareev, 1994: 17–18)

So Sergei Mareev describes the last days of Russian philosopher Evald
Ilyenkov.[3] Although the text presents an individual's recollections, it is
nevertheless an instance of collective remembering, a contribution to a joint
endeavour: remembering Ilyenkov. Such biographical writing, however
personal in mood, is a social utterance in a social medium (language
mediated by specific narrational devices), addressed to others and subject
to their scrutiny. It contributes a part to a picture that is collectively
sustained, and its significance depends on that wider picture.

Biography is, of course, just one of innumerable ways we sustain an
image of our past. Through the written word, photograph, film, audio and
video recording, ritual and memorial, and so on, the past is constantly
made present. This is no small fact, but a defining feature of the human
condition as it now is.

Collective remembering, no less than experiential memory, pertains to
matters of identity. The question, 'Who was Ilyenkov?', may only be
explored by engaging in practices of collective remembering that aspire to
tell the story of his life and work. In a sense, Ilyenkov *just is* the focus of
that narrative. Of course, after Ilyenkov's death, all that remains is the
story of his life. But that story was hardly less crucial when he was alive,
for Ilyenkov was *for himself* the subject of his emerging life-story. So we
all see ourselves, as we aspire to live meaningful lives. As Alasdair
MacIntyre has stressed (1981: ch. 15), the integrity of an individual's life
depends on its being seen as a narrative which runs from birth to death.

MacIntyre, we might note, has sympathies with the Greek view that
the character of a person's death – the point of closure – is a crucial factor
giving shape to her life as a whole. Thus we might surmise that Ilyenkov
felt the narrative coherence of his life demanded his suicide, or perhaps it
was a belief that his life had ceased to constitute a meaningful narrative
that provoked his death. The issue is contestable, and might remain
so even if we had access to Ilyenkov's testimony. The special relation of an
individual to the events of his life provides no guarantee that his version
of events is authoritative, as those who mourn Ilyenkov have reason to
lament.

The social and the individual: priority disputes

We might say that our examples illuminate distinct species of memory,
related to different aspects of identity. On the one hand, there is the 'inner-
worldly', 'first-personal' acquaintance with the past that sustains our
identities as enduring subjects of experience; on the other, there are the

public, 'third-personal' practices of collective remembering, vital to our identities as subjects of lives lived in social space. It is tempting to keep the two phenomena apart, arguing that they represent contrasting modes of awareness of self in time.

Yet this manoeuvre obscures the fact that the individual and social dimensions of memory are so evidently interrelated. Collective remembering depends, obviously, on episodes of first-personal awareness. Mareev's account, for instance, is composed of reports of experiential memories, supplemented by factual memories (I doubt he actually heard the pathologist's remark). It is part of a narrative presentation of Ilyenkov's life, but of course its focal point is a subject of experience. And Mareev's account stands or falls on the evidence of experiential memory, which plays a key role in the epistemic evaluation of narrative.

At the same time, experiential memory, as we possess it, depends on our ability to place memory images into context. Without a framework in which to locate the deliverances of memory, only fractured presentiments, disconnected images and stark propositions would remain. Voluntary acts of remembering would be impossible. Thus the socially entrenched skills that structure collective remembering are implicated in the possibility of experiential memory. We might speculate that a being unable to see itself as the focus of a life-story could not have experiential memories as we understand them. Thus our identities as self-conscious subjects of experience depend on our identities as 'narrative selves'.

It is nevertheless inviting to try to subordinate the social dimension of memory to the individual, or vice versa. Traditionally, psychology has treated personal memory as the primary notion. It is awfully tempting to try to turn the tables and argue that all memory, even in its most intimate personal aspects, is imbued with the social. Such a position might be developed from Vygotsky's writings,[4] or discerned in views inspired by him, such as social constructionist and discursive psychology, and my focus here – Jerome Bruner's cultural psychology.

One argument for the primacy of the social takes up the idea that experiential memories are nothing without interpretation. We talk as if self-interpreting images pop up on the mind's stage. But this, it is argued, is Cartesian claptrap. There are no self-interpreting images and no theatre of the mind for them to populate. The self is not a passive spectator of the mind's show, but an active interpreter. And interpretation involves skills of classification and narrative that are socially forged and sustained. The mind's objects are thus, in a significant sense, fashioned by cultural 'tools' and all memory is thereby imbued with sociality.

This position is insightful, but flawed. Consider again the *All my Lovin'* example. This involuntary remembering yields a sensation with an obscure content that I must respect. Because it is obscure, I have to deploy powers of thought and interpretation that are, no doubt, culturally mediated. But my memory experience is not itself a social or cultural construct, for it is not a construct at all. It is a presentiment of the past that *warrants* one or other interpretation. The same is true of many less curious memory experiences. The past intrudes upon us in personal memory (I almost mean that literally), and our beliefs and interpretations must conform to its deliverances.

This might suggest that I am reinventing the idea of 'the given' in the domain of memory. Such a strategy, it will be argued, is hopeless, for there are no 'raw' memory images, no 'bare presences' like the sense data of old. Anything contentful before the mind is already conceptualized, construed, interpreted. This is as true of memory (truer?) as of perception.

I am no advocate of the myth of the given. I do think, however, that we need to revise the pictures of the relation of mind and world that influence much debate about social memory, in particular the assumption of the ubiquity of interpretation that informs much cultural and constructionist psychology (e.g., Bruner, 1991: 8–9). We must abandon the idea that what the mind confronts is the product of interpretation, together with the key metaphor that motivates it: the idea of the mind as organizing experience. To see why, consider how these problematic ideas figure in Bruner's work.[5]

Cultural psychology on the road to irrealism

Bruner presents cultural psychology as an alternative to two psychological orthodoxies. The first is Piaget's universalistic view of psychological development, which, Bruner argues, fails to appreciate that psychological development involves the acquisition of a variety of domain-specific capacities designed for tasks that are, to a large degree, culturally defined (Bruner, 1991: 2–3). We must recognize that culture is a repository of psychological skills (a 'tool kit'), a support-system for the acquisition of mental powers, and a site of distributed knowledge. Piaget's approach is also scientistic, portraying all knowledge as scientific theory building and casting children as little mathematicians, logicians, scientists. This is a poor basis to explain their developing knowledge of social reality and of other minds, which involves normative modes of explanation, narrative structures of interpretation, empathy and hermeneutical sensibilities.

The second rejected orthodoxy is the legacy of the cognitive revolution, which ousted behaviourism only to substitute a no less impoverished view of human beings as information-processors (Bruner, 1990: ch. 1). This, Bruner argues, renders psychology unable to understand *meaning*, a concept crucial to any plausible theory of mind. Meaning is no by-product of formal systems, but something *made* by human agents as they navigate cultural reality. We will never understand children's 'entry into meaning', their knowledge of the minds of other 'meaning makers', unless we look beyond the head and explore how meaning is culturally created, sustained and negotiated.

In all this, Bruner preserves the metaphor of the mind as organizing experience. He simply argues that many resources for the organization of experience reside in the culture and must be appropriated therefrom. Bruner sometimes seems to accept a relatively traditional dualism between the 'inner world' of the mind and the external world beyond its frontiers. In *In Search of Mind*, for example, he writes that:

> The metaphor of an 'outer reality' that could never be directly known and an inner one that one 'constructs' to represent it has always been a root one for me – the drama of Plato's prisoners in the cave. (Bruner, 1983: 134)

For Bruner in this mood, cultural psychology's principal insight is that the conceptual scheme that defines the structure of mind, and which shapes the 'construction' of our conception of the world, cannot be understood without essential reference to culture.

Increasingly often, however, Bruner appears to advance a more radical position, one that plays up the sceptical theme implicit in the quotation above. Bruner argues that our 'folk psychology' is an ineliminable aspect of our self-understanding (1990: ch. 2). He takes a richer view of folk psychological explanation than many writers, arguing that it includes not just explanation in terms of the propositional attitudes, but an appreciation of the cultural context of behaviour and a facility with narrative. Nevertheless, he endorses the mainstream belief that folk psychology is primarily a tool for the explanation of behaviour, a device for organizing our experience of behaviour. This inclines Bruner to a constructivist view of mental states and the 'self' that possesses them. Mental states are seen as creatures of attribution, and the self is portrayed as an explanatory construct. Earlier, we saw how we are led to view the self as an active interpreter. Now we find ourselves saying that its essence is to exist for-itself as an object of its own interpretation: the narrative self is all. The self is a virtual object, an artefact of strategies of self-interpretation. It exists, in Dennett's words, as 'a centre of narrative gravity', akin to a fictional character, as much made by meaning as making it (Bruner, 1995: 26–7).

There is something ironic in this progression of ideas. A primary objective of Bruner's position is the *repersonalization* of psychology. He aims to make possible a new psychology of the individual that ousts the dominant, dehumanizing models of mind and to put personal meaning at the foundation of mind. Yet Bruner's willingness to fictionalize the self undermines this objective. The self is restored to psychology only to be declared a mere artefact, less than wholly real.

Some would say that Bruner's position is yet more radical, representing a full-bloodied constructivism where everything 'real' is, in a sense, an artefact of our modes of interpretation and categorization. Bruner insists that there is no 'aboriginal reality': the world as we encounter it is a product of the organizing power of mind, of the 'narrative construction of reality'. So we do not diminish the self by admitting it is artefactual. For even science, on this radical reading, is just one more set of discursive practices which 'structure reality', one more 'way of worldmaking'.

With this, the idea that the mind organizes experience has led us down the well trodden path to global irrealism. The resulting position is fashionable, particularly when endowed with postmodern flourishes, and convenient, since it allows the cultural psychologist to write off criticisms from mainstream psychology, which can be dismissed as labouring under the delusion that there is a 'real' mind to study.[6]

McDowell: navigating the space of reasons

I think this irrealism is profoundly misguided. I believe we should aspire to a vision of mind and world which countenances the reality of personal being in, and in cognitive contact with, an enduring world which, for the most part, is not of our making. The task is to embrace this realistic vision while giving full weight to the sociocultural dimensions of mind.

What alternative is there to the idea that, since experience is organized by the mind, the reality we encounter in experience is a product of inter- pretation? Here I draw inspiration from John McDowell's *Mind and World* (1994). McDowell argues that epistemology has typically been caught between two unsatisfying views of experience. First, there is the position pejoratively called 'the myth of the given', where sensations are portrayed as providing the basis for belief. The problem for this position is to provide a satisfying account of how my receiving impressions of such and such a kind is supposed to *ground* my belief that things are thus and so. For if impressions are conceived as they typically are – as raw sensory 'feels', nonconceptual in nature – then it is hard to see how their occurrence could constitute *reasons* for belief. That I receive certain impressions might *cause* me to form certain beliefs, but it could not justify them, for only something conceptual in structure could do that. So conceived, experience is part of the causal order but lies outside (what McDowell, following Sellars, calls) 'the space of reasons'.

It is tempting to recoil from this picture into a form of coherentism that admits that nothing can provide a rational warrant for belief but another belief. Thus if we continue to represent experience as a causal impingement on the mind, we are forced to argue that something must be 'done' to the deliverances of experience before they present themselves to the mind. We are brought to the view that experience must be conceptualized, inter- preted and organized to enter the economy of thought.[7] This is Bruner's position. But now we have to admit that the results of this process of inter- pretation are at several stages removed from 'reality' itself. Indeed, this coherentism makes it hard to see how thought can be rationally constrained by reality at all. Bruner's response to this problem, as we have seen, is not to care.

The novelty of McDowell's stance is that he denies that these two posi- tions exhaust our alternatives, for we can think of experience, not as the result of the organizing of raw sensation, but as an *openness* to reality. What experience yields are *appearances of how things are*. Such appearances have no special epistemic privileges; nothing guarantees they are correct. They must be scrutinized in light of our existing system of concepts and beliefs. But when experience correctly presents how things are, thought reaches right out to reality. There is no gap between mind and world; the world is present to us in thought.

McDowell's position depends on the idea that the deliverances of experience are already conceptual in nature. Experience is not an apprehension of raw data, but an awareness *that things are thus and so*. In other words, the deliverances of experience are already within the space of reasons. (In Kantian terms, the receptivity of experience and the spontaneity of reason form an indissoluble unity.) What experience yields is already fit for our concepts and hence nothing need be done to experience before it can represent reality to the mind. Thus the world we experience is not, on McDowell's view, at a distance from the world as it is.

Many will argue that we cannot think of experience as simply offering the world to the mind. Meaning is the currency of the mental, but the world beyond the mind is empty of meaning, or 'disenchanted', in Weber's famous phrase. The 'external world' is the domain of objects interacting according to natural, causal laws, and nothing in that domain need be explained by appeal to meaning. It follows that nothing can be conveyed from the 'realm of natural law' into the 'space of reasons' without first being endowed with meaning. That is why we must see conceptualization or interpretation as the world's passport into the mental realm.

McDowell urges us to drop the view that reality is disenchanted as one more scientistic presumption. We must not confine the conceptual, the meaningful and the rational to a bounded domain called 'mind' and set this against the meaningless 'external' realm of the causal, the natural, the nomological, as if nature stops where the space of reasons begins. We must rather see how the conceptual permeates the natural, and vice versa. In this, I see a striking parallel between McDowell's position and Ilyenkov's work on 'the problem of the ideal'. Both seek to 're-enchant' reality to avoid the dilemma that philosophy must either bridge the gulf between mind and world, or declare the world a construct of mind.[8]

McDowell's account of experience is focused largely upon perception. But just as he would have us see perception as an openness to reality, so we can portray memory as affording an openness to the past, to how things were. Of course, in memory the mind does not (directly) receive something from beyond its frontiers. But memory is nevertheless analogous to sense experience – indeed it is a genuine form of 'receptivity'. As the *All my Lovin'* example illustrates, memories are often brought to mind by causal processes no more under rational control than sense experience. Indeed, memory underscores how the contrast between mind and world does not coincide with the contrast between the rational and the natural, for the contrast between phenomena within the 'realm of law' and those in 'the space of reasons' arises *within* the mind. McDowell's position allows us to see memory experiences as examples of how things meaningful can impinge upon us in experience, presenting us with glimpses of how things are or were which warrant the formation of certain beliefs.

But what of the sociocultural dimension of experience in general and memory in particular? Significantly, McDowell's position continues to afford a central role to the notion of culture. Both he and Ilyenkov see an individual's ability to inhabit the space of reasons as requiring the possession of sophisticated conceptual skills acquired through the child's assimilation of culture. These skills are aspects of our 'second nature' and their acquisition brings the child into contact with the *world*, with its ever-receding horizons, rather than a merely local environment. Such is the character of *human*, rather than merely animal existence.

In my view, it is in the exploration of these thoughts, rather than in a global cultural constructivism, that the future of cultural psychology resides.

Enabling versus constitutive views of culture

Both McDowell and Ilyenkov represent culture as *enabling* the emergence and exercise of mind. For them, the child's inauguration into culture represents the acquisition, or actualization, of conceptual powers that make possible experience of the world. A being that has these powers is a fully fledged inhabitant of the space of reasons; that is, it is able to organize its activity in response to rational requirements on belief and action. Such a being guides its thought by good reasons for belief, and acts in the light of good reasons for action, and only such a being can be said to have a conception of the world and to be the subject of a life conceived as a story played out within that world.

McDowell argues that the crucial component of the process in which the child assimilates culture, or *Bildung* as he calls it, is the acquisition of language, conceived 'as a repository of tradition, a store of historically accumulated wisdom about what is a reason for what' (McDowell, 1994: 126). Initiation into language is initiation into a medium that already embodies conceptual relations and which enables the exploration of the geography of the space of reasons. Ilyenkov takes a broader view, urging us to see that assimilation into culture involves the appropriation of many forms of socially significant activity that are nonlinguistic in kind and which form the basis for the subsequent development of language. For Ilyenkov, what is at issue is the infant's emerging capacity to guide her behaviour by norms, so that her behaviour is not simply called forth by biological imperatives. This process begins with the manipulation of arte-facts, of objects that elicit behaviour because they are seen as significant, and occurs far earlier than language acquisition.

The differences between McDowell and Ilyenkov on this point are impor-tant, for the central task of any cultural psychology must be to provide a rich and satisfying account of *Bildung*. Both agree, however, that initiation into culture is a precondition of the possibility of the emergence of mind. Hence, to say that, on this position, culture *enables* mind is not to say that initiation into culture merely assists the exercise of capacities that could be exercised independently of the influence of culture. Rather, entry into culture makes possible the very 'responsiveness to meaning' that is the quintessence of human mentality (McDowell, 1994: 123).

Another crucial point of agreement is that what we acquire through our initiation into culture is the ability to respond to rational requirements on belief and action, to guide our activity by rational norms. These rational requirements are thought of as objectively binding, as 'there anyway' whether we recognize them or not. Culture's gift is to make available to us the contours of the space of reasons, to enable us to see reasons that have force regardless of whether that force is perceived.

Contrast this idea with what I shall call a *constitutive* view of culture's influence. On the constitutive view, what is a good reason for belief or action is held to be so because it conforms to accepted practices in the culture, because it coincides with what the community *counts* as a good reason. Here, the practices of the community simply constitute the norms of rationality – what the community does defines the space of reasons – and the individual is required to conform to those practices to count as rational.

The constitutive view naturally entails that the assimilation of culture, in the sense of conformity to the community's practices, is a precondition of mindedness, and hence it appeals to some who seek a philosophical rationale for cultural psychology. In addition, it has a certain philosophical pedigree. It appears in influential readings of Wittgenstein and of Richard Rorty's critique of traditional philosophy.[9]

The constitutive view is, in my view, a disastrous basis for cultural psychology. It does violence to our conception of ourselves and our relation to the world to think that what constitutes a compelling reason for a belief or action is ultimately a matter of communal agreement. This represents the community as policing the requirements of rationality and ultimately truth (or even worse – as constituting the requirements they police). It thus fails to do justice to the idea, which is a precondition of all our reasoning and enquiry, that thought is answerable to a world which is not of our making.[10]

The attractions of the constitutive view have so eclipsed alternatives that the McDowellian position is only just being entertained. I think there are three principal reasons why the constitutive view is so attractive.

The first derives from the power over us of a certain kind of scientific naturalism, one which embraces the disenchanted conception of reality (McDowell, 1994: lecture V). In the grip of that conception, we search in desperation for an account of the place of reasons, values, meaning in the world. How, deploying only resources available from the disenchanted perspective, can we give an account of responsiveness to reasons? The only option, it seems, is to construct the rational out of patterns of behaviour, patterns that conform to the majority practice. But this is to suggest that mere behaviour could be turned into something rational simply through coincidence with the mere behaviour of others. And, to turn to parallel concerns about meaning, that the mere noises that issue from a person's mouth are made meaningful in virtue of their congruence with the mere noises made by others. The whole doomed project is misconceived, for it is driven by an unduly austere conception of what is real.

Second, I believe the constitutive picture appeals to those who are over-impressed by sceptical arguments. In the midst of our practices, we typically have a strong sense of what constitutes a good reason for some belief or action, and we understand the character of disputes about whether some purported reason is in fact a good one. For example, my reason for believing that I am presently typing at my computer is that I see the keyboard and feel the keys, my action upon the keys produces exactly the effects I expect, and so on. In short, everything in my present experience speaks in favour of this belief, and nothing against it. I understand how one might dispute whether, say, unusual fluctuations in the weather are a reason to believe in the deleterious effects of global warming, but not whether things as I presently take them to be constitute grounds to believe I am working on my computer. Traditional epistemology, however, counsels us not to rest content with reasons of the latter variety, because they can be attacked by sceptical arguments of the Cartesian kind. We are thus urged to look for further reasons that are immune from sceptical attack and serve to justify those we typically adduce.

It is now widely agreed, of course, that those who seek a foundational rebuttal to scepticism will be disappointed: there simply are no reasons that are immune from sceptical attack and sufficiently substantive to provide the foundation for everything else we believe. The fact that sceptical concerns cannot be answered leads many to dismiss the sceptic's arguments as in some way misconceived and, indeed, to ridicule the pretensions of the foundationalist (Rorty's critique is an obvious example). They find it difficult, however, to rid themselves of the idea, implanted by the sceptic, that there is something lacking in the reasons we normally give. Unable to supplement these reasons by philosophical argument, they find the necessary addition in the endorsement of the community. On this view, what makes such-and-such considerations a reason for a particular belief is that these kinds of considerations are counted as a reason for belief among members of our epistemic community. Agreement thus becomes the ultimate epistemic warrant. But the idea that there is a place to be filled here by communal agreement is a mistake, and one that is a legacy of scepticism. The trick is to recognize that our normal modes of justification stand in no need of supplementation, either by foundational epistemology or 'post-foundational' conventionalism.

Third, and finally, there is a streak of self-aggrandizing anthropocentricity in the constitutive view. It makes human beings arbiters, indeed creators, of the true, the rational, and (no doubt) the good. Such a view seems empowering, but it really bespeaks immaturity: an inability to come to terms with a properly secular world-view. For the constitutive conception cannot free itself of the idea that truth, rationality and value are ultimately expressions of *personality*. I believe this is an illusion, and a dangerous one.

It might be replied that the real attraction of the constitutive view is that it enables us to appreciate the extent to which communally accepted practices deeply influence what we are and what we may become. Only it can fully capture the extent of the social construction of identity. But this too is a mistake, for the opposite is true. We can only appreciate the extent to which the community influences us, for good or ill, if we preserve a robust sense of how things are. For among the things that participation in the practices of our community empowers us to do is to navigate an independent course through life, responding in our distinctive way to reasons that have a force independent of communal assent. And among the ways our participation can diminish us is because the community distorts or obscures truths which are not of its making. We cannot hope, for example, to illuminate the phenomenon of collective memory unless we keep a firm grip on the idea that our practices do not 'construct' the past, but illuminate and disclose or distort and conceal it. Those practices issue in reasons for belief and our guiding light in assessing those reasons is the idea of accountability to the way things were.

Conclusion

This last thought returns us to the theme of memory, with which this paper began. Memory is a topic that vividly displays both the promise of cultural psychology and the complexities it faces. Although mainstream psychology has typically treated memory in extremely individualistic fashion, the sociocultural dimensions of memory are not hard to see. And once perceived, they appear to be of enormous import for psychology. Memory, after all, is crucial to identity. The problem, however, is to find a way properly to accommodate both the individual and the social dimensions of memory in a plausible account of the integrity and persistence of the self. It is, I believe, a criterion of adequacy for any cultural psychology that it give credence to the sociocultural character of mind while preserving due sense of the inner, intimate and private dimensions of our mental lives. But this is a difficult criterion to meet, for cultural psychology cannot proceed by simply grafting a number of hitherto overlooked sociocultural factors onto an individualistic picture of the mind inherited from some existing branch of the cognitive sciences. Cultural psychology requires us to rethink our very conception of mind and its place in the world, to reconceive the relations we bear to nature and to each other. It demands a conceptual – a *philosophical* – transformation.

Bruner understands this as well as anyone, for he has always been aware of philosophy's importance. This is not because he looks to philosophy to provide a foundation for psychology, but because he has always recognized the power of speculative enquiry to illuminate and enthuse, to counsel and inform, and because he holds psychology to especially high ideals. For Bruner, psychology's object is self-understanding, the attainment of a satisfying picture of our place in nature, and, moreover, one which will inspire us to live better. It might be said that, for Bruner, psychology is a kind of empirical philosophy, a contemporary descendant of the 'moral sciences' that should never lose sight of its speculative roots.

I have tried to show that, although Bruner appreciates the importance of philosophical enquiry, his own philosophical sensibilities incline him towards positions that represent an untenable premiss for cultural psychology. Bruner's commitment to the dualism of scheme and content leads him to embrace, or at least to flirt with, forms of radical cultural constructionism and philosophical irrealism that fail what I take to be a second criterion of adequacy for any cultural psychology: that it acknowledge the social dimensions of the mind without forsaking a sensible realism in which minded beings inhabit a world which is, to a large extent, not of their making. I suggested that the seeds of a more satisfactory vision of the relation of mind and world can be found in the recent work of John McDowell, which has interesting parallels with the ideas of Russian philosopher Evald Ilyenkov. Both reject the dualism for a view that, in favourable circumstances, perception is an awareness of how things are and thought makes contact with an independent reality.

As we saw, both McDowell and Ilyenkov attribute a vital role to culture in the development of mind, for they argue that initiation into culture enables the individual to acquire the cognitive powers to navigate the space of reasons. Moreover, we might add that their positions are entirely compatible with the view that 'cultural tools' mediate our awareness of reality. We must simply be clear that the 'mediational means' do not somehow get between us and reality itself. Rather, their use serves to bring reality within our reach. In this, it is important to take the tool metaphor seriously. Just as the use of a hammer does not somehow remove us from the object on which we are working, so our concepts, models, theories and so on need not create a barrier beyond which we cannot see. We use them to disclose the world to us, not to obscure it. Such a view is, I believe, precisely what Vygotsky had in mind when he invoked the concept of mediation, though this is often lost on his Western followers. I conclude, therefore, that though much remains to develop in McDowell's position, it is a promising ally of cultural psychology.

While I am sure that Bruner will find much to argue with in the case I have made, I am equally certain that he will welcome efforts such as this to re-examine critically the guiding metaphors of cultural psychology and the pictures of mind and world that inform its research. For he appreciates more than anyone that such speculative reflections are not just a preliminary to the 'real' research, but an integral part of mature psychological enquiry. And there is no greater advocate of such enquiry than Jerome Bruner himself.

Notes

Earlier versions of this paper were presented at the Small Group Meeting on Collective Memory in Bari in May 1997, and at the Queen's University Philosophy Colloquium. I am indebted to the participants at these events for their comments and criticisms, and to Shaun Maxwell for his insightful commentary at the Queen's Colloquium. I am grateful to the Social Sciences and Humanities Research Council of Canada, and to the Principal's Development Fund at Queen's University, for supporting the research presented here.

1   An experiential memory is one which essentially involves memory experience or imagery. When A experientially remembers O, A has a memory experience of O, and O's having been the case is appropriately related to A's present experience of O (e.g., that O was the case is part of the explanation of why A now has memory experiences of O). Experiential memory is to be contrasted with 'propositional' or 'factual' memory: memory that *p*. I remember that my parents moved to such and such an address before I was born, or that Napoleon was born in Corsica, without bringing to mind experiences of the events or persons remembered, or indeed any experiences at all.

Experiential memory involves (in some sense) 'reliving' the past. Thus, David Wiggins writes that remembering once climbing the stairs of the Eiffel Tower involves rehearsing to oneself 'something and enough of that climbing of those stairs … rehearsing it from the point of view of the climber' (Wiggins, 1992: 339). This is obviously close to the truth, but some qualifications are necessary. First, we are prone to think that experiential memory is like a mental videotape of events, but the imagery that comprises experiential memories is often fragmented and disjointed, and sometimes pertains to the mood of the events or states of affairs remembered. Second, Wiggins may be wrong to imply that experiential memories must represent the past events from the point of view from which the events were originally experienced by the rememberer. Sometimes, our experiential memories (like our dreams) represent us as we were from a *third-person* perspective, although such images are often juxtaposed with others that are first-personal (e.g., I see myself as a little boy riding a tricycle in the garden from the perspective of a spectator, while at the same time remembering how the pedals felt, how the handlebars looked as I rode, etc.). It is too quick to rule out these third-personal representations of self as not genuine memory experiences on the grounds that they are obviously constructions (perhaps based on stories we have heard about the events in question). After all, many first-personal memory images also involve significant elements of construction; moreover, the constructions in question may themselves have been formed at the time of the original events (perhaps we often form a (usually unconscious) representation of our body as if from a third-person perspective), and hence our present awareness of these images is related to representations of events causally grounded in past experience in a way that is, arguably, sufficient to count as experiential remembering of how things were.

It would be a mistake sharply to counterpose experiential and factual remembering, for many cases of remembering involve both propositional and experiential dimensions. Memories that *p* are often engendered by, or engender, experiential memories.

2   This is not to say that I hold a 'psychological continuity theory' of personal identity, according to which a person, A, is the same person at time, t2, as at an

earlier time, t1, only if there is the right kind of continuity, underwritten by A's memory, in A's mental states (beliefs, desires, memories, dispositions of character, etc.) between these times. I hold only that psychological continuity is an important dimension of our conception of (normal) personhood, not that it is a strict condition of personal identity.

3 Mareev's book (1994) is a collection of personal reminiscences about Ilyenkov. It was published by Znanie in an edition of 250 copies, a poor reproduction of a rough typescript, barely superior in quality to a *samizdat*, and evidence of the fragility of collective memory.

4 Vygotsky's view of memory, and how it might be enhanced by the work of Voloshinov and Ilyenkov, is the subject of Bakhurst, 1990.

5 The metaphor of the mind 'organizing' experience – central to many empiricist views, and to neo-Kantian versions of the dualism of 'conceptual scheme' and 'sensory content' – takes various guises in Bruner's work. In *In Search of Mind*, for example, Bruner describes 'the world we perceive directly' as 'a filtering, a sorting out, and finally a construction' and writes that '[t]he nature of the filter and of the construction processes that work with it – these constitute the *real* philosopher's stone. It does not turn base metal into gold, but turns physical "stimuli" into knowledge, a much more valuable transformation' (1983: 66). For a lengthier treatment of Bruner's position (which also includes a discussion of the relevance of Ilyenkov's philosophy to Bruner's views), see Bakhurst, 1995a.

6 Not that Bruner himself seeks to insulate cultural psychology from serious engagement with the mainstream. Some of his many followers, however, are wont to do so.

7 I am aware that in this chapter I run together the *conceptualization* and the *interpretation* of experience. This conflation is one I suppose (perhaps unjustly) my opponents to make (sliding, for example, from the idea that the theory-ladenness of scientific observation means that there is no uninterpreted data to the idea that sensory experience is never encountered in an uninterpreted (rather than unconceptualized) form). A fuller treatment of the issue will need to substantiate that supposition, and to distinguish clearly the respective contributions of these two activities of mind.

8 Those familiar with Ilyenkov's work, particularly as I present it in Bakhurst, 1990, might be puzzled by the harmony I detect between Ilyenkov and McDowell. McDowell wants to hold that experience yields some kind of direct access to reality. But Ilyenkov, in his work on ideality, seems to argue that the world becomes a possible object of thought only in virtue of its endowment with meaning, or 'idealization' by human activity. Does it not follow from Ilyenkov's view that the mind has access only to the world insofar as it is mediated (constructed?) by activity and hence that we lack access to reality as it is in itself? I have tried in many writings to give a negative answer to this question (e.g., Bakhurst, 1991: ch. 6, 1995b, 1997 (the latter takes up the congruencies and differences between Ilyenkov and McDowell)). I believe Ilyenkov thinks of the mediating power of activity as bringing us into contact with the world as it is, rather than engendering an object of thought which somehow comes between us and things as they are. I return to the concept of mediation in the conclusion to this chapter.

9 For such readings of Wittgenstein see, e.g., Wright, 1980: ch. 11 and Kripke, 1982, and compare McDowell, 1994: 92–4 and 1998: ch. 12. (The interpretation

of Wittgenstein I develop in Bakhurst, 1995c, embraces the constitutive view as a transcendental thesis, which, I there argue, is none the less compatible with empirical or 'internal' realism. I now think this strategy is to be avoided.)

Rorty's position is complex. Although he writes that 'there is nothing to be said about either truth or rationality apart from descriptions of the familiar procedures of justification which a given society – *ours* – uses in one of another area of inquiry' (1991: 23), he would deny that he embraces the constitutive view. The latter, he would argue, is a misguided attempt to provide a philosophical theory of the nature of rationality and truth. Better to give up the hope of any such theory and let justification rest with an appeal to 'the ordinary, retail, detailed, concrete reasons which have brought one to one's present view' (Rorty, 1982: 165). One may nevertheless suspect that Rorty's constant references to society and solidarity are a vestige of the constitutive view, or something like it, according to which our everyday reasons need a social warrant to be the reasons they are.

10   McDowell himself invokes a similar distinction between 'enabling' and 'constitutive' questions and explanations in McDowell, 1998 (ch. 16), in a discussion of the explanations of mental content. Note, however, that in that context McDowell identifies an enabling explanation with a causal one. In my version of the distinction, an enabling explanation need not be causal in any straightforward sense of the term.

References

Bakhurst, D. (1990) 'Social memory in Soviet thought', in D. Middleton and D. Edwards (eds), *Collective Remembering*. London: Sage.

Bakhurst, D. (1991) *Consciousness and Revolution in Soviet Philosophy*. Cambridge: Cambridge University Press.

Bakhurst, D. (1995a) 'On the social constitution of mind: Bruner, Ilyenkov and the defence of cultural psychology', *Mind, Culture, and Activity*, 2 (3): 158–71.

Bakhurst, D. (1995b) 'Lessons from Ilyenkov', *Communication Review*, 1 (2): 155–78.

Bakhurst, D. (1995c) 'Wittgenstein and social being', in D. Bakhurst and C. Sypnowich (eds), *The Social Self*. London: Sage.

Bakhurst, D. (1997) 'Meaning, normativity, and the life of the mind', *Language and Communication*, 17 (1): 33–51.

Bruner, J.S. (1983) *In Search of Mind: Essays in Autobiography*. New York: Harper & Row.

Bruner, J.S. (1990) *Acts of Meaning*. Cambridge, MA: Harvard University Press.

Bruner, J.S. (1991) 'The narrative construction of reality', *Critical Inquiry*, 18: 1–21.

Bruner, J.S. (1995) 'Meaning and self in cultural perspective', in D. Bakhurst and C. Sypnowich (eds), *The Social Self*. London: Sage.

Kripke, S. (1982) *Wittgenstein on Rules and Private Languages*. Oxford: Basil Blackwell.

MacIntyre, A. (1981) *After Virtue*. London: Duckworth.

Mareev, S. (1994) *Vstrecha s filosofom E.V. Il'enkovym (An Encounter with E.V. Ilyenkov)*. Moscow: Znanie.

McDowell, J. (1994) *Mind and World*. Cambridge, MA: Harvard University Press.

McDowell, J. (1998) *Mind, Value, and Reality*. Cambridge, MA: Harvard University Press.

Rorty, R. (1982) *Consequences of Pragmatism*. Minneapolis: University of Minnesota Press.

Rorty, R. (1991) *Objectivity, Realtivism, and Truth. Philosophical Papers*, Vol. 1. Cambridge: Cambridge University Press.

Wiggins, D. (1992) 'Remembering directly', in J. Hopkins and A. Savile (eds), *Psychoanalysis, Mind and Art: Essays for Richard Wollheim*. Oxford: Blackwell.

Wright, C. (1980) *Wittgenstein on the Foundations of Mathematics*. London: Duckworth.

12

IN RESPONSE

Jerome Bruner

Reading oneself through the eyes of others has something of the excitement of reading poetry. It makes the familiar strange again, quickens what once might have seemed self-evident. Sometimes the version of yourself that comes through others' perspectives produces a shock of recognition, of *self-recognition*, and leaves you bemused. How could someone know better than you did what you meant when you originally set pen to paper?

Yet, as this volume reminds us, a corpus of ideas exists not in some one person's expression of them, but in an interpretative community. The essays in this book are products of such a community. Its members do not just live with each others' ideas; we also 'try on' each others' conceptions to see how they fit our own predilections, arriving at perspectives that are new but still communally viable. In time, we even lose track of who proposed what. What matters is the body of conjectures that started and sustained the discussion: what got asked more than how it was answered. Many of those conjectures have been with us for ages; the real issue is how they come in and out of discussion and in what forms they resurface. The function of an interpretative community is to keep teasing at fundamental conjectures in an effort to refresh them and make them answerable in the light of new ideas.

This collection happens to be organized around my work, but it could just as well have focused on others among the book's authors – Clifford Geertz, Michael Tomasello, David Olson, Judy Dunn, and on through the members of our interpretative community. Perhaps it would not have been so different had it done so! My advantage as the book's focus is, as they say in the military, my service record: not just service stripes, but campaign ribbons and even Purple Hearts for 'wounded in action'.

In reply to the essays, I want to concentrate on a few of the fundamental conjectures with which I (and my fellow book-mates) have struggled over the years. I shall forgo commenting directly on points raised in particular chapters, though what follows is organized to address matters they raise.

The founding conjectures I shall explore are these. I shall start with the question of how culture affects mind, then consider how 'culture' should be understood. I shall proceed to the origins and development of language, and conclude with some reflections on why cultural psychologists tend to favour a constructionist view of 'reality'.

The culture–mind nexus: five views

How does culture relate to mind? It is both a product of mind and, plainly, it affects mind. This is not an unusual circumstance – products often affect their producers – but the culture–mind nexus is special.

All of us, I am sure, were deeply impressed at some point by Alfred Kroeber's axiomatic claim about the 'superorganic' nature of culture, that it has an 'existence' beyond what is in the minds of the individuals who live in it and can be said to 'know' it (though we should note the truism that nobody in a culture ever knows the whole of it).

Kroeber, of course, was not first to proclaim this axiomatic difference between the concepts of culture and of mind. Emile Durkheim and Max Weber had each enunciated it in different ways. But whether superorganic or historical or collective, culture was assumed to find its way into the minds of those who participated in it, affecting how they thought about themselves, each other, and the world. There was much rhetoric on this issue, but surprisingly little light shed on how, say, ritualized Balinese 'culture' found its way into Balinese 'minds', save perhaps to note that young Javanese girls learned their dances in a semi-hypnotic, ritual way. When Clifford Geertz did his justly famous study of the Javanese cockfight, he took its 'rules' to reflect a local, communal expression of more general tensions in Javanese culture. It was at the level of such local instantiations that culture expressed itself in individual minds. But the vexing question remained of *how* the culture-at-large managed to work its way into the desperate economy of cockfight betting.

One can, I think, discern several quite different approaches to the culture–mind nexus. Let us look at them critically.

The first saw culture as a repository of basic myths, founding ideas and symbol systems that, through instantiation in everyday practice, found their way into our thinking, feeling, acting, and so on. The most rigorous account of how this occurred was the Humboldt–Whorf–Sapir mega-hypothesis. Individual mental reality reflected, or was shaped by (depending upon how strong a Whorfian position one took), one's local language. It was further deemed self-evident that language either reflected or was shaped by culture (depending upon how strong a version, this time, of Humboldt's hypothesis). It was probably Saussure, with his emphasis on the systemic interconnectedness of the categories in *la langue*, that gave this culture–language–mind mega-theory its cachet. But it was never clear to anybody (including Saussure) how the abstractions of *la langue* work their way into the pragmatic, highly localized versions of *la parole* that people actually speak in interpersonal relations.

I find less rigorous versions of how a cultural repository of myths and story-forms get into individual minds more promising, though none has the elegance or force of Humboldt–Whorf–Sapir. Their promise typically lies in their framing the elements of such a repository in a narrative form that expresses the normatively driven action sequences that define people's interactions with each other and the world.

Kroeber himself favoured a more cautious approach to the culture–mind nexus, one faithful to his 'superorganic' axiom. How a culture's mythic or linguistic or belief structures affected individual praxis, and how praxis affected mind, remained a puzzle for him. He had been trained in psychoanalysis – which he had practised for several years – and was chary about claims that a culture's generalized body of founding beliefs and myths 'got into' individual minds in any straightforward way. As he comments in his writing – and as he remarked to me during his year at Harvard in the 1950s – there is something incommensurate between cultural facts and the facts of individual mental content.

Kroeber was at that time one of the most revered living anthropologists, full of years and honours, and I a brash young psychologist working principally on social and motivational influences on perception. He was warning me, I felt, to steer clear of assigning causal status to cultural facts in the operation of mind. For him, culture and mind remained incommensurate in some deep way, and he was plainly worried about the psychologizing of anthropology.

This brings me to a second approach to the culture–mind problem – one that also reflected a Kroeber-like caution – Wilhelm Wundt's. Wundt went so far as to urge that there were two 'psychologies': a naturalist, positivist, experimental psychology of the individual mind, and a 'folk psychology' given to the study of cultural products, such as music, myth and law. Folk psychology was descriptive rather than explanatory, more like history than experimental science, more a *Geisteswissenschaft* than a *Naturwissenschaft*. For Wundt, the two approaches were immiscible if not incommensurable. He spent the first half of his professional life studying the experimental psychology of perception, memory and thought, the second studying folk psychology. He made few efforts to relate them systematically, save to note the constraints of folkways and technologies on how people used their minds. Had Wundt the theoretical sophistication of his successors a half century later, he might have formulated something like a principle of complementarity: just as there is no translatability between wave and particle theories of light, both of which are 'true', so there is no translatability between individual and folk psychology. Obviously, folk psychology depends upon the existence of individual minds, but the two do not reduce to each other.

Yet, there were those who, though they adopted a somewhat similar view, believed that they saw a way out of the immiscibility. One of them was a Polish Jew who had fled to France in 1905 to escape Polish anti-Semitism, studied medicine, then switched to psychology under the influence of the leading French Gestaltist, Paul Guillaume. Ignace Meyerson soon became interested in 'historical psychology', in how periods created different *mentalités*. His work has now been rediscovered by psychologists in France and is undergoing a renaissance. I say *re*discovered by psychologists, for in fact Meyerson's work had already been an inspiration to the distinguished historians of the Annales school, whose basic idea is that history should concentrate not just on kings, dynasties, wars and constitutions, but on changing conceptions of the ordinary and their influence upon *mentalités*. Yet, despite his many years as editor of the leading French psychological journal, the *Journal de Psychologie*, to whose pages Meyerson brought such celebrated humanists as the historian François Furet and the archaeologist Jean-Pierre Vernant, mainstream French psychology paid little heed to the new 'historical psychology'. Unfortunately, virtually nothing of Meyerson's has yet been translated into English.[1]

His basic premiss is that a society and its institutions have *oeuvres* ('works') as their principal output (an echo of Wundt here: Meyerson was acquainted with his *Volkerpsychologie*). Such oeuvres rely on traditions of creation, and depend upon a division of labour in which no individual 'does the whole thing', or even knows how to. But once an oeuvre is created and enters praxis, it begins to shape the ways of thinking and acting of all who are affected by it, use it and come to need it for getting on in the life of society. Oeuvres vary from musical scales and well-honed folktales to national constitutions, bodies of scientific theory and even forms of wagering on cockfights. They also include such mundane things as corporate organizations and such odd ones as conceiving of France in the shape of a hexagon, each side of which has a unique frontier facing outward to the world.[2] Mind, or *mentalité*, comes increasingly to be formed by using, adjusting to, even rebelling against such oeuvres – or rather, against their local manifestations in family, town, school, and so on. The local is highly important not only in Meyerson's historical psychology, but in the thinking of the Annales historians.

In a word, then, Wundt introduced a note of incommensurability into the culture–mind nexus, which Meyerson sought to overcome by arguing that a society in its collectivity produces 'works' that channel the way mind works and develops. Culture does not influence mind: its *products* used by individuals do.

Let me turn to another approach to mind and culture, one whose popularity rests, I sometimes despair, on obscuring many of the issues we have been discussing. It is the 'interiorization' position associated with Vygotsky and his followers.[3] This view takes it as given that every culture has various distinctive forms that have developed historically, especially its language and other traditional symbolic forms. Not much is said about what these forms might be. As for mind, it begins its life with an internal stream of mental activity which, presumably, is autochthonous. Part of its unenculturated activity consists of generating 'inner speech', defined negatively simply as not being outer-directed lexico-grammatical speech. Culture affects mind when 'outer speech' and other cultural forms, like scientific concepts, become incorporated or 'interiorized', displacing 'inner speech'. This displacement goes on through one's whole education – as when one goes, say, from using simple arithmetic to algebra.

What is missing in this view is any serious effort to characterize the forms of a culture independently of their 'interiorization' in particular minds. And since no serious effort is made to specify what a culture is, how it comes to be known and transmitted historically, this position strikingly fails to illuminate the culture–mind nexus. Indeed, interiorization theory obscures the vexing question of the commensurability of culture and mind by simply asserting that the latter 'interiorizes' the former. Vygotsky and Vygotskians have provided rich accounts of how the child's mind grows and how it uses 'external' forms, but they have had little to say about how this is accomplished.

This question, however, has by no means gone unattended by advocates of other approaches. Two French anthropologists have made the try in a big way, each in flat-out opposition to the other. Together, they represent a fourth approach to the culture–mind nexus. Claude Lévi-Strauss rests his argument on a two-pronged approach, one directed at culture, the other at mind. Culture has a structure that emerges out of four obligatory 'exchange' systems for managing scarce resources. One relates to goods and services, a second to prestige and status, a third to eligible mates for marriage, and a fourth to the symbolic means of exchange itself. Cultures evolve efficient forms for managing these exchanges. The psychological side of the picture is quite different. It consists of such presumably 'universal' mental tendencies as seeing the world in binary contrasts (inferred, following Roman Jakobson, from how human beings process the sound system of language). Individual minds, on this account, 'process' the structure of the supra-individual culture in terms of the binary distinctions to which they are disposed. Culture emerges in the human mind in exaggerated mental structures that operate on their own contrastive principles.

I oversimplify, of course, but I think this brief account catches the gist of Lévi-Strauss's position. The opposition to it comes from Daniel Sperber, who finds Lévi-Strauss's approach too rigid about exchange systems, too unmindful of the nature of cultural change, and psychologically too specialized on binary contrast. Sperber proposes an 'epidemiological' model. Human minds, he argues, have evolved susceptibilities to certain symbolic forms. Symbolic representations that match these evolutionarily determined susceptibilities, whether generated within a culture or impinging from outside, are adopted and become part of the culture's ways, while serving, as it were, the mental needs of those within it. Certain cultural forms, then, are contagious, and find their way (in different variants) into virtually all cultures and the minds of those under their sway.

We need not pause long over these views. I mention them only to bring out the nature of the fourth position. It assumes certain requirements for the existence of a culture as a superorganic entity – certain critical exchanges in one case, certain evolutionarily imposed orientations in the other. It further assumes certain features of mind, which Lévi-Strauss construes as independent of cultural requirements, and which Sperber portrays as closely linked to them. For Sperber, human beings are simply subject to contagion by belief systems that promote the superordinate cultural good. Our minds are tuned to favour our survival as a culture. Sperber thus represents the fourth view in a sociobiological, evolutionary form. The great problem with all such neo-Darwinian theories is that they so easily spin into circular reasoning about what is causing, and what is being caused by, what.

The fifth and final view of the culture–mind nexus contains a normative element. Its basic premiss is that culture is an idealized or canonical set of norms imposed on individual thought and behaviour. It was in this sense that Durkheim intended his famous phrase about cultures having 'exteriority and constraint'. Max Weber's elaborate system of sociology also rests heavily on this normative doctrine, as does much British social anthropology with its heavy emphasis on institutional forms. All of these stances posit some sort of individual need that matches the distinctively normative structure of the culture, though few have much to say about it.

One exception were the psychological theories that placed the 'need to conform' at the very heart of social behaviour. The most notable was Floyd Allport's 'J-curve' theory of conformity. Whereas most 'natural' behaviour is distributed normally in the usual binomial distribution, 'social' behaviour is distributed with a tight cluster around a norm, the J-curve. But J-curves and cultural analysis were never really serious bedfellows. The early Allport was a flat-out behaviourist who would have rejected Durkheim's 'collective representations' as so much 'Group Mind' twaddle, much as the behaviourists dismissed McDougall for his book on the Group Mind.[4]

Those, then, are my candidates for the big five 'solutions' of how to deal with culture's influence on mind. All of them are still with us in spirit. I dare not label them for fear of creating a nominal magic. The tribulations of these positions highlight the difficulties in bringing together 'facts' from individual psychology, on the one side, and culture, on the other. Should we conclude, then, that 'cultural psychology' is doomed, as its central ideas are either muddled or strangled in incommensurability? Certainly not! I simply want to make us wary of the usual ways of formulating the relation of culture and mind. This wariness has, at least, led me to some energizing conjectures (or prejudices). Let me conclude this section with a few of them.

To begin with, concepts like 'culture' and 'mind' are constructed rather than discovered. With all due respect to Lévi-Strauss, the exchange systems that characterize a culture are not natural kinds. They are pragmatically useful ways of categorizing activities in the social world. The same can be said for any concept of mind. As Geertz long ago reminded us, our conceptions of mind are themselves cultural products, constructed with the ends of predicting, understanding, controlling, of 'keeping some practical show on the road'. Where the human sciences are concerned, I have long since given up the vanities of positivism, the idea that there is a uniquely knowable mental or cultural world 'out there' that can be characterized in an abstract way, independently of the contexts in which 'subjects' are situated and in terms of which they act.

All human action takes place in some cultural context, and the shape of that action is to some degree a function of that context. Equally, the nature of a cultural context is in crucial measure determined by those operating within it. Does this force us into hopeless circularity? Again, I think not. There is no more circularity here than one encounters in any hermeneutic or interpretative analysis. To put it more concretely, to understand how an individual mind is affected by some cultural context, one must determine what that particular mind makes of the context. To understand that (and to escape provisionally from the hermeneutic circle) one must also determine the way in which that context is interpreted by those with whom the individual in question interacts.

Cultural psychology is an *interpretative* discipline. Its strategies are hermeneutical rather than causal or correlational. This does not mean that crops do not fail, droughts do not destroy habitation patterns, or that years of schooling do not correlate with income. What leads Balinese villagers to place such ruinous wagers on the outcomes of cockfights is their interpretation of the meaning of such cockfights in their communal lives. And that interpretation derives from a communal conception of how Balinese society operates, which in turn, can be further clarified by understanding the 'superorganic' history of Balinese society – its power structure, its treasury of narrative forms, its founding myths, and the like. So too with droughts and years of schooling. Obviously they can be 'measured' and correlated with other 'variables'. But in a deeper sense, there are no truly independent variables, ones completely independent of the interpretations placed upon them by those 'subjects' (as psychologists like to call people) whose reactions constitute our dependent variables. This does not mean that we cannot use statistics or our beloved analysis of variance, but that one needs to interpret what such methods yield in more than an off-the-cuff spirit.

Having said that, it becomes obvious that some things are fundamentally amiss in the classical approaches to the relation of culture and mind. First, all the approaches we considered commit the sin of *reification*: they treat both culture and mind as though they were independent or autonomous things. Even renditions of the culture–mind nexus inspired by the Sapir–Whorf hypothesis tend to omit the interactive aspect of language, its *pragmatics*. When you are concerned with pragmatics – the uses to which utterances are put – you cannot treat language as just an autonomous syntax, semantics and lexicon.

Second, all the classical approaches are *unsituated*, even Meyerson's, despite his sensitivity to how a culture's oeuvres affect the mental lives of individuals who make use of them. Let me offer an example, albeit a rather contorted one, of what I mean by 'situatedness'. Hebrew religious practice in pre-Inquisition Spain had an interesting conceit. Interpretation of the Torah, whether in the freer style of Maimonides or the more literal one of conservative *midrash*, always began by reference to specific words and expressions in the Torah itself. Perhaps to honour this ancient precept, Torah reading was always done with the aid of a pointer. In opulent pre-Inquisition Spain, this pointer was a fine silver tapered rod tipped by a tiny human hand with index finger extended, the rod itself exquisitely engraved and about a foot and a half in length. I take its symbolism to be 'nothing is too elegant and fine a means for tracing the words and phrases in the Holy Scroll'. I had never known of such 'Torah pointers' until, on my first trip to Spain, I came across one in a traditional and up-market antique shop in Madrid. When I asked the proprietor what it was, he told me simply that it was used by pre-Inquisition Spanish Jews for 'reading their Bible'. I bought it, knowing virtually nothing of the cultural-historical background just related. The more I have learned about Spanish history and culture, the more it has told me about my Torah pointer and, through it, about the world. I discovered through a silversmith, for example, that it was made in the late seventeenth or early eighteenth century, more than a century *after* the Inquisition and after the expulsion of the Jews from Spain, presumably for the use of the *converso* community who had been converted to Christianity as the price for not being expelled as Jews. The more I learned, the more *situated* that pointer became in the context of the cultural history of Spain. The pointer, of course, is one of Meyerson's œuvres. The more I learned, the further I got from a cause-and-effect explanatory account of things, and the better I understood them (to invoke von Wright's compelling distinction between 'understanding' and 'explanation').

To return to the main argument, it is increasingly clear that one does not *explain* how culture affects mind but *interprets* its influence in some under-standable way. In our example, the task is to make sense of why Torah pointers were used in post-Inquisition Spain by *conversos*, why they took the risk of having them made, what they told themselves, why they didn't just migrate as so many *conversos* did, and so on. How culture influences mind in particular instances seems better told in a series of connected narratives, likeness among them suggesting the generality of a *genre* rather than an explanatory theory.

Finally, the classic approaches typically neglect or misconstrue the insti-tutional constraints that impose themselves on individual minds. The Inquisition did indeed lead to Christian conversions and the creation of a *converso* subculture, which in turn led many young *conversos* of the next generation or two to be 'tempted' to emigrate to the New World where traditional ways were less firmly established and opportunities greater. Indeed, as Tzvetvan Todorov has argued, it may have been the cosmopolitan perspective of post-Inquisition Spain, *conversos* included, that made possible Spain's New World conquest. So, should we not include cosmopolitanism and its consequences among the effects culture may have on 'mind'?

Which brings us to the question: What is culture?

What is culture?

Clyde Kluckhohn and Alfred Kroeber once prepared a learned monograph reviewing some 171 different definitions of culture which they duly sorted into 13 categories. Reflecting on that original 1950s compendium (which he was assigned to critique as a young graduate student), Clifford Geertz writes:

> The vicissitudes of 'culture' (the *mot*, not the *chose* ... *there* is no *chose*) ... were in fact only beginning. Everyone knew that the Kwakiutl were megalomanic, the Dobu paranoid, and the Zuni poised.... We were condemned, it seemed, to working with a logic and a language in which concept, cause, form, and outcome had the same name. (1999: 10–11)

So why, then, would anybody want to take such a raggetyandy of a concept and create a 'cultural psychology'?

I have recently written – in collaboration with my law professor-activist colleague, Anthony Amsterdam – a rather large book, *Minding the Law* (Amsterdam and Bruner, 2000), which devotes two chapters to expounding a perspective on culture and applying it to the operation of the American legal system as it reveals itself in US Supreme Court opinions over the last century of racial discrimination cases from *Plessy v. Ferguson* to *Hopwood v. Texas*. While it steers clear of trying to characterize culture-in-general (and avoids the culture-and-mind issue), the book does try to forge the concept of culture into something usable for legal interpretative analysis.

For one, it forswears the old idea of culture as a 'unified whole' held together in stable equilibrium. For our purposes, culture represents a balance between what a wider community takes as canonical or predictable social reality, and what individuals or groups within that community conceive as possible worlds alternative to the canonical one. We thus treat 'culture' as a dialectical interplay between the canonical, usually hardened into institutional forms, and possible worlds generated by interests at variance to the canonical, but also sometimes institutionalized in, for example, theatre, criticism or fiction. Partly at the goading of constitutional lawyer David Richards, we came to speak of the canonical as existing in a noetic space of possibilities. In time, the noetic even comes to unseat and replace the canonical, as when Harriet Beecher Stowe's *Uncle Tom's Cabin* sparked opposition to institutionalized slavery in America or when the writings of the Harlem Renaissance undermined the form of American racism that had led the Supreme Court to invoke the segregationist 'separate-but-equal' doctrine in *Plessy* v. *Ferguson*. We trace the dialectic between two 'foundational' beliefs in American popular thought – The American Creed ('the land of opportunity for all') and The American Caution ('keep your powder dry and don't let others take advantage of you') – to show how they were constantly at loggerheads with each other. There are no inevitabilities in this account of change: neither Harriet Beecher Stowe nor Langston Hughes and Richard Wright were 'necessary' consequences of anything. And the war against Hitler, which further made America wary of racial segregation and more sensitive to our own home-grown racism, was not a necessary condition for predisposing the Supreme Court to make its holding in *Brown* v. *Board of Education*. Our only claim about culture in this account is that it provides an orderly way of describing the contending forces in a continuing American dialectic over race, segregation, justice-for-all.

Quite plainly, not all of the individuals involved in the desegregation struggle of the 1950s were aware of all facets of this dialectic. How could they have been, for some of its facets were truly obscure? Take Lord Mansfield's famous (for constitutional lawyers, anyway) decision in *Somersett's Case*, which was a crucial factor in establishing a line of precedent for *Brown*. Lord Mansfield held in his mid-eighteenth-century decision (using Montaigne as his authority), that man's natural state was free and that it required a local ordinance to hold anybody in bondage. Therefore, Somersett, a slave escaped from his American master visiting in England, was a free man, in the absence of any local ordinance permitting bondage in England. *Somersett's Case* is simply part of Anglo-American common law and, as such, can be used as precedent in the tradition of *stare decisis*. But it took Thurgood Marshall to cite it in his oral argument before the Court – *that* made a difference. But can we claim that, without Thurgood Marshall, the Court would have found differently in *Brown?*

Once again, culture is not a causal concept. All one does in cultural analysis is search for congruence in how events work themselves out, in the 'sense' that people make of them. It was congruent enough for Marshall to cite *Somersett* as an element in the dialectic. But how wide-ranging should such congruences be? What forms should they take? To what should they relate? Should we look for evidence of the corruption of Roman moral responsibility to account for the fall of that great empire, as Gibbon urged us to do in the eighteenth century, or look to the inherent growth of self-promoting self-interest in Rome's military bureaucracy policing the Empire's 3,000-mile frontier, as Hugh Elton urged nearly two centuries later? Assume that both Gibbon and Elton were right. Which gives a more congruent context to the Fall of Rome and the barbarian invasion that triggered it, domestic moral slackness among the elite at home or self-serving bureaucratic wrangling at the frontier of empire?

Do we have to choose? If I were giving a course in 'Bureaucracy', I'd want Elton. In Moral Philosophy, perhaps Gibbon. Is this to say that one's emphasis in choosing a pattern of cultural congruence has rhetorical or even political motivation? Well, possibly. But here again pragmatics. Most cultural analyses are carried out with something in mind, even those conducted in classrooms. Not all of them are convincing, for congruence in a cultural account is itself governed by cultural canons.

Now to our next 'founding conjecture': In what fashion is language an expression of culture? How is its acquisition related to mastering a culture's practices? And (half in jest) of what does language consist?

Language, mind and culture

First I must answer some complaints made in earlier chapters. One of them is that I have a hidden soft spot for nativist conceptions of language: I assume that there is something like LAD, Chomsky's Language Acquisition Device, that steers the mastery of language or that the forms of language are determined by a self-sufficient 'language organ' rather than a long, historical process of development and change. Such assumptions, several authors point out, are inconsistent with other positions I have taken. I want to deny these charges, though I remain something of a Hamlet on such questions.

My working hypothesis is that human languages are not comprehensible without considering the parallel development of our unique, species-linked capacity for intersubjectivity, our ability to 'read' each others' minds. I believe that intentionality itself – the 'standing for' relation of arbitrary symbols to their referents – is impossible without such intersubjectivity.

'Mind-reading' is inferential in its very nature. We are not telepathic, the contagion of empathy being as close as we get to 'direct' mind-reading. The rest is based on inference from contextualized action and expression. I think, moreover, that we are sensitized by our evolutionary past to draw inferences about others' mental states with respect, principally, to the possible actions they may bring about – the so-called 'arguments of action'. We seem preternaturally disposed to recognize agency, action intended, goal sought, instrumentality and the effect of setting. In a word, we organize our perception of others as involving an Actor, a circumscribed Act directed to some Goal and employing certain Means, all constrained by a particular kind of Setting. We take it as given that these 'arguments of action' are influenced, or even determined, by the so-called intentional states of others – their beliefs, intentions, wishes, fears and so on. We are incorrigible mentalists: for us, naïvely, people act in certain ways because they want to, desire certain outcomes, believe certain states of affairs compel them to, etc. We believe the same of ourselves.

Further, we see people as 'responsive' or 'sensitive' to our communicative acts. That is the criterion by which we distinguish 'real' Others from things (and thereby we often fall into animism, for our category of Others may include such inappropriate objects as dogs, clouds and even flowers (as my daughter once insisted in justifying why she talked to sunflowers on the south wall of our garage)). We communicate with others with the goal of affirming or altering their intentional states, and thereby to influence their actions, and our communicative strategies are shaped by the fact that we organize our conception of actions in terms of Agency, specific Acts, Goals, Means and determinative Setting. All of the above begins ontogenetically (and probably phylogenetically) before we master lexico-grammatic speech. It provides, as it were, the *pragmatic* substrate of human communication.

It is thus not surprising that when the young child first masters speech, her nonlinguistic communication is already pragmatically adept, devoted to getting things done in the world. And (absent autism) it rapidly gains in pragmatic adequacy. Even young children's bedtime soliloquies are devoted to rearranging how recent actions (particularly communicative acts) fared in the child's world, or to laying plans for future actions and their contingencies. In all of Emmy's 'narratives from the crib', she showed no shred of concern about grammatically well-formed utterances. Her concerns were completely pragmatic (Bruner and Lucariello, 1989).

Moreover, Emmy's seeming readiness to pick up new lexical units or syntactic forms was completely motivated by pragmatic considerations rather than by any interest in the niceties of grammar. She was looking for a convenient way of representing in speech the state of affairs she was trying to clarify in terms of what she did or might do. How is it, then, that natural languages provide the forms for children to use in this effective, pragmatic way?

There are two ways of approaching that famous mystery. One is genetic, the other cultural-historical. The former, as we know well, proposes some sort of grammatical deep structure that expresses itself in local realization rules in particular languages. It is innate and resides in some sort of autonomous 'language organ'. If we give this view a fashionable evolution-ary twist, these rules (like Sperber's contagions) are the beneficent outcomes of natural selection – though given the short life of lexico-grammatical speech on earth, this seems implausible.

The other view is that local languages have the grammatical rules necessary for achieving appropriate communicative ends – pragmatic ends – because that is how languages evolve historically. Michael Tomasello states this view with particular elegance in his chapter. For ease of communication, longer or more cumbersome forms of expression are shortened, standardized and regularized for much the same reason that some forms slowly drop out of a language with disuse.

Hamlet-like, I find myself attracted by both views. I shilly-shally on this issue. I cannot believe, however, that the innate 'deep structure' of lan-guage, if ever it were printed out in celestial space, would be principally about syntax. I confess that, when Chomsky was striking Skinner hip and thigh for his Augustinian account of language learning, I was attracted by his formalism with its tree structures. But increasingly I have moved to the view that the structure of languages derives from other innate, not very well-formed readinesses to structure experience in ways that, for interpersonal convenience, can be represented linguistically, with minimum effort, and in a syntactically regularized manner. My chief candidate for this form of innateness is our readiness to see the world in terms of the 'arguments of action'. And, like Charles Fillmore, I see these as being time marked either by aspect or by tense. That is the way experience plays out; that is what we are looking for in any system of linguistic representation. And that is what the history of linguistic usage is about: ways of representing Agents, finite Acts, desired Goals, appropriate and inappropriate Means, and constraining Settings.

But there is at least one element missing from this account. And here I introduce a matter so primitive, and so embedded in communication, that it is difficult to make explicit. It is *deixis* – how we locate ourselves linguistically in interpersonal, intersubjective space-time. I take its most primitive expression to be what Daniel Stern called the 'attunement' between mother and child: they 'take turns' vocalizing or expressing themselves facially or posturally, position themselves 'appropriately', follow each others' line of regard. They form a deictic unit before ever they master the subtleties of such deictic linguistic contrasts as 'here–there', or 'in front of–behind', or such anaphoric distinctions as 'a–the' or how to manage 'marked and unmarked' forms. I see this capacity for deixis as an evolutionary step that marks us off drastically from our primate ancestors. It is difficult to imagine that it has no innate, biological basis.

A word about the human capacity for narrative. As I have argued elsewhere, our predisposition to structure interpersonal experience in terms of the arguments of action makes narrative recounting inevitable, and makes our susceptibility to narrative explication incorrigible. All one needs to generate narrative is some 'canonical' expectancy about how action plays out in the world and some setback or violation of that expectancy.

To return to the question which began this section, I see no compelling evidence that language as such, or its acquisition, is a simple unfolding of a programme in some biological organ in the brain, unaffected by the pragmatic push to influence things in the interpersonal world. On the other hand, any form of human activity that plays out so automatically must have some predisposing neurobiological support. We talk like tournament tennis is played or expert fencing fenced: fast and almost faultlessly. Does that kind of performance require some analogue of an upright posture, a human pelvic girdle, a locking knee? Neurobiological support, yes, but surely not an autonomous 'language organ'! It is also inconceivable to me that social practice does not have a major effect on how language is formed and changed over generations.

Finally, and most decidedly, I do not find it very convincing that the so-called 'universals' of language issue from a programme stored in a language organ in the brain. The commonality of human plights in no matter what culture, the vicissitudes of human intersubjectivity, our sensitivity towards the acts and the intentional states of others, even the exigencies of communicating rapidly about certain classes of events in the world – these provide a far better account of the vast array of language universals. I am prepared to admit that there is something about the nature of figure–ground perception that predisposes us to topic–comment structures in speech. But figure–ground perception is far more ancient than speech, and remote from the kind of 'innate structures' envisaged by the linguistic nativist.

Construction and reality

Finally, a word about 'constructivism'. As an amateur 'psychological historian', I attribute allegiance to contructivism or realism to sheer temperament. Typically, one's stance on this matter has its source in one's early reading (or misreading) of seminal sources – in my own case, Ernst Mach's *The Analysis of Sensation* (though my friend Gerald Holton would doubtless assure me that I had misread Mach if he turned me into a constructionist). And reading Kant also fixed me in my stance.

But my variant of constructivism is not Kantian. Nelson Goodman cured me of that. I take the view that there is no single 'basically true' version of reality. 'Reality' is always relative to a stance one takes towards the world, and one can take many different stances, all of them selective and organized by different principles. I cannot believe a priori that all versions of reality are translatable into each other, or that any of them is, as it were, all-purpose. Building a house, for example, we take a 'carpenter's view' and go about the job depending upon tape measures and T-squares. There are myriad pragmatic rules that are confirmed in the process. These 'rules of use' happen also to be exquisitely represented by arithmetic, geometry and physical principles. It is all very comforting. But the moment we look at the task of construction in the light of whether, say, we have assured sufficient privacy for those who will inhabit the house, things change. Then we become concerned about whether rooms are sufficiently isolated from one another, yet connected by common space so as not to be little coventries. When we think about 'living patterns' and aesthetic considerations, the model we have in mind is not buttressed by physical metrics like centimetres, grams and seconds.

It is comforting but misleading for a psychologist to draw the Lockean conclusion that the spatial reality is 'primary', the habitational one 'secondary'. In use, the two depend equally upon a pragmatic criterion: Do they work for particular ends? In both domains, the physical and the habitational, we rely on certain basic forms of logic to get to our conclusions – though the premises from which we draw the logical conclusions may be different. There are also points at which we must be careful about applying 'standard' logics loosely. Just because it follows that if A is bigger than B and B bigger than C, then A is bigger than C, it does not follow, for example, that if somebody likes Room A better than Room B, and Room B better than Room C, they will like Room A better than Room C. They may be using different criteria in the A–B, B–C, and A–C comparisons. Must we assume that the preference scaling would become more 'real' if the person judging could be made to employ a single criterion? Can we legislate such matters from a pinnacle above all forms of 'reality', from a 'view from nowhere'?

These are the kinds of conjectures that both realist and constructivist struggle with, neither with total success. For a cultural psychologist, the underlying task is to give some descriptive and analytic structure to the realities we construct in different cultures or under varying conditions of social life. We cannot see our own children simultaneously in the light of love and the light of justice (as Roscoe Pound once famously said about lawyers in litigation, their forte is that they can think separately about things that are inextricably linked). Indeed, one of the most useful features of narrative mental structures is that they permit the recounting of facts in a way that isolates them from things that might bring their narrative necessity into question. Try to convince consumers of standard American narratives that Abraham Lincoln's principal motive in signing the bill establishing Land Grant Colleges in 1962 was to get farmers behind Union efforts in the Civil War. 'That doesn't sound like Lincoln', they will tell you. To convince you of my interpretation of the 'facts' in this matter, I would have to tell you some tales about Lincoln as 'fixer', lawyer, politician in Illinois, tales that would set you off on another narrative track.

I have never felt the almost religious attachment to constructivism that some 'social constructionists' do. Nor towards a pragmatic account of truth (or reality, or whatever it should be called). Like Goodman, I feel it something of a pity (and part of the burden of being a human being) that we make claims about 'reality' and, having done so, are compelled to admit that our 'realities' are made, though we go on cherishing the illusion that there must be some methodological trick whereby we could find reality directly. Ontology, to my sceptical way of thinking, is an artefact of epistemology. It is a curious game, making claims about the reality of our proposed realities. I think it a more grown-up pursuit just to make claims about their usefulness.

And usefulness varies. The usefulness of legal tender (what makes it 'real' money) depends on people's beliefs – that they can exchange it for gold, which in turn they believe they can trade for goods, and so on 'all the way down'. Legal tender is a 'real' social construction. It has a lot of other 'realities' attached to it in the law. If you steal it, if you borrow it and fail to repay it, if you falsely promise it for your advantage in exchange for goods or services, if you defame another and reduce their power to earn it, you are likely to get hauled before a real court and may end up spending real time behind real steel bars. Only a fool would deny that this is the same as the 'reality' or verifiability of an atomic theory, demonstrated, say, in a cloud chamber and then in an atomic explosion. But why should we insist at this point that nature and culture are either totally alike or totally different? The worlds of law and finance are very different from the world of physics, and require different ways of using mind and organizing social effort. Doubtless, atoms (our construct of something in nature) are not influenced by our confidence in them. But financial deals literally float, as it were, in a medium of mutual confidence.

Our task as human scientists is to explicate *for each other* how human living arrangements work. Our explanations often have powerful effects on those very arrangements, for we, as human scientists, are part of the 'reality' that we seek to understand. The irony is that it was physics that taught us the advantages of leaving behind the kind of positivist realism that hampered efforts to understand the natural world. Without some conception like constructivism we would be totally the victims of reductionist dogmatism.

One last point. Constructivism invokes pragmatic criteria: Does the 'reality' one postulates succeed in achieving certain desirable ends? Is it stable enough, does it generate believable accounts of particulars? Does it generate a logic and a working language that is generative? I recognize, of course, that the necessary and sufficient criteria of a pragmatic standard (whether it works) are also culturally established. There is no platinum metre-rule that can measure whether a postulated 'reality' is adequate pragmatically. All of which is just to say that the measure of adequacy of any particular theoretical construct, like the construct itself, is a human, cultural product.

Coda

This concludes my reflections on the questions posed by this book. I do not apologize for the reckless claims and overarching generalizations I have set forth in this chapter, but offer them in the spirit of combating the tendency we often feel to be overcautious in our public pronouncements. I loved the other chapters in this book. You'll see echoes of my answers to the questions they pose in things to come.

Notes

1 It was quite by luck that I was thrust into Meyerson's work. In the mid-1990s, as part of the Meyerson renaissance, a colloquium was organized in Paris to celebrate his works and honour the opening of a Meyerson archive at the University of Nanterre. I was invited as an overseas struggler in the vineyard of cultural psychology. The organizer, Françoise Parot, kindly sent me a bushel of Meyerson's writings, wryly informing me that it was time for me to catch up. My paper was published as Bruner (1996).

2 I choose this odd example for good reason. I have many friends in France, and all of them adhere to images of their country based on this classic hexagon, in

much the same way that long-resident New Yorkers divide the United States, on first cut, between 'this side' of the Hudson and 'that side'.

3   I have discussed this position more fully elsewhere in an effort to discover what is reconcilable in the views of Piaget and Vygotsky (Bruner, 1997).

4   I am leaving out of my account both McDougall and Freud, since I see both of them as more interested in how our psychological dispositions (stemming from 'human nature') put their shape on culture. For the same reason, I am passing over the curious intellectual movement that went by the name of 'culture-personality' theory.

References

Amsterdam, A. and Bruner, J.S. (2000) *Minding the Law*. Cambridge, MA: Harvard University Press.

Bruner, J.S. (1996) 'Meyerson aujourd'hui: quelques reflexions sur la psychologie culturelle', in F. Parot (ed.), *Pour une psychologie historique: Ecrits en hommage à Ignace Meyerson*. Paris: Presses Universitaires de France.

Bruner, J.S. (1997) 'Celebrating divergence: Piaget and Vygotsky', *Human Development*, 40: 63–73.

Bruner, J.S. and Lucariello, J. (1989) 'Monologue as narrative recreation of the world', in K. Nelson (ed.), *Narratives from the Crib*. Cambridge, MA: Harvard University Press.

Geertz, C. (1999) 'A life of learning'. The Charles Homer Haskins Lecture for 1999. American Council of Learned Societies, Occasional Paper.

INDEX

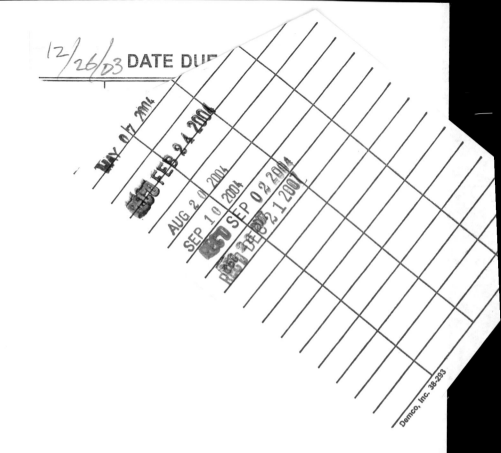